CARMEN DE TRIUMPHO NORMANNICO

–

THE SONG OF THE NORMAN CONQUEST

Carmen by Bishop Guy d'Amiens

Transcribed and translated by Kathleen Tyson

x.xv.mmxviii

ISBN-13: 978-1492704751

The consecration of William the Conqueror by Norman and Anglican bishops - attributed to Matthew Paris

CONTENTS

Introduction

Carmen de Triumpho Normannico
- The Song of the Norman Conquest

INTRODUCTION

True and complete history is never possible; better history is always possible. Better history requires an open mind and objective weighing of what we think we know against new information being revealed by science, archaeology and comparative historiography. This 2017 revised transcription and translation of the *Carmen Widonis* and the related material in the appendices offer new insights about the motivations, geography and method of the Norman Conquest. The translation is more literal than earlier editions, but it is also enriched with insights from a wider range of sources, sciences and disciplines.

The *Carmen Widonis* is a Latin verse history of 835 lines that records the earliest account of the Norman Conquest. The song was written by a Gallic bishop to be sung by bards for the entertainment of the victorious warriors and to publicise the Norman Conquest in the courts and abbeys of Gallic Europe and Rome. It now provides important guidance on early English geography, politics and ecclesiastical influence at a time when England was transitioning from Anglo-Danish to Anglo-Norman rule. The Battle of Hastings was the last great battle between sea armies of Gallia and the Danes for imperium in Britain, a contest that had begun thousands of years earlier.

The *Carmen* is the most detailed account we have of the Norman Conquest. It survives as a single untitled and unattributed manuscript in a composite collection of poetry and miscellany from the abbey of Saint Eucharius-Matthias at Trier. A fragment of the first 66 lines is also preserved, but is clearly a copy of the earlier work. I am grateful to the Royal Library of Belgium for digital photographs of the manuscript for a new transcription and providing access to the original during my researches.

The manuscript of the *Carmen Widonis* is untitled. It became known as the *Carmen de Hastingae Proelio* in the twentieth century, but that name is too narrow for an epic scope embracing the launch of the

Norman fleet from Dives in early September 1066 to the coronation of William the Conqueror on Christmas Day in Westminster. This edition is titled *Carmen de Triumpho Normannico – The Song of the Norman Conquest* to recognise the wider scope.

The *Carmen* was composed in 1067, possibly for the Easter celebrations at Fécamp Abbey in Normandy. The work is attributed to Guy of Ponthieu, bishop of Amiens, a kinsman of the contemporaneous Count Guy of Ponthieu. The evidence for authorship comes from two later original sources for the Norman Conquest. Orderic Vitalis names Guy twice as the author of an admirable verse history in his *Historia Ecclesiastica Normannorum*, and Robert of Torigni similarly refers readers to Guy's *Carmen* in his revision of the *Gesta Normannorum Ducum*. The *Carmen* was also a likely source for William of Poitiers' *Gesta Guillelmi*, the Bayeux Tapestry and Baudri of Bourgueil's *Letter to Adela*, although each provides a slightly different view of events. Guy d'Amiens had long known both King Harold and Duke William personally, so we gain a first-hand insight into the men through the song.

Very likely the verse history was commissioned by Queen Mathilda, as it was her duty as royal consort to commission songs from bards of the day to celebrate the martial feats of her husband. Orderic Vitalis recorded that Guy was appointed chaplain to Queen Mathilda and accompanied her to England in 1068, which confirms a close, cooperative relationship which may have started with the commissioning of the *Carmen*. Queen Mathilda would have been responsible for planning the Easter 1067 homecoming and victory celebrations at Fécamp, and she might reasonably commission the *Carmen* as one of the entertainments.

By 1066 Guy d'Amiens had overreached and was out of favour with the pope; his episcopal powers had been restricted. He may have accompanied his martial kinsmen and written the *Carmen* to win favour from King William or the influential Abbot Lanfranc, to whom the foreword is addressed for correction. Guy may also have sought to promote the interests of Count Eustace of Boulogne or the heir of Count Guy of Ponthieu, both of whom are characterised as heroic in the battle narrative.

As the earliest account, the *Carmen* is unique among contemporary histories for sharing credit for the victory far more widely than later accounts. All allies would have joined at Fécamp for the celebrations and sharing out of the war booty, so this pan-Gallic cast may have been deliberate diplomacy. Indeed, any bias favours Ponthieu, Boulogne and the Mediterranean archers rather than Normandy. Later works by Normans were more narrowly partial to Normandy.

King Harold is treated respectfully, although described as an oathbreaker, adulterer and usurper. Bishop Guy d'Amiens, Count Guy of Ponthieu, Count Eustace of Boulogne and *Haroldi ducis* all witnessed a charter in 1056 for Count Baldwin V at the Flanders court. Witnessing charters together indicates a degree collaboration, probably arising from shipping and trade. Count Eustace and Count Guy's son are said to be among the warriors with Duke William when King Harold is killed in battle. Both might have hoped a greater share in the rewards of conquest. A disappointed Count Eustace of Boulogne attempted to seize Dover Castle in 1068, and relations between Normandy and counts of Ponthieu were always turbulent.

There have been two critical editions of the *Carmen* published with English translations under the title *The Carmen de Hastingae Proelio of Guy Bishop of Amiens* by editors Catherine Morton and Hope Muntz (Oxford Medieval Texts, 1972) and Frank Barlow (Oxford Medieval Texts, 1999). While this edition varies from the earlier translations in many respects, these earlier editors suggested many insights and interpretations I would have missed otherwise. I initially started translating a few lines of the *Carmen* because I felt the earlier editors had misconstrued the navigation and negotiations with besieged Londoners, and changes to these accounts are perhaps the most important contributions of the current edition. I also sensed the lively humour, character sketches and drama had been muted or missed by earlier editors. It was only when new information emerged from the text, and original research revealed new motivations and a new geography for 1066, that I fully appreciated the scale of the editorial charge I had too lightly undertaken.

What started as the endeavour of weeks became the passion of years. I first translated the *Carmen* in 2013, amateurishly in hindsight, and have been diligently improving the translation and interpretation ever since. In 2015 I took a sabbatical to gain an MA in Medieval History from King's College London. This 2017 edition benefits from all the instruction I received on my courses, but especially the diligent and enlightened editing of the *Carmen* translation by Dr Daniel Hadas, my lecturer in Latin at King's College London. If the text and translation are not yet perfect, they are now metrically and grammatically defensible. Dr Hadas has also given me a grounding in what academics expect of a critical edition, although this text is still intended to be enjoyed by a wider reading public. The formatting has been changed from intralinear translation to facing pages. Explanatory notes on editing are with the Latin text and footnotes explaining historical context are now with the English translation. As even Dr Hadas was uncertain of some ungrammatical lines and colloquial words, any remaining errors and infelicities are entirely my own.

The translation is quite literal, but with some less common interpretations. Latin has just 7,000 non-unique words, where English has over 80,000. Latin words often had multiple meanings which poets used artfully for emphasis or satirical effect; interpretation can depend on context. Certain words used in connection with navigation or the church had distinct connotations I believe relevant to the *Carmen* narrative. Examples are *sinu placido* for 'calm basin' at line 128 and *coloni* for 'ecclesiastical tenants' at lines 127, 637 and 667. Some corrections to the manuscript vary from earlier texts as well. I have rejected some earlier amendments by editors as unjustified. Where I have amended a word in the Latin transcription, the correction is in angled brackets or footnoted. Where I have introduced words to clarify meaning in the English translation, the additional words appear in grey to distinguish them from literal translation.

Perhaps the most meaningful change in this edition is a recasting of the narrative of the 118 lines on the siege of London – lines 635-752. Augustine Thierry first published the *Carmen* in his 1825 *History of the Conquest of England by the Normans*. Ignoring the London Charter of Liberties as a settlement of the siege, and altering one word of the Latin text in his desire to make sense of line 688, he misconstrued the offer of a 'better separation' for London and confused the urban magistrate receiving the offer of truce with *Ansgardus*. He suggested *Ansgardus* might reference Esegar the Waltham-based Anglo-Danish staller. English historians made his supposition into orthodoxy, establishing Esegar the Staller as the defender of London in 1066 histories ever since. There is no pre-1825 record the venerable and provincial Danish retainer Esegar lived to 1066 or ever held authority in urban, multi-cultural, mercantile London. Any urban office for Esegar is very unlikely as his father had long before fallen out of royal favour, and proud, multi-cultural Londoners had an elite garrison of professional warriors and a veteran portreeve to command the citizen brigades in 1066.

This edition translates line 688 literally, respecting the text of the manuscript, as offering the citizens of London a 'better separation'. This interpretation is consistent with known facts. King William ceded London as a semi-autonomous commonwealth with his first act, the London Charter of Liberties. The recipient of the offer of truce and the charter was the Norman portreeve, the chief urban magistrate, Godfrey de Magnaville. *Ansgardus* is now translated as Edgar the Aethling. The *Carmen* presumably uses the Germanic name given the boy at his christening in the Slavo-Dacian court of Hungary. The Saxon name Edgar was not used in Hungary, and neither of the boy's parents spoke any English or knew any Englishmen before 1056. The infant's Germanic name was probably Anglicised after his 1057 arrival in England to make him more acceptable as a potential royal heir, or even after the Norman Conquest when he allied with Scots and rebels. A Frankish bard would prefer the boy's Germanic christening name.

Godfrey de Magnaville remained London's portreeve and chief secular magistrate from 1051 until his death in 1100. Godfrey commanded and trained the citizen militia and oversaw maintenance of the city's walls, barbican and keep. He also collected taxes and promoted effective urban administration as a royal agent in the city. Godfrey may have been known personally to Duke William from the duke's stay in London in 1051 or an earlier military career in Normandy, as the *Carmen* observes approvingly that he 'received many wounds for his homeland' at line 683. Godfrey may even have accompanied Duke William to London in 1051 to reinforce defences in London against the exiled outlaws Godwin and Harold. Duke William brought many Norman veterans to aid his cousin King Edward in briefly asserting royal rule after Godwin and Harold were exiled. Although Godwin and Harold were restored to their earldoms in 1052, relegating the king to a figurehead, Godfrey continued as portreeve. London alone was allowed as a sanctuary for Gallic citizens, and London's Norman bishop was the only Gallic prelate restored to office. As a Norman and the royal agent in London Godfrey was the most eligible correspondent for negotiations between King William and the citizenry in 1066.

Taking *Ansgardus* as the boy-king of London completely changes the *Carmen* narrative, which now aligns more closely with accounts of London given by William of Poitiers, Orderic Vitalis and Baudri of Bourgueil. The London Charter of Liberties is rendered a proximate result of negotiations for peace between king and city. London remained a semi-autonomous commonwealth until 1693, proving through its urban development and prosperity the good sense on both sides in agreeing a truce in 1066. London then was a multi-cultural, mercantile, self-ruled canton separate from a more dangerous and unstable hinterland, like early New York, Singapore, Hong Kong or Cape Town, and served the same purpose of promoting and protecting multi-cultural emigration, mercantile commerce and financial prosperity.

Other insights in this edition may be initially controversial but appear well supported by context, other original sources and confirmatory evidence:

- The allies brought an effective military force of 6,000 experienced and well-armed Gallic warriors. This number is given as an exact formula at line 96 when understood with reference to a medieval mathematics text.

- The fleet crossed the Channel on a single tide, anchored off-shore within sight of land, and waited sunrise and the next flooding tide. The ships rafted together in the 'sea-harbour' formation perfected in Norman Mediterranean campaigns. This detail clarifies the Bayeux Tapestry, suggesting *Pevenesæ* was a familiar fleet anchorage in the seascape and not a place in the landscape.

- The Norman landings, fortifications and camp at *Hastinge portus* were in the Fécamp Abbey estate *Rameslege*. The port is now the Brede Valley, but in 1066 it was the Brede Basin with a great eight mile long estuarine port or loch. The entrance to the 'calm basin' was bracketed by tidal islands Rie and Iham, now Rye and Winchelsea. This geography at last makes sense of the place name *Senlac* preferred by Orderic Vitalis. *Senlac* simply means 'sandy loch' or 'sandy lough', a very apt topographic name for a long, sandy, tidal arm of the sea above the sea-ford anchorage at *Pevenesæ*.

- The *diruta castella* – ruined fortlets – at the landings were likely Fécamp Abbey monastic cells with signal beacons at *Peneuessel* (now

Udimore) and Iham (now Winchelsea). The difference in elevations is 30 metres today. In 1066 the two beacons could be aligned to guide navigation from the Gallic coastal anchorages at Wissant, Boulogne and Le Touquet opposite. The invading Normans first landed at *Peneuessel*/Udimore, where they built and garrisoned a watchtower as a signalling station, gaining wide views of any approach by land or water. The Norman fleet then crossed the shallow basin and camped securely at *Hastinge portus*, now the Icklesham ridge, restoring the Fécamp cell on Iham. Normans knew they would find fresh water springs, silage for horses, and charcoal bloomeries for cooking and iron forges. The fleet of ships was secured in a sheltered harbour that served as a wine and oil port for continental merchants for at least 1500 years.

- Both Norman and English armies were on the march when they met, so the battlefield might be near a Roman road linking the cape of Hastingas to the hinterland Sussex Weald. While Battle is not an impossible location, there is no archaeological evidence for a battle there after more than a century of investigation. It is more likely the abbey was situated on Battle Hill so it could be seen at the top of the Brede Basin by all mariners entering the Brede Basin port. This follows medieval custom and has the advantage that watchmen at the abbey could signal an attack on the port to the wider region. Anyone walking the public footpath between Icklesham and Udimore today can still see Battle Hill from the centre of the Brede Valley. Anyone standing on the gate tower at Battle can see the turbines of the wind farm on Winchelsea Sands and the manor churches at Brede and Udimore. The *Carmen* describes an uncultivated *mons* above the valley for the battle, but other accounts use *collis*, a hill, ridge or mound. The battlefield need not be very great in height, although the great ridge above Hastings should not be discounted as impossible. Fécamp Abbey erected St Helen's Church at Ore after the battle, symbolising the restored communion of England with Rome.

- King Harold's dismemberment and burial under a hilltop cairn on unhallowed ground was consistent with his status as a tyrant and excommunicant under canon law. The *Carmen* gives us the words inscribed on Harold's grave at lines 591-92, which William of Jumièges confirmed were in jest. The inscription enjoins the usurper's spirit to guard the sea on one side and the strand on the other, consistent with the summit of Hog Hill above Icklesham, with views of both the Normandy coast and the Brede Basin.

- The five boroughs targeted for urban submission in the *Carmen* had all been contested trading cantons, and all were important to English Christian communion with Rome:

  o Dover was the site the first minster in England ceded by royal grant to Rome and was the Romano-Gallic port emporium *Dubris*. 2nd century King Lucius was the first British convert to Roman Christianity and endowed papal envoys a church in Dover Castle with revenues of the port.

  o Canterbury was the archiepiscopal see of Pope Gregory the Great's envoy to the Anglians and was the Romano-Gallic emporium *Cantium*. King Aethelberht, who had lived in Neustria and married a Neustrian queen, settled a church with port revenues on Saint Augustine in 598. This diverted Pope Gregory's mission from Anglia and instead established the Roman Church's British archiepiscopacy in Kent.

  o Winchester was the royal seat, royal minster and episcopal see of the kingdom of Wessex and was the Romano-Gallic emporium *Venta Belgarum* for the port at *Magnus Portus*. The borough was ceded by the king of Wessex as an episcopal see to the papal envoy Birinius in 634. Winchester also held a papally-privileged Benedictine monastery founded by King Alfred the Great to confirm Wessex communion with Rome.

  o Westminster was the site of the first royal foundation abbey of the East Saxons on the site of the Romano-Gallic trading canton at Thorney Island. King Edward the Confessor re-founded the abbey as a Benedictine order with a school for secular clerics, a royal treasury, and his royal palace. Westminster Abbey was privileged by the pope in 1051 when King Edward briefly re-confirmed English communion with Rome. Roman communion was overthrown in 1052 when exiles Godwin and Harold returned, Anglo-Dane Stigand appointed himself archbishop, and the Frankish Archbishop Robert of Jumieges was driven into exile.

- ○ London was the Romano-Gallic emporium *Londinium* which became the episcopal see of Mellitus, a companion of Saint Augustine, and was privileged by Pope Gregory as a metropolitan reserved to direct papal authority.

- The submission of urban boroughs in the *Carmen* at lines 613-22 completes the conquest left unfinished after the battle. King William only succeeded to King Harold's royal demesne by conquest; he had to secure boroughs and privileged ecclesiastical estates by oath. The *Carmen* tells us that burgesses and magistrates renewed oaths of loyalty to the new king to retain royal protections and privileges. Recording urban oath-taking in the *Carmen* reinforced King William's legitimacy as ruler of all England.

- At Winchester King William granted Queen Edith and the two prelates, bishop Stigand and the abbot of New Minster, the privilege of retaining tributary taxes and paying only market tolls. This represents a valuable concession that may have been precedent for King William's later offer to London's magistrates and citizenry.

- The siege of London is resolved by recognition of London as a semi-autonomous Anglo-Frankish commonwealth, consistent with its early history as a Romano-Gallic emporium, a Roman imperial municipality, a metropolitan reserved to the Holy See by Pope Gregory the Great, a Danish canton under truce with King Aethelred from 1012, and the privileged Danish military and financial capital of England from 1017. In this edition the narrative of the siege is light-hearted, both sides prospering from truce.

- William, bishop of London, is identified as the metropolitan bishop 'equal in rank' holding King William's left hand in the coronation procession. The equality of the metropolitan bishops of London and York was laid down by Pope Gregory the Great in a letter to Saint Augustine reproduced by Bede, and was re-confirmed by the Council of London led by Lanfranc as archbishop in 1072. The excommunicate archbishop of Canterbury, Stigand, was ineligible for participation.

- The coronation rite in the *Carmen* is now better aligned with Frankish rites in translation. The king petitions for communion with the Roman Church, a prerequisite to consecration. The public election and confirmation customary in the English ritual follow. This better reflects the canon law purpose of royal consecration as committing the monarch to protection of the church.

Appendices address 'Imperium in Britain to 966', which provides an overview of several thousand years of sea army conquests, and 'Imperium in England 966 to 1066' which is the backstory of Saxon, Frankish, Norman and Danish rivalries in the century before the Norman Conquest. 'The New Geography of the Norman Conquest' moves the landings, camp and battle into the Brede Basin. 'Royal, Papal, Urban and Ecclesiastical Jurisdiction' attempts to explain the patchwork of rights, jurisdiction and privileges held variously by kings, bishops, abbots, and urban boroughs in pre-feudal England.

Coming late to history as a second career, I owe a great debt to many dedicated and tolerant academic historians and others with specialist knowledge. In addition to Daniel Hadas, who has first claim on my gratitude, I am particularly grateful to Elisabeth van Houts, John Gillingham, David Bates, Simon Keynes, Peter Heather, David Carpenter, Rory Naismith, and Julia Crick, who have all by turns been justly critical and encouraging. I am also grateful to Patrick Gautier Dalché for his published transcription of the coastal navigation guide *De Viis Maris*, David Georgi for his thesis on Norman French, Paul Hughes for his expertise on coastal and cross-Channel navigation, Sally Harvey for her insights about medieval horses, and Charles Stanton for his history of the Norman naval conquest in the Mediterranean. Many others have spurred further researches. I am grateful for Brede Basin local expertise to Richard Comotto of Winchelsea Archaeological Society, Philip Merricks of Icklesham and Richard Merricks of Udimore. For youthful inspiration I am grateful to late Professor George Kish who taught me long ago that geography is inseparable from history.

Most of all I am grateful for the patience and support of my sons, father and partner, who were forced to cede their just claims on me to an unreasonably demanding 11th century Gallic bishop these past four years.

Kathleen Tyson
London
October 2017

Image from the 12th century manuscript of the *Carmen Widonis*, Brussels, Royal Library of Belgium, MS 10615-729, ff. 227v – 230v

CARMEN DE TRIUMPHO NORMANNICO

PROEM

Quem probitas celebrat sapientia munit et ornat •

   Erigit et decorat •   Lanfrancum Wido[a] salutat •

Cum studiis clarus videaris lucifer ortus •

   Et tenebras pellis radiis dum lumina spargis •

---

[a]   Just the initials L and W are preserved in the manuscript, but *Lanfrancum* and *Wido* are metrically and historically appropriate.

THE SONG OF THE NORMAN CONQUEST

PREFACE

Whom honesty celebrates, wisdom fortifies and adorns, honours and glorifies.

Lanfranc[1], Guy[2] greets you.

When seen through your endeavours, you are as the bright morning star, and casting rays you banish darkness while spreading light.

---

[1]   Lanfranc (c.1005 – to 1089) was a lawyer and administrator from a powerful family in Pavia who became a monk after travelling widely. He rose to great influence as the Prior of Bec. Many bishops, abbots and even Pope Alexander II were among his students. Duke William appointed Lanfranc the first abbot of the Abbey of Saint-Etiènne at Caen at its founding in 1059 after Lanfranc secured his restoration to communion with the church. Lanfranc became archbishop of Canterbury from 1070, overseeing reform and re-establishment of the English church in communion with Rome.

[2]   Wido or Guy d'Amiens (c. 1014 – 1074) was a Frankish nobleman of Ponthieu and bishop of Amiens renowned for his poetry. Only the *Carmen* survives. Guy had incurred papal displeasure in a dispute with the abbey of Corbeil. He may have been seeking favour with Count Eustace, King William, or the pope through Lanfranc. His success can be measured by his appointment as Queen Mathilda's chaplain by 1068.

Per mare nec fragilis • si^a sit tutissima navis •   5

  Te precor ad portum carmen deducere nostrum •

Invidie ventis^b agitari nec paciaris •

  Nec boreae flatum timeat sed litus amoenum

Remige te carpat ne laesum rupe labescat •

  Sis judex illi justus de more^c magistri •   10

Quod minus est addens et quod super obsecro radens •

  Nullus credo sibi sub te tutore nocebit •

Sic tuus incipiat fieri meus iste libellus •

  Ut careat viciis • et laudibus amplificetur •

Evitare volens dispendia disidiose •   15

  Mentis et ingeniis placeant cum carmina multis •

Carminibus studui Normanicca bella reponi •

  Elegi potius levibus cantare camoenis •

Ingenium mentis vanis quam subdere curis •

  Cum sit et egregium describere gesta potentum •   20

Finibus occiduis quae gessit regia proles •

  Willelmus titulis commisi posteritatis •

Nam sibi sublatum regnum virtute redemit •

  Et victor patrios extendit trans mare fines •

Ergo decet memorare suum per secula factum •   25

---

^a Altered to s*ed* in earlier editions.
^b Manuscript has *mentis*; Barlow suggests *ventis*.
^c Corrected from *morte*.

That it may be as the safest ship on the sea, not frail,
I pray for you to pilot our song to port.

Neither permit the craft to be shaken in envious winds,
nor let it dread a northern gale, but beach it on a
pleasant strand, yourself as helmsman, lest struck on
a rock it founder.

Be a just critic to this, in the manner of a teacher.

I pray you add what is lacking and remove what is
excessive.

I believe none can injure himself under you as tutor.

Thus may my small book begin to become yours, that it
may lack flaws and be exalted in praises.

Wishing to avoid idly wasting mind and talents while
songs may please many, I strove to record the Norman
Conquest in verse.

I deemed it better to sing in melodic poetry than to apply
my genius to frivolous pursuits, and also verse is
superior to describe the feats of the mighty.

What William the royal heir accomplished in western
lands I have etched in the books of posterity.

For by force he recovered a kingdom stolen from him,
and as conqueror extended the borders of his realm
across the sea.

Therefore it is proper to commemorate his feats through
the ages.

CARMEN

Justiciae cultor • patriae pax • hostibus hostis •

    Tutor et eccleasiae rex benedicte vale •

Amodo torpentes decet evigilare Camenas •

    Et calamos alacres[a] reddere laude tua •

Mutasti comitis regali nomine nomen •   30

    Quod tibi nobilitas contulit et probitas •

Julius alter enim cujus renovando triumphum •

    Effraenem gentem cogis amare jugum •

[a] *Calamos* translated as 'pen' in earlier editions.

THE SONG

Cultivator of justice, peace of the fatherland, foe of the
  enemy, defender and blessed king of the church,
  farewell!

For now it is fitting the dreamy Muses awaken and
  make their pipes spirited in your praise.

You exchanged the title duke for a royal name because
  nobility and integrity united in you.[3]

Indeed another Caesar,[4] in renewing whose triumph,
  you compel an unbridled people to love the yoke.

---

[3] William the Bastard, Duke of Normandy, was a direct descendent
of Rollo or Robert I, the first duke of Normandy. Rollo was a Norse
sea-lord who raided France repeatedly in the late 9th and early 10th
centuries with a mixed band of enterprising Norsemen, Danes and
Anglo-Danes from East Anglia and Northumbria. They devastated
wealthy abbeys, priories and market towns as far as Paris. Rollo
was given the duchy of Normandy under treaty with King Charles
the Simple in 911 in exchange for limiting his raiding to foreign
lands and protecting France from rival sea-armies. William was the
only son of Duke Robert the Magnificent by his mistress Herleva. He
was confirmed as heir before his father made pilgrimage to
Jerusalem. Robert died on the return journey in 1035. Duke
William was known as William the Bastard before his conquest of
England gave him the preferred sobriquet of William the Conqueror.

[4] The Normans identified strongly with Julius Caesar, believing
Normandy was formerly privileged by him as *Belgium Julii Caesaris*.
They may have studied *Commentaries on the Gallic Wars* in
preparation for the conquest of England. Like Caesar, Duke William
originally planned to use the highest tides around the September full
moon to cross the Channel by night, moor off-shore, then enter an
estuarine port at daylight on a flooding tide.

Innumerus terrae populus nec perfida nautis •

    Aequora • nec litus saxa nociva ferens •   35

Incumbens hyemis nec te deterruit horror •

    Quin ab avis peteres regna relicta tibi •

Posteritate favet tibi jus legis quoque summa •

    Ergo tibi terror omnis ademptus erat •

Tempore sed longo te trans freta ducere classes •   40

    Tempestas prohibet imber et assiduus •

Dum prestolaris ventorum prosperitatem •

    Et mare turbatum cogit abire retro •

Eurus et equoreas crispabat flatibus undas •

Not the countless people of the land, nor seas
treacherous for mariners, nor the looming rocky coast,
nor dread of impending winter discouraged you from
seeking the kingdom bequeathed to you by your
forefathers.

Justice favours your inheritance, likewise the highest
law,[5] therefore fear of each was cast away from you.

But for a long time storms and incessant rain prevent
you leading the fleets across the strait.

While you wait a favourable wind, both raging sea drives
you to back and tossing surf curls in the east wind.

---

[5] William had several claims to the crown of England. Marriage
articles between Richard II of Normandy and King Aethelred II of
England for Emma of Normandy provided that her children would
have precedence over sons by his first wife, as she was married in
the Christian rite and consecrated queen, and that descendants of
Richard the Fearless, her father, would succeed to the English
throne if Aethelred had no surviving sons. William of Poitiers says
that King Edward formally adopted Duke William as his heir.
William of Malmesbury says that Duke William was appointed heir
in 1052 on the advice of Stigand, with the consent of Godwin and
Harold in settlement of their revolt. Edward may even have agreed
the succession with his kinsman before returning to England in
1041, then middle-aged, childless and aware of the brutal fates of
his seven brothers, particularly Godwin's treachery against Alfred in
1036. The *Carmen* suggests the Witans' assent to the succession at
lines 291-94, possibly during William's visit to England in 1051
when the duke visited England or 1052 in settlement of the revolt.
As King Edward sickened he asked for an envoy; dapifer Hubert de
Rie was sent from Normandy and brought back a two-handled sword
from King Edward, possibly signifying the unity of duchy and
kingdom under William's future rule. The *Carmen* says both ring
and sword were sent to Duke William at line 295. Finally, Pope
Alexander II supported William of Normandy's claim in 1066; he
provided a banner and a letter obliging the clerics of England to
recognise William as king in canonical duty.

Tunc tibi planctus erat spesque negata viae •   45

Tuque vellis nolis tandem tua litora linquens •

Navigium vertis litus ad alterius •

Portus ab antiquis Vimaci fertur haberi •

Quae[a] vallat portum Somana nomen aquae •

Docta nimis bello gens est per cuncta fidele •   50

Fluctivagis praebens sepius hospicium •

[a] *Que* in earlier transcriptions.

Then there was lament, and hope of passage was
  denied to you, and like it or not, at last quitting your
  coast you turn the fleet to another's shore.

Vimeu is said to have been a port from ancient times; [6]
  the name of the waters which surround the port is the
  Somme.[7]

The people are exceptionally shrewd in combat,
  thoroughly reliable, often providing hospitality to the
  wave-tossed.[8]

---

[6]   Vimeu was a large barony with its manorial seat 9 miles inland.
Use of the manorial seat in naming the port suggests coastal Franks
retained the Roman naming convention, identifying a port by its
associated fortress or emporium. Such a naming convention would
aid recognition in foreign courts and abbeys where local place names
would be unfamiliar. The emporium of Paris is similarly remote from
the Port de Paris at Saint-Denis. Shakespeare reminds us of a
another Norman naming convention; the battlefield of Agincourt in
Henry V is named for the nearest fortification. Following the same
logic, the Battle of Hastings was named for the nearest fortified
settlement, not the place where the battle was fought.

[7]   Like the Brede Basin opposite on the Sussex coast, the medieval
Baie de Somme reached deep inland as a wide, sheltered, estuarine
basin with many subsidiary creeks. And like Rye, the town of St
Valery was situated on a spur of land enisled at high tide, accessible
by causeway at low tide. The Romans and coastal Gauls preferred
such arrangements for their trading cantons, as islands offered
superior security from hinterland tribes, and mercantile traffic over
causeways or canals was easier to control and tax.

[8]   The description of St Valery residents is likely satirical. The
locals were famous pirates and wreckers. Ships taken by violence,
forced into port by gales, or even wrecked with false lights, would be
plundered for sport and profit. Anyone of high status taken alive
would be held for ransom.

Desuper est castrum quoddam Sancti Walarici •
  Hic tibi longa fuit difficilisque mora •
Nam ter quinque dies complesti finibus illis •
  Exspectans summi judicis auxilium •   55
Ecclesiam sancti devota mente frequentans •
  Illi pura dabas ingeminando preces •
Inspicis et templi gallus qua vertitur aura •
  Auster si spirat laetus ab inde redis •
Si subito Boreas Austrum divertit et arcet •   60
  Effusis lacrimis fletibus ora rigas •
Desolatus eras • frigus faciebat et imber •
  Et polus obtectus nubibus et pluviis •
Desolatus eras • frigus faciebat et imber •
  Et polus obtectus nubibus et pluviis •
Sed Pater omnipotens in quo tibi spem posuisti •
  Tempora qui fecit • temperat atque regit •   65
Qui palmo coelum • terram • mare • ponderat aeque
  Cui proprium constat omnibus esse locis •
Praesentem precibus dedit et calcabile Petro •
  Equor sub pedibus compaciendo sibi •

Above the port is the fortress of Saint Valery.[9] Here the
delay was long and irksome for you. For fifteen days
you occupied those regions, awaiting aid of the
Supreme Judge.

Visiting the church of the saint devoutly, you offer
prayers to Him, redoubled by chastity,[10] while you
watch by which wind the weathercock of the sanctuary
is turned.

If the south wind should blow, you go back joyful
thence; if suddenly the North wind shifts and hinders
the South, you wet your face in streams of flowing
tears.

You had been forsaken. It was cold and foggy, and the
sky was shrouded in cloud and rain.

But the Father is all powerful, in whom you placed
hope.

Who makes the seasons, rules and tempers them also.

He who weighs in his palm sky, earth and sea alike,
whose essence is sure to be present in all places, who
in compassion even granted prayers to Peter, that the
surface of the sea be walkable beneath his feet.[11]

---

[9] The Benedictine abbey and market town at St Valery-sur-Somme
were within a fortified stronghold on a tidal island linked to the
mainland by a causeway, like Rye and Iham opposite in the Brede
Basin.

[10] The prayers of the chaste were deemed more acceptable to God.

[11] Matthew 14:28-29.

Velle tuum tandem pius ut Deus est miseratus •   70
   Pro votoque tibi suppeditavit opus •
Expulit a coelo nubes et ab aequore ventos •
   Frigora dissolvit • purgat et imbre polum •
Incaluit tellus nimio profusa calore •
   Et Phebus solito clarior emicuit •   75
Festa dies Michaelis erat celebranda per orbem •
   Cum pro velle tibi cuncta Deus tribuit •
Protinus una fuit mens omnibus aequa voluntas •
   Jam bene pacato credere se pelago •
Quamquam diversi tamen adsunt laetificati •   80
   Nec mora quisque suum currit ad officium •
Sublimant alii malos • aliique laborant •
   Erectis malis addere vela super •
Plurima cogit equos equitum pars scandere naves •
   Altera festinat arma locare sua •   85
Haut secus invadit classis loca turba pedestris •
   Turba columbarum quam sua tecta petit •

You at last were willing to be dutiful, that God might be
   compassionate, and acceding to your vow,[12]
   He supplied to you the means.

He drove clouds from the heavens and swells from the
   sea.

He diffused the cold. He cleared the sky of rain.

The earth warmed greatly in ample heat, and the sun
   shone forth brighter than usual.

Michaelmas was to be celebrated around the world[13]
   when God granted everything according to your wish.

At once all men were of one mind and like purpose, to
   entrust themselves to the now becalmed sea.

Though spread out, they converge joyfully, nor delay,
   as each man rushes to his duty.

Some step the masts and others labour to rig sails upon
   the raised masts.

Many gather the knights' horses to board the ships.

Others hasten to stow their weapons.

A mob of infantry takes their places in the fleet no
   differently than a flock of doves settles to its dovecote.

---

[12] A deed of Takeley Priory suggests Duke William vowed to found
an order for St Valery in England and fulfilled the vow in 1068.

[13] 27th September 1066.

Scene 37: Loading the ships with armour, weapons and supplies.

O quanto subito fragor illinc ortus habetur •

    Cum nautae remos arma petunt equites[a] •

Hinc resonando tube varios dant mille boatus •   90

    Fistula cum calamis • et fidibus cythara •

Timpana taurinis implent mugitibus auras •

    Alternant modulos cymbala clara suos •

Terra tremit • coelumque pavet • miratur et \<a>equor •

    Quadrupedes fugiunt piscis avisque simul •   95

Quippe decem decies decies et milia quinque[b] •

    Diversis feriunt vocibus astra poli •

---

[a] *Pedestris, nautae* and *equites* evidence early division of Norman military forces into infantry, navy and cavalry.

[b] Jean des Murs in the 1341 *Opus quadripartitum numerorum sive de mensurandi ratione* at line 1075 states *mille cubus sit, ergo decem decies decies* – 'a thousand is a cube, therefore ten times ten times ten'. Missing this simple formula, other editors have come up with highly exaggerated numbers.

Oh, imagine how great the sudden uproar in that place, when mariners take up their oars and knights their arms!

Echoing from here, trumpets sound a thousand different calls, together with reed pipes and stringed harps.

Ox hide drums complement their airs with a rumbling, shrill cymbals accentuating the rhythms.

The earth shakes, the sky quakes, and the sea marvels.

Beasts flee, birds and fish likewise.

Surely ten times ten times ten and five thousand more men in varied voices re-echo to the Pole Star![14]

11c illustration from the Abbey de Saint Aubin d'Angers

[14] Six thousand men would imply 600 to 1,000 ships, consistent with other accounts. Ships would also transport servants, horses, weapons, tools, provisions and non-combatants such as grooms, clerics, cooks, masons and carpenters. All ships of this era also carried small, portable forges and smiths for ironworking.

Sed tu templa petis sancti supra memorati •

   Muneribusque datis curris adire ratem •

Clangendoque tuba reliquis ut litora linquant •   100

   Praecipis et pelagi tucius alta petant •

Hactenus adfixae solvuntur litore pup<p>es •

   Equor et intratur agmine composito •

Iam breviata dies iam sol devexus abibat •

   Cum tua preripuit previa navis iter •   105

Nox ubi caeca polum tenebrosis occupat umbris •

   Et negat obsequium Cinthia tecta tibi •

Imples non aliter facibus rutilantibus undas •

   Sydera quam caelum sole ruente replent •

Quot fuerant naves totidem tu lumina spargis[a] •   110

Impositae malis permulta luce la<n>ternae •

   Tramite directo per mare vela regunt •

[a] A pentameter may be missing at this point in the manuscript.

But you seek the shrine of the above-mentioned Saint
Valery, and after you give offerings, you hasten aboard
your ship.

And sounding the trumpet, you order the rest of the
fleet to leave the shore and prudently strike for
the depths of the sea.

Hitherto moored, the sterns cast loose from the shore,
and take to the open sea in orderly procession.

The days now short, the inclined sun was already setting,
when your flagship in the lead set the course.

When dark night overspread the sky in gloomy shadows,
and the veiled moon denied to you her services, you
overspread the waves with glowing torches, no
differently than the constellations refill the heavens in
place of the fallen sun.

As many as were the ships, so many are the lights you
scatter.

The lanterns raised on masts, by their wide-cast light,
guide the sails on a straight course through the sea.

Scene 38: Ships form a tidy fleet off-shore for the Channel crossing

Sed veritus ne dampna tuis nox inferat atra •

   Ventus et adverso flamina turbet aquas •

Sistere curva jubes compellat ut anchora puppes •   115

   In medio pelagi litus adesse facis •

Ponere vela mones • exspectans mane futurum •

   Ut lassata nimis gens habeat requiem •

At postquam terris rutilans aurora refulsit •

   Et Phebus radios sparsit in orbe suos •   120

Praecipis ire viam committere carbasa ventis •

   Praecipis ut solvat anchora fixa rates •

But fearful lest dark night impose losses on your men, and wind roil the sea in contrary gusts, you order the ships to stations so the curved anchor might restrain their sterns.[15]

In the middle of the sea you make a sea-harbour.[16]

You advise the sails be laid down pending the morning ahead in order that your exceedingly weary people might have rest.

But after reddening daybreak shone on the land, and the sun cast its rays over the world, you gave the command to make way, to set light sails[17] to the winds.

You ordered that the anchor fixing the raft be weighed.

---

[15] *Pevenesæ* in the Bayeux Tapestry and *Pefenesea* in the *Anglo-Saxon Chronicle Version D* for 1066 likely identify an anchorage in the seascape for dropping anchor to muster the fleet while awaiting the flow of the next tide for coastal navigation or estuarine passage inland to port. All variants of *Pefenesea* or *Peuenesae* in the *Anglo-Saxon Chronicle* are for ships mustering, lying to, sheltering or being raided. The 11th century location may correspond to Lydd as lyð meant a sheltered anchorage in Anglo-Saxon. Modern Pevensey was founded in the 13th century and is wholly irrelevant to 1066.

[16] The Normans learned the crescent-shaped 'sea-harbour' formation in the Mediterranean. One ship drops anchor while the sterns of the others are chained together in an arc-shaped raft, bows outward for defence by archers. Smaller vessels are protected within the arc of the larger ships' sterns. Rafting reduces the risk of fouled anchors as the ships resume their course. The maneuver is described by Leo VI in *Taktika,* Constitution XIX.

[17] *Carbasa* are light sails made of linen or flax rather than wool, perhaps preferred for estuarine navigation.

Tertia telluri supereminet hora diei •

Cum mare postponens litora tuta tenes •

E coelo fulgens extenso crine cometes •   125

Anglis fatatum nunciat excidium •

Debita terra tibi pavidis nudata colonis[a] •

Laeta sinu placido[b] teque tuosque capit[c] •

Scene 32: Halley's Comet is seen in England immediately after Harold's usurping the crown

[a] *Colonis* here and at lines 637 and 667 implies settlers or tenants on ecclesiastical lands: Rameslege, Westminster and London.

[b] *Sinu placido et capaci* is similarly used by Pliny the Elder to describe a spacious and placid gulf or basin where whales congregate to breed. *Historiae Naturalis* IV:6.

[c] *Capio* in nautical usage means to reach an intended destination.

22

The third hour of the day overspread the earth when,
   leaving the sea behind, you reach a sheltered strand.[18]

From the sky a gleaming long-tailed comet foretold the
   English doom.[19]

Depopulated of its terrorised settlers,[20] the happy land
   owed to you embraced you and yours in a calm basin.

Scene 39 shows ships being poled to a sheltered strand, masts and rigging being struck,
horses led ashore in knee-deep or shallower water, and oarports opened for inland rowing.

---

[18] These lines describe a placid basin three hours from the sea.
Fécamp Abbey's estate at Rameslege embraced the sheltered and
sandy Brede Basin, almost exactly three hours' tidal navigation from
the breach in the shingle offshore at Lydd. The territory had been
held under charter of King Cnut, confirmed by all subsequent kings,
from 1017 until Godwin and Harold violently seized the port in 1052.

[19] Halley's Comet was taken as a portent of great events. It
appeared during May 1066, however, not September.

[20] The Anglo-Norman clerics and colonists of Rameslege were killed,
enslaved or exiled by Godwin and Harold in 1052.

Rex Heraldus enim sceleratus ad ultima terrae •

   Fratris ad exicium perfida tela parat •   130

Non modicam regni partem nam frater adeptus •

   Tecta dabat flammis • et gladiis populum •

Marte sub opposito currens Heraldus in hostes •

   Non timuit fratris tradere membra neci •

Alter in alterutrum plus quam civile[a] peregit •   135

   Bellum • sed victor proh dolor ipse fuit •

Invidus ille Cain fratris caput amputat ense •

   Et caput et corpus sic sepelivit humo •

Haec tibi praevidit qui debita regna subegit •

   Criminis infesti quatenus ultor eas[b] •   140

[a] St Augustine, Orosius and Isidore of Seville all give *plusquam civile* as one of the four types of war, meaning war between brothers or close kinsmen.

[b] A foreshadowing of Harold's beheading and anonymous burial seems more appropriate than earlier editors' interpretation of the agency of God as avenger. Traitors, oathbreakers and excommunicants were dismembered and given anonymous burials on unhallowed land to reinforce the severity of their transgression in breaking an oath of allegiance or separating from the church and discourage cults.

For wicked King Harold, at the far end of the land, raised his treacherous blades to cut down a brother, for his brother had occupied no small part of the kingdom,[21] putting roofs to the flame and people to the sword.

Rushing his army under arms against his enemies,[22] Harold did not fear to deliver the limbs of his brother to death.

Each against the other waged internecine war, but alas, Harold was the victor.

That envious Cain severed his brother's head by sword, and so head and body he buried in the earth.

He who subjugated the kingdom owed to you foreshadowed this: what course the avenger of a hostile crime might follow.[23]

---

[21] Tostig Godwinson was stripped of his earldom in Northumbria and exiled following a revolt by northern thegns in 1065 against oppressive taxation and violence against churches. Tostig's kinship to Duke William by marriage may have been a factor in Harold's alienation from his brother. Tostig took refuge in Bruges and sought an alliance of Flanders and Normandy against Harold. Tostig raided the south of England from the Isle of Wight in the spring of 1066 with a mercenary fleet from Flanders, then raided Norfolk and Lincolnshire, where he lost men and ships. He spent the summer in Scotland with King Malcolm III before joining forces with Harald Hardrada, king of Norway. They defeated northern defenders at the Battle of Fulford on 20th September, but were defeated at Stamford Bridge on 25th September.

[22] King Harold had raced his army from the south to the north to take the invaders by surprise. He attacked their unprepared camp before dawn, a technique he had practiced in his 1063 Welsh raids.

[23] Tostig's beheading and anonymous burial in unhallowed ground foreshadow Harold's own beheading and shallow, coastal burial.

Litora custodis metuens omittere[a] naves •

  Moenibus et munis • castraque ponis ibi •

Diruta quae fuerant dudum castella reformas[b] •

  Ponis custodes ut tueantur ea •

Non multo spacio tua gens se pace potita •   145

  Invadit terram, vastat et igne cremat •

Nec mirum regem quia te plebs[c] stulta negabat •

  Sons perit juste vadit et ad nichilum •

Ex Anglis unus latitans sub rupe marina •

  Cernit ut effusas innumeras acies •   150

Et quod agri fulgent pleni radiantibus armis •

  Vulcano flammis depopulante domos •

Perfidie gentem ferro baccante perire •

  Quasque dabant lacrimas cede patrum pueri •

Scandere currit[d] equum • festinat dicere regi •   155

---

[a] Amended from *amitere* by earlier editors.

[b] *Castellum* designates an auxiliary fortlet, cell or signal beacon, wheras *castrum* – as used at line 52 (St Valery-sur-Somme) and line 605 (Dover) – denotes a principal or head fortification. *Castella* cannot mean Pevensey Castle, being both plural and diminutive. Fortlets, cells or beacons at *Peneuesel* (Udimore) and *Hastingeport* (Iham or Icklesham) would be auxiliary to Fécamp Abbey, so a proper use of the plural diminutive.

[c] The use of *plebs* contrasts with the use of *colonis* for the rightful settlers at line 127, perhaps implying trespass.

[d] Here and at line 494, *scandere currit* – 'he runs to mount' – is translated as 'swiftly mounts'.

26

You secure a beachhead, fearing to lose the ships, and
fortify it with palisades, and pitch the camp therein.[24]

You restore the strongholds that were lately destroyed.[25]

You station garrisons that they may defend them.

Not much space has been occupied by your men in
peace; they invade the countryside, they lay waste and
put to the torch.

No wonder! Because the foolish commoners defied your
rule, the guilty die justly and go to annihilation.[26]

One Englishman kept hidden under the sea cliffs.

He sees the countless ranks stream forth, and the fields
that shine full of gleaming weapons, homes devoured
by blazing flames, the tribe of treachery done to death
in a frenzy of steel, and the tears which children shed
at the slaughter of their fathers.

He swiftly mounts a horse. He hastens to tell the king.

---

[24] Wace in his 12th century *Roman de Rou* says palisade panels were
brought in the ships to be fixed together with pins to quickly secure
the camp compound. This suggests the Normans selected their
campsite in advance and knew the ruined state of fortlets or cells.

[25] Cells of Fécamp Abbey were presumably destroyed by Godwin in
1052 when he seized Rameslege.

[26] Settlers on Fécamp Abbey lands in 1066 may have been regarded
as traitors or trespassers by returning Normans.

Scene 47: Homes burnt, maidens and children are taken captive.

Rex redit a bello praemia laeta ferens •

Nuncius occurrit quae fert hoc in ordine pandit •

Rex tibi pro certo nuncia dira fero •

Dux Normannorum cum Gallis atque Britannis •

Invasit terram • vastat et igne cremat • 160

Milia si quaeris tibi dicere nemo valebit •

Quot mare fert pisces tot sibi sunt equites •

Et veluti stellas coeli numerare nequires •

Ejus sic acies nec numerare vales •

Captivos ducit pueros • captasque puellas • 165

Insuper et viduas • et simul omne pecus •

The king had returned from war laden with rich spoils.[27]

The messenger rushed to meet him; what he brought he explained in this order:

"King, for certain I bring you dire tidings: the Duke of Normandy, with both Gauls and Bretons, has invaded the land. He is laying waste and putting to the torch.

"If you ask to be told his thousands, none can be sure. As many as the sea bears fish, such are his cavalry; and as you could not count the stars in the sky, just so, neither can you count his infantry.

"He leads boys as captives, while girls are seized as well as widows, and likewise all the cattle."[28]

Scene 40: The knights swiftly sack *Hestinga* to pillage supplies.

---

[27] Geoffrey of Monmouth in *Historia Regum Britanniae* suggested King Harold's refusal to return the spoils of Stamford Bridge to northern towns and thegns, or even share it generously with his own southern army, caused widespread disaffection, discouraging some forces from joining at Hastings.

[28] Slavery for war captives was customary in Anglo-Saxon England and Nordic realms but had been outlawed in France since King Dagobert in the 7th century. The Normans would outlaw slavery in England too within a generation.

Rusticus haec retulit rex contra sibilat illi •

   Quamvis haec timeat velle tamen simulat •

Advocat ipse duces comites terraeque potentes[a] •

   Verbis ut fertur talibus alloquitur •   170

Miliciae pars summa meae magnatibus orta •

   Solus non bello vincere cui pudor est •

Nothica quos misit per te superavimus hostes •

   Et per te nostrum • stravimus equivocum •

Nutrivit proprio matris[b] quem[c] lacte papilla •   175

   Tu mihi praesidium murum et auxilium •

Audisti nostrum quod gens Normannica regnum •

   Intravit praedans • pauperat • exspoliat •

Hoc Willelmus <audet>[d] qui te sibi subdere querit •

   Nomen habet magnum • cor tamen est pavidum •   180

Est vafer • et cupidus nimiumque superciliosus •

   Nec novit pacem • nec retinere fidem •

Si possit leviter molitur tollere nostra •

   Sed Deus Omnipotens non erit hoc paciens •

[a] Harold's army was led by earls and urban garrison commanders of
the fraternal order of Huscarls. Under reforms instituted by King
Cnut, thegns had become subordinate to earls. Only the elite
Huscarls directly served the king.
[b] Amended from *matrum* by earlier editors.
[c] Amended from *quam* by ealier editors.
[d] *Agit* added by earlier editors to complete the metre.

What the peasant reported the king hissed at scornfully.

Although King Harold might dread the news, he yet
pretended to welcome it.

He summoned the earls, thegns and nobles of the land.

As it is told, he addressed them in such words:

"My noblest warriors, sired by great men, to whom it is
shame only to win without combat!

"Through you we vanquished the enemy whom Norway
sent,[29] and through you we have laid low another such
of our own, him who suckled milk at my own mother's
teat.[30]

"You are to me a garrison, a barricade and a reserve
army!

"You have heard that the Normans invade our
kingdom.

"They pillage! They plunder! They despoil!

"William dares this, who asks that you submit to him.

"He has great repute, yet his heart is trembling.

"He is sly and greedy and arrogant beyond measure.

"He knows not peace nor will he keep faith.

"He designs lightly, if he can, to take away what is
ours.

"But God Almighty will not let this stand!

---

[29] King Harald Hardrada of Norway claimed the crown of England as
successor to his father, King Magnus. King Harthacnut had agreed
by treaty with King Magnus in 1040 that the survivor of the two
should reunite the Nordic kingdoms. After King Harthacnut's death
King Magnus ruled Denmark and extended his claim to England as
part of the Danish realm.

[30] Tostig Godwinson, Harold's brother.

Quantus erit luctus • quantus dolor et   185
    pudor ingens •

    Regni quanta lues quam tenebrosa dies •

Si quod querit habet • si regni sceptra tenebit •

    Hoc omnes fugiant vivere qui cupiunt •

His ita prolatis • quaerit responsa suorum •

    Scrutantur taciti dicere quid valeant •   190

Nascitur extimplo clamor qui perculit astra •

    Et vox communis omnibus una fuit •

Bella magis cupimus quam sub juga colla reponi •

    Alterius regis • vel magis inde mori •

Exultans fatuus rex grates reddidit illis •   195

    Insuper hoc unum concilium retulit •

Primum legatos decet ut mittamus ad illum •

    Illi qui dicant si placet ut redeat •

Pacificum si vult nobiscum foedus inire •

    Vestro consilio non ego reiciam •   200

Sin aliter • non sponte sua mea litora linquet •

    Desinat hoc quod agit trans freta regna petat •

Aequo consultu majorum nec ne minorum •

    Providus eloquio monachus eligitur •

Exploret qui castra ducis qui credita caute •   205

    Verba sibi referat regis ab imperio •

Acceleravit iter pedibus transvectus equinis •

    Sub tunica nigra verba uerenda gerens •

"How great will be the grief, how great sadness and
monstrous shame, how great the scourge of the
kingdom, how dark the day, if he gains what he seeks,
if he possesses mastery of the realm!

"Let all shun this who wish to live!"

This thus laid before them, Harold asked his men's reply.

They weighed in silence what they might wish to say.

Presently a battle-cry rose that echoed to the heavens,
and one voice became common to all:

"We spoil for war rather than place our necks under
the yoke of the foreign king!

"We prefer even death!"

Jubilant, the foolish king gave them thanks.

In addition he tendered this one condition:

"First, it is fitting that we send envoys to him, who are
to treat with him if he agrees to return.

"If he is willing to undertake a peace treaty with us, by
your counsel, I would not spurn him.

"If otherwise, not leaving my shores of his own accord,
he must quit this course that he has driven.

"Let him seek his kingdoms across the Channel!"

By counsel of the great and the lowly alike a sage monk
of eloquent speech was chosen who would seek out the
camp of the duke, who might securely carry thence the
words entrusted to him by command of the king.

He hastened along the intervening road by sure-footed
horse, carrying under his black tunic the menacing
words.

Dux erat in castris intrans haec monachus inquit •

   Est opus ut nostrae sic valeas patriae •   210

Rex et primates regni quoque[a] jura tenentes •

   Praecipiunt dicto quod cicius redeas •

Mirantur super his de te quae fama reportat •

   Quod sine re[b] regnum ducis ad excidium •

Captivos reddas • et quicquid vi rapuisti •   215

   Indulget si vis cetera damna tibi •

Aetati parcit • morum parcit levitati •

   Olim quae fuerat parcit amiciciae •

Si contra dicis • ut si sua reddere tardas •

   Bella tibi mandat • Ergo decet caveas •   220

Miliciam vix ipse suam populumque cohercet •

   Gens est quae nullum novit habere modum •

Nam Dominum testor bis sex sibi milia centum •

   Sunt pugnatorum proelia qui siciunt •

[a] *Quod* in earlier editions.
[b] Corrected from *te* by earlier editors.

The duke was in camp; reaching this the monk spoke:

"It is prudent that you bid farewell to our land!

"The king and nobles of the realm who rule lawfully order you return more quickly than I speak the words.

"And also they are amazed at what rumour reports of you, that you lead the kingdom to ruin without cause.

"Return the captives and whatever you have seized by force.

"If you will, the king pardons your other damages.

"He allows for age.

"He allows for capricious ways.

"He allows for the friendship that once was.

"If you say otherwise, or if you hesitate to return what is his own, he commands war against you.

"Thus it is fitting you be cautious.

"He himself can scarcely restrain his warriors and his people.

"This people is such as are famed to brook no bounds.[31]

"God as witness, there are twice six hundred thousand for him.

"They are fighters, who spoil for battle!"

---

[31] King Cnut had spread Anglo-Danish imperium from Iceland to St Petersburg in his lifetime, so the Anglo-Danish overlords of England in 1066 might well view themselves as knowing no borders or bounds.

Scene 46: Harold's envoy speaks to Duke William

Talibus objectis mutata leonis imago •   225

    Pondus virtutum • miles et intrepidus •

Dux floci pendens quicquid sibi vana cuculla •

    Attulerat • fatuas approbat esse minas •

Verba tua regis dixit non sunt sapientis •

    Nil latitare procul poterit hoc sapiat •   230

Excessi puerum • leviter nec regna petivi •

    Defunctis patribus debita jure mihi •

F<o>edus[a] amiciciae nostrae dissolvit inique •

    Dum tenet injuste quae mea jure forent •

Quod monet ut redeam furor est dementia summa •   235

    Tempus enim prohibet et via non facilis •

[a] Earlier editors suggested *sedus*. *Foedus* preferred here and at 279 as Old French *foedes* meant allies or collaborators and medieval Latin in other Frankish texts uses *fedus* as pact or truce.

At such reproaches the face of a lion emerged, befitting a knight, virtuous and fearless.

The duke held immaterial whatever the vain monk had brought him, deeming such empty threats.

"Your words are not those of a wise king," he said.

"He will not be able to remain in hiding at a distance.

"Let him understand this:

"I am past youth.

"Nor did I capriciously claim the realm owed in justice to me on the deaths of my forefathers.

"Our pact of friendship he villainously violated when he unfairly seized what ought justly to be mine.

"Insofar as he warns I ought to withdraw, he is raving; it is utter madness.

"Indeed the season forbids it, and the journey is not easy.

Scene 33: Harold is consecrated king by Stigand

Inmerito quamvis commitere bella minetur •

    In Domino fidens gens mea non refugit •

Nescit quae[a] furtiva mihi perjuria fecit •

    Nec penitus recolit quod meus iste fuit •   240

Si perjura manus nondum dampnata resultat •

    Divino tamen est jam rea judicio •

Si querit pacem • si vult delicta fateri •

    Indulgens culpae parcere prom\<p>tus ero •

Terram quam pridem tenuit pater hanc sibi   245
    reddam •

    Ut meus ante fuit si meus esse velit •

[a] Corrected from *quod*.

Scene 23: Harold swears vassalage on chests of holy relics in Normandy.

"However unjustly he threatens to wage war, trusting in the Lord, my people will not back down.

"Does he not know he broke his oath, stealing what is mine?

"Or has he forgotten altogether that he was made my vassal?

"If his perjured hand does not yet restore all things ill-gotten, even now the sinner is arraigned for divine trial.

"If he wants peace, if he will confess his crimes, I would readily pardon him, forgiving his offences.

"Such land as his father formerly held I will restore to him, if he wishes to be my vassal, as he was before."[32]

---

[32] According to Norman sources and the Bayeux Tapestry Earl Harold became William's sworn vassal in Normandy.

Monachus accelerat reditum • Dux praeparat arma •

   Heraldi mentem noverat atque dolum •

Admonet • inflammat • confortans corda suorum •

   Francia quos genuit nobilitate cluens •   250

Belligeri sine felle viri famosa juventus •

   Quos Deus elegit • vel quibus ipse favet •

Fama volat quorum per climata • quattuor • orbis •

   Invictusque manens miliciae titulus •

Gensque Britannorum quorum decus exstat   255
   in armis •

   Tellus ni fugiat est fuga nulla quibus •

Viribus illustres Cenomanni gloria quorum •

   Bello monstratur per probitatis opem[a] •

Apulus et Calaber Siculus[b] quibus jacula fervent •

   Normanni faciles actibus egregiis •   260

[a] There is no entirely satisfactory translation for this unusual phrase, which recurs at line 334. It seems to convey an early concept of chivalry, the noble use of force.

[b] Pope Nicholas II had invested Robert Guiscard of Normandy with a kingdom of Apulia, Calabria and Sicily in 1059 by the Treaty of Melfi, granting him a papal banner to carry against the Saracens. The successful Mediterranean conquests and restoration of the pope to Rome may have inspired the Norman invasion of England, as well as providing experienced mercenaries, mariners and artillerymen.

The monk hastened back.

The duke prepared his forces.

He knew Harold's mind and also his trickery.

He rouses, he rallies, emboldening his men's hearts:

"Renowned for nobility, the knights whom France begets are famed men of war, without malice, whom God has preferred, or indeed those He himself favours!

"Fame of whom has spread to the four corners of the Earth, so they hold the military accolade 'invincible'!

"And people of Brittany, the dignity of whom stands forth in arms; unless the earth itself should give way, none puts such men to flight!

"Illustrious men of Maine,[33] the glory of whom is displayed in war through feats of chivalry!

"Apulian, Calabrian, Sicilan! Whose flying darts swarm![34]

"Normans! Ever-ready to achieve the extraordinary!

---

[33] Duke William's first conquest was the neighbouring county of Maine in France, which he annexed to Normandy in 1064. He followed this by defeating Conan II of Brittany and allying Brittany to Normandy in 1065, aided by Harold Godwinson.

[34] Mariners, archers and crossbowmen from the Norman campaigns in the Mediterranean were recruited in 1066. Normans in the Mediterranean had proven the effectiveness of artillery and cavalry against massed infantry and had mastered sea transport of men, materiel and horses in great fleets.

Falsus et infamis, perjurus rex et adulter •

  Molitur nobis tendit et insidias •

Ejus enim mos est non vis • vincere fraude •

  Spondendoque fidem porrigit ore necem •

Ergo cavere decet ne decipiamur ab illo •   265

  Ni simus risus ludus et in populo •

Mandamus vobis quapropter castra tueri •

  Irruat in castris ne malus ille latro •

Sed cras si dignum vobis videatur et aequum •

  Contra quem misit vana referre mihi •   270

Reddere legatum pro verbis verba paratum •

  Illi mitamus qui minimum timeat •

Scene 15: Harold spurns both church and noble wife.

"False and infamous, a perjured king and adulterer,[35] Harold soothes us even as he prepares ambush.[36]

"Indeed, it is his practice to conquer not by force but by deceit,[37] and a pledge of faith from his mouth tenders murder.

"Therefore it is fitting to be wary lest we be deceived by him, and lest we become the butt of jokes among his people. Wherefore we charge you to protect the camp, lest that evil brigand breach our stronghold.

"But on the morrow, if you deem it fit and proper, in exchange for the one he sent to bring empty words to me, we should return an envoy prepared word for word, that one who fears least.

---

[35] Calling Harold 'adulterer' may refer to Harold's betraying a noble Norman wife or fiancée. Walter of Coventry in the *Memoriale Fratris* says that Harold was married to William's half-sister in 1064, bringing her to England but then repudiating her. Wace's *Roman de Rou* suggests betrothal to William's young daughter, with marriage to follow when she was of age. Either rite celebrated in the church would render Harold's marriage to Edith of Mercia in 1066 adulterous.

[36] The risk of siege by land and sea is consistent with a camp on the on the cape of Hastingas, where Harold's fleet could blockade the Normans' retreat through the Rye Camber while a land army blocked advance over the isthmus to the mainland.

[37] Harold preferred surprise attacks on enemy camps, using a series of night attacks in Wales in 1063 and a daybreak attack on the unprepared camp at Stamford Bridge in 1066. His father Godwin similarly preferred surprise night attacks in his Baltic campaigns.

Monachus est nobis quo non moderancior alter •

    Et nulli cedens rhetoris officio •

Signifer insignis ni regula sacra negaret •   275

    Si vobis placeat hic mea dicta ferat. •

Dixit et est actum • complevit et actio dictum •

    Monachus accitur • nec mora carpit iter •

Interea f<o>edes[a] fuscatae fraudis et heres •

    Nocte sub obscura furis in arte vigens •   280

Rex acies armare jubet • ducis atque latenter •

    Mandat ut invadant agmina si valeant •

Estimat invigiles prosternere fraudibus hostes •

    Fallere dum querit fallitur atque ruit •

Dux quia directo legato pervigil exstat •   285

    Ejus et ingenio conscius artis erat •

Divertens legatus iter per devia terrae •

    Nescius accessit rex ubi furta facit •

Pro merito de parte ducis rex inquit aveto •

    Quem non ex aequo cogis inire malum •   290

Hoc quia perplures testantur et asserit idem •

    Assensu populi consilio procerum •

Etguardus quod rex ut ei succederet heres •

    Annuit • et fecit teque favente sibi •

---

[a] Barlow suggested *sedes* for *fedes*. *Foedes* preferred on same
rationale as at 233.

"There is a monk than whom no other among us is more self-controlled, and he yields to none in courtly rhetoric, fit to be a standard-bearer if not barred by sacred vow. If it please you, let him bear my words."[38]

As it was said it was done; the action fulfilled the word. The monk was fetched; he took the road without delay.

Meanwhile the ally and heir of veiled treachery, under dark night's cover, was active with a thief's craft.

King Harold ordered his men to arms while still concealed from the duke. He ordered them to attack the duke's troops if they could.

He reckoned to overthrow an unwary enemy by stratagem. While seeking to surprise, he was yet taken by surprise – and ruined.

Having dispatched his envoy the duke remained vigilant and by nature was wary of trickery.

The envoy, detouring through byways, approached unseen where King Harold was preparing his ambush.

As is fitting he said:

"I bring greetings on behalf of the duke, O King, whom you compel unjustly to cause harm.

"Because very many witness this, and he claims likewise, with agreement of the people on advice of the nobles, King Edward declared him heir that he might succeed him, and he made this so himself with your favour.[39]

---

[38] Wace identifies Huon Margot, a monk of Fécamp Abbey.

[39] William of Poitiers reported that Godwin and Harold confirmed William as heir in settlement the 1052 rebellion.

Anulus est illi testis concessus et ensis •   295
    Quae per te nosti missa fuisse sibi •
Est igitur servanda fides • jurata teneri •
    Nexibus atque sacris dextera stricta manus •
Ergo decet videas ne te perjuria laedant •
    Et jurata tene salvus ut esse queas •   300
Heraldus vultu distorto colla retorquens •
    Legato dixit • vade retro stolide •
Judice cras domino regni pars justa patebit •
    Dividet ex aequo sacra manus Domini •
Ille retro gressum vertens per devia rursum •   305
    A quo missus erat huic maledicta refert •

Scene 48: William's army advances along a road

CARMEN DE TRIUMPHO NORMANNICO
CARMEN DE TRIUMPHO NORMANNICO

"The ring and sword bestowed on him are his tokens of faith,[40] which you know through you were conveyed to him.[41]

"Faith is well-served that is held to as it was sworn, and so your right hand binds you in sacred bonds.[42]

"It is fitting therefore you beware lest perjury condemn you, and hold to your vow, that you may be saved."

Neck twisting, face distorted, Harold said to the envoy:

"Go back, fool!

"By the Lord as judge tomorrow lays plain the rightful claim to the kingdom.

"Let the sacred hand of the Lord apportion justly!"

Retracing his course back, again through byways, the monk carried these taunts to him by whom he was sent.

---

[40] The ring and sword are two of the five royal regalia: ring, sword, crown, rod and sceptre. A gift of ring and sword would have been powerful evidence of King Edward's intent for the succession.

[41] Harold's trip to Normandy may have accompanied the return of envoy Hubert de Rie, who brought a two-handled sword and other gifts from King Edward as described in annals of Colchester Abbey.

[42] Norman accounts say Harold was knighted by Duke William after the campaign against Conan II of Brittany, accepting vassalage and swearing loyalty on caskets of holy relics to William as his future king.

47

Imperiale decus • dux • pax • et gloria regni •

    Praevius incedens ante suas acies •

Aggregat et strictim compellit abire quirites •

    Et faciles hasta conglomerare facit •   310

Legati facies nativo cassa rubore •

    Pallor et ostendit proxima bella fore •

Dux ait • Est ubi rex • Non longe monachus inquit •

    Dixit in aure sibi signa videre potes •

Plurima verba fero • quae censeo non referenda •   315

    Illa tamen dicam quae reticere nocet •

Ex inproviso sperat te fallere posse •

    Per mare • per terram praelia magna parat •

In mare quingentas fertur misisse carinas •

    Ut nostri reditus praepediatur iter •   320

Quo graditur silvas plani deducit adesse •

    Et per quae transit flumina sicca facit •

Scene 49: William views the English with the envoy from a height

48

In imperial splendour, the duke, peace and glory of the realm, proceeding before the ranks of his army,[43] convened his commanders,[44] gathered them slightly forward, and bade them assemble loosely by his planted lance.[45]

The face of the envoy was drained of its ruddy hue; his pallor foretold the battle to be imminent.

The duke asked, "Where is the king?"

"Not far," said the monk. He spoke in his ear, "You can see his standards."

"I bring many words I deem unimportant, yet I will tell what might damage left unsaid.

"He hopes he may ambush you.

"He prepares great battles by sea and on land. It is said he has sent five hundred vessels[46] to sea so as to hinder our course of return.

"Where he advances the forests are levelled to the plain and he makes dry the rivers which he crosses.[47]

---

[43] The Normans are already mounted and on the march.

[44] *Quirites* were those promised land and title in exchange for military service and tribute.

[45] *Hasta* – referencing a planted lance – here and at line 447 calls the commanders to assembly, consistent with Roman military practice.

[46] *Carinas* were smaller, faster, dual-purpose ships used for military transport, raiding and trade, an Anglo-Saxon variant on the Nordic *knorr*. They had a single sail amidship and a row of oars, adaptable to either coastal or estuarine navigation.

[47] Juvenal, *Satires*, x. 173, and Justin, *Epitome*, ii.10. William of Poitiers uses the same analogy in the *Gesta Guillelmi*, ¶16, having used the *Carmen* as one of his sources.

Fors numerum metues • Numerus sed viribus expers •

   Plurimus a minimo s<a>epe repulsus abit.

Est sibi milicies unctis depexa capillis •   325

   Feminei juvenes Martis in arte pigri •

Et quot sunt ovibus • totidem sunt aequiparandi •

   Ut vulpes pavidi fulguris ad sonitum •

Nobilium memor esto patrum dux magne tuorum •

   Et quod fecit avus quodque pater facias •   330

Normannos proavus superavit avusque Britannos

   Anglorum genitor sub juga colla dedit •

Et tu quid facies nisi quod majora parando •

   Succedas illis per probitatis opem •

"Should you fear their great number? Their forces are numerous but lack experience.[48]

"The greater number will often fall away, thrust back by the smaller force.

"His noble warriors have combed oiled tresses; they are girly-youths inept in the arts of Mars.[49]

"And as many as they are, they are to be reckoned as the same number of sheep, taking fright at the crash of thunder, like foxes.

"Be mindful of your noble forefathers, great Duke, and do as your forefathers have done. Your great-grandfather conquered the Normans, and your grandfather the Bretons.

"The tribe of the English yields its neck to your yoke.

"And you also will prevail, if not surpass themyou're your greater preparation.

"You may excel them through noble feats!"

---

[48] Duke William recruited experienced warriors from all Norman and Frankish parts of Europe, where King Harold had to fight with such Huscarls, thegns, bondsmen and fyrd as he could raise locally, supplemented by Danish mercenaries. Many English were poorly equipped. They also lacked wide experience of war. In battle the English fought shield wall to shield wall, or surprise attacks as Harold practiced in Wales and Stamford Bridge. The Normans were much better armed, better disciplined in combat, and practised in wreaking havoc on massed infantry, alternating artillery barrages with cavalry and infantry charges.

[49] The Normans considered long hair as unmanly and untrimmed beards as brutish. Normans kept their hair cut quite short at back and sides, and facial hair was kept well-trimmed. Short hair had a practical advantage in making chain mail and armour more comfortable to wear.

Paulo conticuit faciens et se remoratum •   335

   Armatas acies ordinat imperio •

Praemisit pedites commitere bella sagittis •

   Et balistantes inserit in medio •

Quatinus infigant volitancia vultibus arma •

   Vulneribusque datis ora retro faciant •   340

Ordine post pedites sperat stabilire quirites •

   Occursu belli set sibi non licuit •

Haut procul hostiles cuneos nam cernit adesse •

   Et plenum telis irradiare nemus •

The duke was silent awhile and composed himself.

He arrayed the armed forces in his command.

He sent archers before infantry to start the battle, and placed the crossbowmen[50] in the centre, that flying bolts might drive into faces, and wounds inflicted in their front rank might force a retreat.

He intended to station his commanders behind the infantry, but confronted with war this was not allowed to him, for he discerned the enemy columns approaching from not far off and the forest shimmering, full with weapons.

Scene 51b: The archers and crossbowmen in the middle of cavalry

---

[50] Ths is the first use of the crossbow in England, brought by Norman allies from Mediterranian campaigns. Heavy iron bolts could pierce armour and shields from afar, weakening the massed English front line prior to cavalry and infantry charges. The Gallic allies thus remained safely beyond reach of hand weapons and javelins in the early battle while causing carnage from below.

Mars deus o belli gladiis qui sceptra coherces •   345

    Corpora cui juvenum sanguinolenta placent •

Et cruor effusus per multa cede virorum •

    Quis tibi tunc animus quanta cupido[a] mali •

Cum medius saevas acies miscere jubebas •

    Quo potius nullum te juvat excidium •   350

Ex quo Pompeium superavit Julius armis •

    Et romana sibi moenia subripuit •

Compulit atque metu vili transire per amnem •

    Nulla reor cedes tam tibi grata fuit •

Nec juvenile decus nec te reverenda senectus •   355

    Nec peditum vilis et miseranda manus •

Flectere nec valuit te nobilitudo parentum •

    Quin ageres quicquid mens tua torva cupit •

Caecatos miseros radiantia trudis in arma •

    Et veluti ludum cogis adire necem •   360

Quid moror in verbis cum jam furor extat in armis •

    Exple velle tuum Mars age mortis opus •

---

[a] Amended from *cupiendo* by earlier editors to fit the metre.

Mars, O God of War! You who delimit sovereignty by
   swords, to whom the bleeding bodies of youths and gore
   poured forth by great slaughter of men give pleasure!

How greatly then your spirit thirsted savagery when
   amidst them you ordered the fierce battle lines engage.

Than which no ruin has better pleased you since Julius
   Caesar conquered Pompey in arms, and seized the walls
   of Rome for himself, and too drove Pompey in vile fear
   across the river, I think no slaughter has been so
   welcome to you.

You respect neither youthful virtue nor venerable old age;
   neither the lowly and wretched band of foot-soldiers nor
   those of noble birth have power to sway you.

Rather you spur any course your savage nature craves.

You thrust blinded wretches into shining armour and drive
   them to venture on murder as if a game.

Why linger with words when fury stands ready in arms?

Satisfy your will, Mars, bring forth the work of death!

Ex inproviso diffudit silva cohortes •

Et nemoris latebris agmina prosiliunt •

Monsª silvae vicinus erat • vicinaque vallis •   365

Et non cultus ager asperitate sui •

Anglis ut mos est densatim progredientes •

Haec loca praeripiunt Martis ad officium •

Nescia gens belli solamina spernit equorum •

Viribus et fidens heret humo pedibus •   370

Et decus esse mori summum dijudicat armis •

Sub juga ne tellus transeat alterius •

Ascendit montem rex bellaturus in hostem •

Nobilibusque viris munit utrumque latus •

In summo montis vexillum vertice fixit •   375

Affigique jubet caetera signa sibi •

Omnes descendunt et equos post terga relinquuntᵇ •

Affixique solo bella ciere tubis •

ª Until the 18th century *mons* might be used for hills or lower
elevations if they were prominent in the surrounding terrain.
Other accounts use *collis*, meaning hill or high ground.

ᵇ Corrected from *relinqunt*.

Suddenly the forest poured forth the English battalions
  and the columns rushed from cover in the woods.

Nearby to the forest was a hill and a neighbouring valley,
  and the terrain lay uncultivated for its ruggedness.[51]

As is the custom for the English, pressing forth crowded
  together, they seized this place for the service of Mars.

A people ignorant of war, they spurn the comfort of
  horses, and confident in their strength, they stand
  their ground on foot, and they think it the highest glory
  to die in arms lest their country be placed under the
  yoke of another.

King Harold ascended the hill to wage war against the
  enemy and he protected both his flanks with his
  noblemen.

At the summit of the hill he fixed his standard and
  ordered the other standards planted by his own.[52]

All dismount, and they leave the horses behind their
  backs.

And so standing their ground, they sound the call to war
  with trumpets.

---

[51] This description is consistent with the Brede Valley below the
Sussex Weald even today, but when the basin was tidal, the
marginal hills would have been even more barren.

[52] The Bayeux Tapestry shows Harold's standard as a Dacian red
wolf-skin, the same as illustrations in manuscripts for Danish kings.

Scene 52a: The English shield wall defies the Norman missiles.

Dux humilis dominumque timens moderantius agmen •

   Ducit et audacter ardua montis adit •   380

Praelia precurrit[a] pedites miscere sagittis •

   Quadratis jaculis scuta nihil faciunt •

Festinant parmas • galeati jungere parmis •

   Erectis astis hostis uterque furit •

Ut canibus lassatus aper stans dente tuetur •   385

   Oreque spumoso reicit arma pati •

Non hostem metuit nec tela minancia mortem •

   Sic plebs Angligena dimicat inpavida •

Interea dubio pendent dum proelia marte •

   Eminet et telis mortis amara lues •   390

a   *Prelia precurrunt* in earlier editions.

The duke, humble and God-fearing, leads his column ahead better composed, and boldly approaches the steep slope of the mountain.

The infantry advance ahead to engage battle with artillery.

Shields are as nothing to squared bolts![53]

The English, having lowered their helmets, hurry to join shield to shield.

Each army rages at the army opposite with raised spears.

As a wild boar, wearied by hounds, takes a stand, brandishes its tusks, refuses with its foaming snout to suffer weapons – it neither fears the foe nor blades menacing death – so the English masses endured peril fearlessly.

Through this time they hang on in doubt, as long as the battle might go either way, while a bitter plague of death-dealing darts hurls forth.[54]

---

[53] *Quadratis jaculis* – literally squared darts – were the deadly iron bolts projected from crossbows. Scene 52a of the Bayeux Tapestry shows a square-based bolt flying toward the English shield wall.

[54] The Norman cavalry and infantry remained safely beyond the reach of English javelins and archers during the early battle. The English, having brought only what they could carry on a long march, might soon exhaust their missiles. Having drawn the English to their ground, the Normans were able to resupply throughout the battle from their camp and even reuse missiles thrown at them from above. When the Norman cavalry and infantry finally charge the shield wall they will be at less risk from missiles coming up the slope if English arrows and spears are nearly exhausted.

Histrio cor audax nimium quem nobilitabat •

  Agmina praecedens innumerosa ducis •

Hortatur Gallos verbis et territat Anglos •

  Alte proiciens ludit et ense suo •

Anglorum quidam cum de tot milibus unum •   395

Ludentem gladio cernit abire procul •

Milicie cordis tactus fervore decenti •

  Vivere postponens prosilit ire mori •

Incisor ferri mimus cognomine dictus •

  Ut fuerat captus pungit equum stimulis •   400

Angligenae scutum telo transfudit acuto •

  Corpore prostrato distulit ense caput •

Lumina convertens sociis haec gaudia profert •

  Bella principium monstrat et esse suum •

Omnes laetantur[a] Dominum pariter venerantur •   405

  Exultant ictus quod prior extat eis •

Et tremor • et fervor per corda virilia currunt •

[a] Corrected from *letantur*.

A troubadour, whom greatly daring heart ennobled,
  advancing before the countless columns of the duke,
  cheers the Gauls and taunts the English in verse.[55]

He mocks them, throwing high his sword.

A single Englishman among the many thousands
  resolved from afar to die by the mocking sword, stirring
  due admiration in martial hearts.

Neglecting to live, he rushed toward death.

The juggler, called by the nickname Taillefer, thus being
  confronted gave spur to his horse.

His sharp lance pierced the Englishman's shield.

His sword severed the head from the fallen body.

His eyes turned back to the allies proferring this source
  of joy: that the very first battle augured their victory!

All rejoiced and together they called upon God.[56]

They thrilled that the first mortal blow was theirs, and
  trembling ardour coursed through manly hearts.

---

[55] William of Malmesbury suggests Taillefer sung the *Song of Roland*.

[56] The Norman battle cry was *Dix aie*, meaning 'God decide'.

Scene 52b: The first cavalry charge against the English shield wall.

Festinantque simul jungere scuta viri •
Invadunt primi peditum ceteras[a] pharetrati •
  Eminus et jaculis corpora trahiciunt •   410
Et balistantes clipeos ad grandinis instar •
  Dissolvunt quaciunt ictibus innumeris •
Sed laevam Galli dextram petiere Britanni •
  Dux cum Normannis dimicat in medio •
Anglorum stat fixa solo densissima turba •   415
  Tela dat et telis et gladios gladiis •

[a]   Corrected from *cetus.*

And at the same time the men hasten to join shields.

The foremost of the Gallic infantry attack the opposing
English archers, and at a spear's throw away they
pierce their bodies with javelins.[57]

And crossbow bolts dissolve shields like a hail-storm,
striking countless blows.

But also the Gallic cavalry charge to the left, the Bretons
to the right, while the duke with the Normans charge
up the centre.

The thick mob of English stand fixed to the ground.

They give both spears for spears and swords for swords.

---

[57] The targeting of the few English archers would weaken the English
ability to counter cavalry and infantry charges.

Spiritibus nequeunt frustrata cadavera sterni •

   Nec cedunt vivis corpora militibus •

Omne cadaver enim vita licet evacuatum •

   Stat velut illesum possidet atque locum •   420

Nec pentrare valent spissum nemus Angligenarum •

   Ni tribuat vires viribus ingenium •

Artibus instructi Franci bellare periti •

   Ac si devicti fraude fugam simulant •

Rustica letatur gens et superasse putabat •   425

   Per tergum nudis insequitur gladiis •

Amotis sanis labuntur dilacerati •

   Silvaque spissa prius rarior efficitur •

Conspicit ut campum cornu tenuare sinistrum •

   Intrandi dextrum[a] quod via larga patet •   430

Perdere dispersos variatis cladibus hostes •

   Laxatis frenis certat utrumque prius •

---

[a] *Dextrum* and *sinistrum* have caused confusion because they could modify either *campum* or *cornu*. *Sinistrum* is taken here as modifying *campum*, so the breach opens on the left flank of the Norman charge. *Dextrum* is taken as modifying *cornu*, so the right-most of the charging Norman wedge seize the opening gap. Alternatively, orienting toward Rome, the English line thins to the north and the Normans come charging from the south.

Bereft of life, dead bodies are unable to lay out, nor yield their place to living warriors.

Indeed each corpse, although bereft of life, stands as if unharmed and holds its place.

Nor could the allies break through the dense wood of the English unless a trick disperses their forces into lesser bands.

The Franks are experts in the arts of waging war by sly methods, and so they falsely pretend flight, as if defeated.[58]

The simple peasants, rejoicing, reckoned they had triumphed, chasing after the retreat with bared swords.

The fit withdrawn, the maimed are left to fall.

The once dense wood is made sparse!

When the Norman charge notices the left battle-line thinning, the right-most penetrate the wide gap lying open.

Each man vies first to destroy a disordered enemy in scattered defeats with loosened reins.[59]

---

[58] The *Battle Abbey Chronicle* attributes the French feint to Count Eustace of Boulogne.

[59] Gallic battle horses were small, 11 to 13 hands, so fighting with loose reins was quite practical. Horses gave advantages of speed, balance and stamina when carrying heavy weapons such as lances and broadswords into battle. Resting heavy weapons on horses allowed warriors to engage longer with the enemy without tiring.

Quique fugam simulant instantibus ora retorquent •

Constrictos cogunt vertere dorsa neci[a] •

Pars ibi magna perit • pars et densata resistit •   435

Milia namque decem sunt ibi passa necem •

Ut pereunt mites bacchante leone bidentes •

Sic compulsa mori gens maledicta ruit •

Plurima quae super est bello pars[b] acrior instat[c] •

Et sibi sublatos pro nichilo reputat •   440

Anglorum populus numero superante repellit •

Hostes vique retro compulit ora dari •

Et fuga ficta prius fit tunc virtute coacta •

Normanni fugiunt dorsa tegunt clipei •

---

[a] This line is added to the manuscript in a different hand.

[b] Corrected from *pars bello* for metrical reasons by earlier editors.

[c] Earlier editors understood *pars* as referring to some of those who
     pursued the French feint, but modified by *acrior bello* – wiser in
     war – it seems to better describe those English who were not
     lured into breaking ranks. This larger, better-disciplined mob on
     the hill repel the Normans who had taken advantage of the
     breach. Standing firm and pressing ahead they force the Norman
     cavalry from the ridge by weight of their greater numbers.

And those Franks feigning flight suddenly face about.

They drive the mob to yield their backs to death.

A large part perish there, while a part closing ranks
make a stand.

Indeed ten thousand suffered death there.

As sheep are savaged by the wild lion, so the cursed
people are overcome, driven to their deaths.

Wiser in war, the greater part remaining above stand
firm, and reckon those lured away as nothing to them.

The English mob push back, gaining the upper hand by
superior numbers, and by force their enemy is
compelled back, losing face.

And flight, before a fiction, is then made fact by might.

The Normans flee; their shields protect their backs.

Scene 53: The Normans are forced off the ridge by the English mob.

Dux ubi perspexit quod gens sua victa recedit •   445

   Occurrens illis signa ferendo manu •

Increpat et cedit retinet constringit et hasta •

   Iratus galea nudat et ipse caput •

Vultum Normannis dat verba precantia Gallis •

   Dixit quo fugitis quo juvat ire mori •   450

Quae fueras victrix pateris cur victa videri •

   Regnis terrarum Gallia nobilior •

Non homines sed oves fugitis frustraque timetis •

   Illud quod facitis dedecus est nimium •

Scene 55: The duke speaking and Count Eustace with the Norman standard

As soon as the duke perceived that his people were giving way, vanquished, he was rushing to them bringing the standard to hand.

He protests; he passes them and halts; and he bars them with his lance.

Enraged, he himself bares his head of his helmet.

Facing toward the Normans he spoke imploring words to the Gauls.[60]

He said: "Where are you fleeing?

"Where will it please you to meet death?

"You who have been victorious, why allow yourselves to be seen defeated?

"Gaul is the most noble among realms of all lands!

"You flee not from men but sheep, and fear needlessly.

"That which you do here is grievously shameful.

---

[60] While facing the Normans, the duke seems to be addressing all the assembled cavalry as Gauls, including Bretons and Franks.

Est mare post tergum maris est iter ad remeandum •455

    Per grave^a mare quod vobis tempus et aura negat •

Ad patriam reditus gravis est, gravis et via longa •

    Hic vobis nullum restat et effugium •

Vincere certeris^b solum si vivere vultis •

    Dixit et extimplo serpit ad ora pudor •   460

Terga retro faciunt vultus vertuntur in hostes •

    Dux ut erat princeps primus et ille ferit •

Post illum reliqui feriunt ad corda reversi •

    Vires assumunt reiciendo metum •

Ut stipulae flammis pereunt spirantibus auris •   465

    Sic a Francigenis Angelica turba ruis •

Ante ducis faciem tremefactum labitur agmen •

    Mollis cera fluit ignis ut a facie •

Abstracto gladio galeas et scuta recidit •

    Illius et sonipes corpora multa fe<rit>^c •   470

^a *Grave* is inserted above *mare* in the manuscript.
^b *Certetis* in earlier editions.
^c *Fac'* in the manuscript.

"The sea is behind; back by sea is the way to return –
through heavy seas – which the season and the winds
will deny you.

"Return to the homeland is perilous; the journey is
perilous and long.

"And here for you there is no escape.

"You must fight to win if you wish only to live!

He spoke and immediately shame flushed over faces.

They turned back the other way, facing toward the
enemy.

As the duke was their leader he also struck first.

Behind him the others struck. Having regained heart,
the rallying forces now scorned fear.

As stubble is consumed by flames in gusts of wind, so
you English mob are ravaged by the Franks.

The battle-line gives way, trembling before the duke.

It melts back like wax from advancing fire.

He cuts away helmets and shields by his drawn sword,
and his charger tramples many bodies.

Heraldi frater non territus ore leonis •

   Nomine Gernt regis traduce progenitus •

Librando telum celeri volitante lacerto •

   Eminus emisso cuspide corpus equi •

Vulnerat atque ducem peditem bellare coegit •   475

   Sed pedes effectus dimicat et melius •

Nam velox juvenem sequitur veluti leo frendens •

   Membratim perimens haec sibi verba dedit •

Accipe promeritam nostri de parte coronam •

   Si periit sonipes hanc tibi reddo pedes •   480

Dixit et ad bellum convertit protinus actum •

Harold's brother is unafraid in the face of the lion.

Named Gyrth, he was born of a royal lineage.

Launching a javelin from his swiftly swinging arm, he
   wounds the body of the horse from a distance with the
   hurtling blade, and so forces the duke to fight as a
   footsoldier.[61]

But made a footsoldier he fights even better, for he
   swiftly chases after the youth as if a ravening lion.

Destroying him limb by limb, he spoke these words:

"Accept a well-earned crown from our portion!

"Since my horse is dead, I render this to you a
footsoldier!"

He speaks and promptly turns his action to the battle.

Scene 56b: Death of Gyrth by wounded horse

---

[61] As war horses were then quite small, there was less risk of injury
falling or being thrown than today.

Obstat et oppositis viribus Herculeis •

Hos truncos facit • hos mutilos • hos devorat ense •

   Perplures animas mitit et ad tenebras •

Per medias strages equitem dum prospicit ire •   485

   Ex Cenomannorum progenitum genere •

Infecto gladio cerebro vel sanguinis unda •

   Innuit ut veniat • et sibi subveniat •

Ille timens cedem negat illi ferre salutem;

   Nam pavitat mortem • ceu lepus ante canem •   490

Dux memor ut miles subito se vertit ad illum •

   Per nasum galeae concitus accipiens •

Vultum telluri plantas ad sydera volvit •

   Sic sibi concessum scandere currit equum •

And he stands against the opposing men with Herculean strength.

Some he beheads, some he maims, some he devours with his sword, and very many souls he sends to the darkness.

While engaged in slaughter he spies a knight riding by, born of the noble race of Maine.

With a sword stained by brains or even flowing blood, he beckoned that knight might come and help him.

But fearing slaughter, that one refuses to bring aid to him, for he trembles before death like a hare before a hound.

The duke, recalling himself as a knight, suddenly spun toward that man.

Incensed, seizing his helmet by the nosepiece, he reels him face to ground and heels to heaven, and swiftly mounts the horse thus offered him.

O coeli rector nostri pius ac miserator •   495

   Nutu divino qui regis omne quod est •

Quas patitur clades Anglorum turma superstes •

   Occidit hic pietas regnat et impietas •

Vita perit mors seva furit bacchatur et ensis •

   Nullus ibi parcit Mars ubi sceptra regit •   500

O Master of Heaven, and our faithful commiserator,

Who in your divine will are ruler of all which exists!

Such slaughter the remaining mob of Englishmen suffer!

Here rightousness is slain and lawlessness reigns.

*Life perishes, savage death rages, and the sword runs
  riot.*

None there shows mercy where Mars rules by his sceptre!

Postquam factus eques dux est mox acrius hostes •

    Vulnerat aggreditur • fulminat insequitur •

Vincere dum certat • dum campum cede cruentat •

    Filius Hellocis[a] vir celer et facilis •

Insidiando ducem tractabat fine gravari •   505

    Sed misso jaculo traditur ictus equo •

Corruit in terram pedes est dux plenus et ira •

    Quomodo se teneat cogitat aut quid agat •

Nam binis miratur equis privatus haberi •

    Heret in hoc paulo sed nihil esse putat •   510

Censet enim virtute sibi fortuna favebit •

    Subveniet votis et sine fraude suis •

Ergo sui mors jurat equi si dextra manebit •

    Non sine vindicta transiet absque mora •

Auctorem sceleris multos inter latitantem •   515

    Longe perspiciens perdere currit eum •

Inpulsu dextrae duro mucronis et ictu •

    Ilia praecidens viscera fudit humi •

---

[a] Many have tried in vain to identify an Englishman named *Helloc* or *Hellox* who might be father to this assailant, but there is no trace of such a man in Anglo-Saxon England. *Hel-locis* may better mean 'strait-places'. *Hellas* in Greek means the same as *hels* in Old Norse – a neck, narrows, pound or strait between two waterways. *Hellocis* was probably the Frankish name for the Dover strait region or the mariners who would later become freemen of the Confederation of the Cinque Ports. The Anglo-Saxon Chronicle Version C for 1052 attests *butsecarlas* – 'ship-warriors' – settled at *Hastingas* on the approach to the Dover strait, and Snorri Sturluson in the *Saga of Harald Hardrada* names the place of the 1066 battle as *Helsingia-port*.

After being horsed, the duke soon wounds his enemies more fiercely.

He attacks. He strikes like lightening. He harries.

As he strives to conquer – while he dyes the field blood-red with slaughter – a son of the strait-places, a man quick and ready, lay in ambush, making it his goal to bring down the duke.

But the strike from his hurled javelin is delivered to the horse.

Thrown to the ground, the duke is again a footsoldier and full of rage.

He considers how to preserve himself, or rather what he might do, for he is amazed to have been deprived of two horses.

He puzzles about this a little but he reckons it as nothing.

Indeed, he thinks to himself, 'Fortune favours the brave', and she will assist his vows without fail.

He therefore vows, if his good fortune continues, his horse's death will not pass unavenged.

Without delay, spying at a distance the culprit of the crime hiding among the crowd, the duke runs to destroy him by a blow of his right hand and the hard thrust of his sword.

Cutting open his groin, he spills his guts to the ground.

At comes Eustachius generosis partibus ortus •

    Septus bellantum multiplici cuneo •   520

Ad ducis auxilium festinat primus haberi •

    Efficiturque pedes dux ut abiret eques •

Miles erat quidam comitis nutritus ab illo •

    Fecerat ut domino fecit et ille sibi •

Talibus auspiciis comes ex dux associati •   525

    Quo magis arma micant bella simul repetunt •

Amborum gladiis campus rarescit ab Anglis •

    Defluit et numerus nutat et atteritur •

Corruit apposita ceu silva minuta securi •

    Sic nemus Angligenum ducitur ad nihilum •   530

Jam ferme campum victrix effecta regebat •

Meanwhile Count Eustace, born of noble pedigree,
   surrounded by a massed wedge of warriors, hastens to
   be first to bring help to the duke, and makes himself a
   footsoldier so the duke might go forth mounted.[62]

There was a certain knight of the count raised by him.

As the count had done for his lord, this one did for him.

The count and duke join forces by such auspicious
   favours.

They return at once to the battle where the weapons
   glitter thickest.

The two swords together thin the battlefield of English,
   and their number ebbs, wavers and wastes away.

Like a wood thins before a relentless axe, so a forest of
   Englishmen is brought to annihilation.

Now he rules the field – the victory is nearly complete!

---

[62] Eustace II, Count of Boulogne, was brother-in-law to King Edward
the Confessor, being the second husband of Goda, Edward's sister.
The praise for the count helps date the Carmen to 1067 as Count
Eustace had his lands and title in England dispossessed in 1068
after he tried to seize Dover Castle.

Jam spolium belli Gallia leta petit •
Cum dux prospexit regem super ardua montis •
Acriter instantes dilacerare suos •
Advocat Eustachium linquens ibi praelia Francis •   535
Oppressis validum contulit auxilium •
Alter ut Hectorides Pontivi nobilis heres •
Hos comitatur Hugo prom\<p\>tus in officio •
Quartus Gilfardus patris a cognomine dictus •
Regis ad exicium quatuor arma ferunt •   540
Ast alii plures aliis sunt hi meliores •
Si quis in hoc dubitat actio vera probat •
Per nimias c\<a\>edes nam bellica jura tenentes •
Heraldum cogunt^a pergere carnis iter •

---

^a Corrected from *cogit* by earlier editors.

Happy Gaul already seeks the spoils of war, when the duke spies the king above on the steep hill,[63] fiercely tearing to pieces his own advancing men.

The duke summons Eustace.

Leaving the battle there to the Franks, he musters strong aid for the oppressed.

Like another son of Actor,[64] the noble heir of Ponthieu, Hugh joined with these, ever eager for duty.

Fourth is Gilfard, called by his father's byname.[65]

The four bear arms to destroy the king.

Although there are many others, these are better than the rest.

If any doubt this, the truth is proven in the deed.

By great carnage, but holding to the laws of war, they compel Harold go the way of all flesh.

---

[63] Those suggesting alternatives to Battle Abbey usually suggest Telham Hill or other great hills. The hill of the battle might be a more modest rise above the Brede Basin floodplain as both armies were on the march when they met and the mounted duke could see the king on the summit once the allies had gained the upper ground. *Mons* can mean any dominant hill on a plain.

[64] *Hectorides* is another name for Patroclus, the ever-eager Trojan hero; he was the grandson of Actor and Achilles' beloved comrade.

[65] The use of surnames was just beginning among Normans. Gilfard (Gifford) was among the first hereditary surnames, as was Taisson (Tyson). Mercenaries who left the lands of their birth to take military service with Normandy would choose a new byname, disassociating themselves from the locative name and loyalties of their birthplace.

Per clipeum primus dissolvens cuspide pectus • 545

Effuso mac<ul>at^a sanguinis imbre solum •

Tegmine sub galeae caput amputat ense secundus •

Et telo ventris tercius exta^b rigat •

Abscidit coxam quartus procul egit ademptam •

Taliter occisum terra cadaver habet • 550

Scene 57: Harold is standing next to a Dacian wolf-skin battle standard when he is slain by lance, axe and sword. The Gauls are already stripping the dead in the lower margin.

a Corrected from *macidat*. *Madidat* suggested by earlier editors.
b Corrected from *extat* by earlier editors.

Shattering his breast through his shield, the first by
lance stained the soil in a vast outpouring of blood.

The second by his sword severed the head beneath the
cover of Harold's helmet.

And the third by his spear poured forth the belly's
entrails.

The fourth hewed off a leg; being removed he drove it
afar.[66]

In this manner the earth receives the slain corpse.

---

[66] William of Malmesbury in his 12th century *Gesta Regum Anglorum*
said the leg was carried away as a trophy to dishonour Harold,
incurring the wrath of the duke. Some have even suggested the
severed limb was a more intimate member. If the hewn leg was
taken up at all, it might have been waved to signal to the English on
the battlefield that their king had fallen, ending the battle in
accordance with medieval rules of war. An alternative interpretation
is that the oathbreaker Harold was beheaded, disemboweled and
quartered – a punishment that would become customary for treason.
Writing in 1070, William of Jumièges says, 'Harold himself... fell
covered with deadly wounds.' The arrow in the eye story, beloved of
Victorian and textbook historians, was quite literally fabricated in a
tapestry described three decades after the battle by Baudri of
Bourgueil in his *Letter to Adela*.

Fama volans Heraldus obit • per praelia sparsit •

  Mitigat extemplo[a] corda superba timor •

Bella negant Angli veniam poscunt superati •

  Vivere diffisi terga dedere neci •

Dux ibi per numerum duo milia misit ad orcum •   555

  Exceptis aliis milibus innumeris •

Vesper erat jam cardo dies volvebat ad umbras •

  Victorem fecit cum Deus esse ducem[b] •

Scene 58a: The English beg parole and yield their backs

[a] Corrected from *extimplo*.
[b] *Necem* is amended in the manuscript to *ducem*.

The flying rumour 'Harold is dead!' spread through the battlefield.

Immediately fear softens proud hearts.

The conquered English refuse battle; they ask for pardon, not expecting to live, yielding their backs to murder.

By rank the duke sends two thousand to the underworld there,[67] besides the other countless thousands.

It was evening; already the day is revolving on its axis to shadows when God makes the duke become a conqueror.[68]

---

[67] The captives may have been decimated, with the highest ranks selected for death, implying 20,000 survivors surrendered. One reason for Norman hatred of Godwin was his killing ninety-nine out of a hundred Normans in the company of Alfred Aethling in 1036 instead of the customary one out of ten for those who surrender.

[68] As skilled navigators influenced by Arab geographers and mathematicians from the Mediterranean, the Normans had already accepted the Earth's rotation on its axis.

Scene 58b: English fugitives flee through steeps and deeps.

Solum devictis nox et fuga profuit Anglis •
   Densi per latebras et tegimen nemoris •   560
Inter defunctos noctem pausando peregit •
   Victor et exspectat lucifer ut redeat •
Pervigil Hectorides sequitur cedendo fugaces •
   Mars sibi tela gerit mors sociata furit •
Duxit ad usque diem vario certamine noctem •   565
   Nec somno premitur somnia nec patitur •

Only night and flight avail the conquered English,
   through hiding places and cover in the dense forest.[69]

The conqueror spent the night encamped among the
   dead and awaited the return of the morning star.

The ever-vigilant son of Actor[70] chases the fleeing
   fugitives.

Mars governs his weapons; Death allied, he rages wild.

He led various skirmishes from nightfall until daybreak,
   neither overcome by sleep nor allowing dreams.

---

[69] There is no mention of the *Malfosse* – 'evil ditch' – described by
Battle Abbey monks in their 12th century Chronicle, where pursuing
mounted Normans tumble into a steep and deep crevasse and the
English make a final stand on its opposite rise. The *Quedam
Exceptiones de Historia Normannorum et Anglorum*, an abbreviated
interpolation of the *Gesta Normannorum Ducum* likely written at
Battle between 1101 and 1103, decades before the Chronicle was
composed, describes a night chase as *per abrupta montium et
concaua vallium* – 'through the steeps of the hills and the deeps of
the valleys' and likewise omits the *malfosse* incident.

[70] Hugh de Ponthieu, referencing line 537.

Illuxit postquam Phebi clarissima lampas •

    Et mundum furvis expiat a tenebris •

Lustravit campum tollens et caesa suorum •

    Corpora dux terrae condidit in gremio •   570

Vermibus atque lupis avibus canibusque voranda •

    Deserit Anglorum corpora strata solo •

Heraldi corpus collegit dilaceratum •

    Collectum texit sindone purpurea •

Detulit et secum repetens sua castra marina •   575

    Expleat ut solitas funeris exequias •

Heraldi mater nimio constricta dolore •

    Misit ad usque ducem postulat et precibus •

Orbatae miserae natis tribus et viduatae •

    Pro tribus, unius reddat ut ossa sibi •   580

Si placet aut corpus puro preponderet auro •

After the brightest lamp of Phoebus shone, and redeemed the world from black darkness, the duke surveyed the battlefield toll, and taking up his own slain men, the duke buried them in the bosom of the earth.[71]

He left the English corpses strewn on the ground to be devoured by worms and wolves, birds and dogs.

The duke gathered Harold's torn body, wrapped the collection in purple linen,[72] and brought it away with him, returning to the seaside camp,[73] in order to complete the customary rites of burial.

The mother of Harold, overwrought by great anguish, sent all the way to the duke, and by her entreaties begged that to her – widowed and miserably bereaved of three sons – for the three one set of bones might be sent back. Else, if it pleased him, he might redeem Harold's body for its weight in pure gold.

---

[71] The speedy burial of so many dead may indicate a sandy reach of land below the steep battlefield, consistent with the western plain of the Brede Basin or the isthmus below Battle.

[72] Purple linen showed due respect for King Harold's remains and may have been an article of royal attire.

[73] *Castra marina* provides further confirmation the Norman camp was remote from the battlefield on land near the port.

Sed dux iratus prorsus utrumque negat •

Jurans quod pocius praesentis litora portus •

   Illi committet aggere sub lapidum •

Ergo velut fuerat testatus rupis in alto •   585

   Praecepit claudi vertice corpus humi •

Extimplo quidam partim Normannus et Anglus •

   Compater Heraldi jussa libenter agit •

Corpus enim regis cito sustulit et sepelivit •

   Imponens lapidem scripsit et in titulo •   590

Per mandata ducis rex hic Heralde quiescis •

   Ut custos maneas litoris et pelagi •

But the enraged duke utterly rejected both, swearing it better Harold were buried promptly on the coast of the port under a heap of stones.[74]

Therefore, just as he had vowed, he ordered the body entombed on the high part of the cliff in the ground at the summit.

Immediately, a certain man, part Norman and part English, a foster-brother of Harold's, willingly carried out the command.[75]

Indeed he swiftly carried up the body of the king and interred it, and placing a stone he wrote an inscription:

"By order of the duke, you rest here, King Harold, that you may remain guardian over sea and strand."[76]

---

[74] King Harold was rightly denied burial in hallowed ground as an excommunicant. Mutilation of the corpse and a shallow grave without benefit of religious rites are consistent with other royal medieval excommunicants. Recording the state of Harold's body and burial serves three purposes in the narrative: it reinforces Harold had been cast out of Christian communion, so damned; it emphasises his illegitimacy as an uncanonical tyrant; and it discourages veneration or remembrance. Although it was also an excommunication offence to bury an excommunicant in hallowed ground or give him funeral rites, the bones may well have been secretly taken up later and reinterred, either at Waltham Abbey or Bosham church.

[75] William of Poitiers identified William Malet. The detail of the men being foster-brothers may indicate they were raised together as youths, perhaps in Flanders.

[76] The inscription is described as a jest by William of Jumièges, ironically enjoining the spirit of King Harold to guard Hastingas from those within Harold's own realm and raiders across the sea – all enemies foreign and domestic. Hog Hill above Icklesham appears the most likely site for the burial, with views over the Brede Basin strand and across the sea to Normandy.

Dux cum gente sua plangens super ossa sepulta •

    Pauperibus Christi munera distribuit •

Nomine postposito ducis • et sic rege locato •   595

    Hinc regale sibi nomen adeptus abit •

Hastinge portus castris tum quinque diebus •

    Mansit et ad Doveram vertit abinde viam •

Nec medium complerat[a] iter cum territus illi •

    Occurrit populus pronus[b] in obsequio •   600

Obtulit et claves castri portasque reclusas •

    Testatur simulans velle sub esse sibi •

[a] Corrected from *comperat* by earlier editors.
[b] *Partus* in the manuscript; *promptus* or *pronus* suggested by earlier editors.

The duke lamenting together with his people above the buried bones disbursed offerings to the poor of Christ.

Setting aside the title of duke, and thus taking his place as king, he departed from here having taken for himself the royal title.[77]

He remained in camp at the port of Hastings[78] for five days, and turned his course from there to Dover.

He had not finished half the journey when a frightened crowd rushed to him, bowing in deference, and bestowed the keys of the castle, and they swore that the gates were laid open, pretending to wish to become his subjects.

---

[77] Once William proclaimed himself king of England at Harold's graveside he succeeded to all royal demesne lands and prerogatives by conquest and was entitled to punish any further English resistance as rebellion. Recording the exchange of titles beside the grave of King Harold reinforces William's divine legitimacy as his successor. By contrast, *Quedam Exceptiones de Historia Normannorum et Anglorum* reports William was proclaimed king by acclamation of his men on the battlefield.

[78] *Hastinge portus* – Hastingaport – is the first use of an English place name. The 12th century coastal navigation guide *De Viis Maris* says the port of *Hastinges* was at *Winchelse* seven miles distant from the coastal castle and town. This aligns with the village of Icklesham above the Brede Basin where a Roman stonework and metalled street crossed by causeway to Udimore. The town of Winchelsea was relocated in the late 13th century to Iham hill after storm surge and flooding destroyed the older settlement. In the foundation charter for new Winchelsea the destroyed old *Winchelse* is described as neighbouring Guestling hundred, also consistent with Icklesham.

Est ibi mons altus strictum mare litus opacum •

   Hinc hostes cicius Anglica regna petunt •

Sed castrum Doverae pendens a vertice montis •   605

   Hostes reiciens litora tuta facit •

Clavibus acceptis rex intrans moenia castri •

   Praecipit Angligenis evacuare domos •

Hos introduxit per quos sibi regna subegit •

   Unumquemque suum misit ad hospicium •   610

Ilico pervasit terror vicinia castri •

   Urbes et burgos oppida queque replens •

---

^a *Tributa* were taxes paid by tributary chieftains, tribes and urban tenants for royal or imperial protection.

In that place is a high mountain, a narrow sea, a shaded shore.

From here enemies more easily attack England, but the castle of Dover hanging from the heights of the cliffs, repelling the enemy, makes the shore secure.[79]

Having received the keys, on entering the walls of the castle the king ordered the Englishmen to leave their homes.

He brought in those by whom he had subdued the kingdom to himself, and sent each and every one to his own lodging.[80]

Immediately panic spread through the surrounds of the castle, filling cities and boroughs and towns everywhere.[81]

---

[79] Dover was important symbolically as the first Christian minster and port endowed to papal legates from Rome by King Lucius in the 2nd century. The minster in Dover Castle was given revenues of the port to support the clerics, a common pattern of endowment for early minsters dominating continental trade.

[80] The choice of Dover as an interim base of administration avenged the burgesses' offence to Count Eustace in 1051 which led to the Godwin and Harold's exile and rebellion. After reinstatement of the outlaws in 1052, Earl Godwin made himself constable of Dover castle. When Earl Harold succeeded Godwin as earl of Wessex, Sussex and Kent, he also became constable of Dover castle and then added the status of *subregulus* or regent.

[81] Cities, boroughs and towns were not royal desmesne; these had to make their own peace with a new sovereign by bringing tribute and renewing oaths of loyalty.

Nobilior reliquis urbs Cantorbeia dicta •

   Missis legatis prima tributa[a] tulit •

Post aliae plures nimium sua jura timentes •   615

   Regi sponte sua munera grata ferunt •

Et veluti muscae stimulo famis exagitatae •

   Ulcera densatim plena cruore petunt •

Undique sic Angli regi currunt famulari •

   Pergit muneribus nec vacuata manus •   620

Omnes dona ferunt et sub juga colla reponunt •

   Flexis poplitibus oscula dant pedibus •

Per spatium mensis cum gente perendinat illic •

   Post alio vadit castra locare sibi •

The city called Canterbury is nobler than the rest.

Envoys having been sent it produced the first tributes;[82]
afterwards other places fearing greatly for their
privileges brought welcome offerings to the king of their
own free will.

And just as swarming flies roused by the spur of hunger
come thick and fast seeking wounds oozing gore, thus
from everywhere the English rush to be servants of the
king.

Nor do they proceed with empty hands.

All bring gifts and place their necks under his yoke.[83]

On bended knee they give kisses to his feet.

The king abided there with his people for the interval of a
month;[84] after this he leaves to pitch his camp
elsewhere.

---

[82] The early capitulation of Canterbury to King William was very
influential. The English church administered many boroughs and
market towns through its churches, minsters and abbeys.

[83] By bringing timely tribute and swearing loyalty to the new king,
the urban clerics, burgesses and magistrates might ensure they
retained their valuable municipal and mercantile privileges.

[84] Dover was a sensible base of royal administration. The port
allowed King William to communicate widely within England by ship
and send tributes received back across the Channel to his exchequer
at Fécamp for distribution at Easter 1067 to the allies.

Guincestram misit mandat primatibus urbis •   625

    Ut faciunt alii ferre tributa sibi •

Hanc regina tenet regis de dote prioris •

    Hetguardi quare dedecus esse putat •

Sic sibi[a] concessam si vadit tollere sedem •

    Solum vectigal[b] postulat atque fidem •   630

Una primates reginae consuluerunt •

    Illaque concedens ferre petita jubet •

Taliter et regis praecepto spirat uterque •

    Nam dominae[c] pariter et sua dona ferunt •

---

[a] Corrected from *tibi* in the manuscript by earlier editors.
[b] *Vectigalia* and *tributa* are taxes dating back to the Roman Republic which carried through to Merovingian, Carolingian and Anglo-Saxon royal administration. *Vectigalia* were tolls or levies on goods traded in an emporium, market or port, while *tributa* were taxes on the urban or manorial tenant community, like poll taxes.
[c] Corrected from *domine*.

He sent to Winchester. He ordered the primates[85] of the city to bring tribute to him as the others were doing.

The queen held this place as a dowry of former King Edward,[86] wherefore King William deemed it would be a disgrace if he advanced to take away a seat thus given to her.

He demanded merely market tolls[87] and also a pledge of loyalty.

The primates of the queen deliberated together with her, and yielding, she ordered those things requested be produced.

And likewise both primates gave their assent to the king's command, for they brought the gifts of the queen and their own together.[88]

---

[85] Winchester had two primates: Stigand, as bishop of the see at Old Minster and the abbot of New Minster, founded by Alfred the Great.

[86] It was traditional to endow a consecrated queen with estates in Winchester as the royal borough of the House of Wessex.

[87] Exemption from borough taxes - *tributa* – paying only customs and market levies - *vectigalia* - was a valuable concession and may have set a precedent for the more generous concessions to London.

[88] Stigand would remain a canonical bishop of Winchester and uncanonical archbishop of Canterbury until April 1070, when he was deposed by papal legate Erminfrid. He died a captive in 1072. Stigand's career from becoming King Cnut's chaplain in 1020 was marked by self-enrichment, looting the church and seizing lands for himself, so that by 1066 his personal wealth was only exceeded by that of King Harold. Excommunicated by five popes, Stigand refused to pay contributions to Rome after usurping Canterbury in 1052. King William and Lanfranc negotiated the amount due to Rome from 1052 to 1070 with Erminfrid and made good the deficit. Stigand's personal fortune probably helped fund the past-due payment.

Rex sic pacatus tentoria fixa resolvit •   635

   Quo populosa nitet Londona vertit iter •

Est urbs ampla nimis perversis plena colonis •

   Et regni reliquis dicior est opibus •

A laeva muris a dextris flumine tuta •

   Hostes nec metuit • nec pavet arte capi •   640

Hanc bello superata petit gens improba sperans •

   Vivere per longum libera tempus in hac •

Sed quia per nimius[a] terror vallaverat omnes •

   Undique planctus erat meror et impaciens •

Una postremum rectores atque potentes •   645

   Tali consilio consuluere sibi •

Scilicet ut puerum natum de traduce regis •

   In regem sacrent ne sine rege forent •

---

[a] *Pernimius* in earlier editions.

Thus pacified, the king took up his pitched tents.

He turned his course to where crowded London gleams.

The city is very large, full of extremely subversive
    citizens, and richer in wealth than the rest of the
    kingdom.

Protected by walls on the left and river on the right,[89]
    it dreads neither foes nor fears capture by cunning.

The disloyal people defeated in battle made for this place,
    hoping to live free in it for a long time.[90]

But because such great terror had overwhelmed all –
    everywhere there was lamentation and unbearable grief
    – the rulers and also the powerful at last united to
    deliberate together in such great council, specifically
    whether a boy born of royal lineage ought to be
    consecrated for king lest they remain without a king.[91]

---

[89] All medieval Christian geography references Rome as the centre of
the world. Facing toward Rome, with London in the foreground, the
Thames is to the right of London and the Roman-era walls are to the
left.

[90] Under canon law, and preserved in early Anglo-Saxon written
laws, renegades or fugitives might gain sanctuary in London,
protected by royal and papal privilege. The king and manorial lords
were barred from pursuit as sanctuary estates were deemed
extraterritorial and inviolable, as embassies are in modern times.

[91] Abbot Aelfric of Eynsham wrote in the late 10th century: 'No man
can make himself king, but the people has the choice to choose as
king whom they please; but after he is consecrated as king, he then
has dominion over the people, and they cannot shake his yoke off
their necks.'

Autumat insipiens vulgus se posse tueri •

    Regali solo nomine • non opere •   650

In statuam regis puer est electus ab illis •

    Cujus praesidium contulit exicium •

Sparsit fama volans quod habet Londonia regem •

    Gaudet et Anglorum qui superest populus •

Interea regni totum qui quaerit habere •   655

    Et votis compos cui favet Omnipotens •

Hostili gladio quae nec vastaverat igne •

    Ut non ingenio vindicat imperio •

Comperit ut factum fatuis quod non erat aequum •

    Praescriptae muros urbis adire jubet •   660

Paruit extemplo celeri velocius aura •

    Agmen belligerum castra locare sibi •

Densatis castris a leva moenia cinxit •

    Et bellis hostes esse dedit vigiles •

The foolish rabble reckoned he would be able to protect them by royal title only, not his works.

The boy was elected as a regal figurehead by those whose guardianship likewise bestowed ruin.

The flying rumour spread that London had a king and the people of the English who had survived were delighted.[92]

Until this ploy, he who sought to hold the kingdom united, and whose vows the Almighty deigned fulfilled, had not laid waste by cruel sword or fire, as he claimed rule by divine authority, not by clever device.

When he learned of this act of fools which was unworthy, he then ordered the walls of the aforesaid city assailed.[93]

A marching column complied at once, swifter than the wind, to lay out for itself a siege-camp.

The army ringed the walls to the left with crowded camps and spurred the enemy to vigilance against attacks.

---

[92] Edgar Aethling, the Hungarian-born son of Edward the Exile, grandson of Edmund Ironside, lacked the other qualities of a medieval king: no martial skills, no men, no treasure, and no allies. His only claim was descent from King Aethelred, twice tainted by the illegitimate births of his father and grandfather. However, just as his grandfather had been briefly preferred to King Cnut by Londoners in 1016, Edgar was now briefly preferred to King William in 1066.

[93] Revolt or treason were among the few justifications a king could claim for invading a territory protected by papal privilege. This line may be providing a canon law defence for the assault on London which follows.

Dimidie leuge spacio distabat ab urbe • 665

   Regia regalis aula decora nimis •

Fertur ab antiquis que Guest[a] vocitata colonis •

   Post Petri nomen duxit ab ecclesia •

Providus hanc sedem sibi rex elegit ad <a>edem •

   Quae sibi complacuit jure nec inmerito • 670

Nam veluti patrum testantur gesta priorum •

   Ex solito reges hic diadema ferunt •

Edificat moles vervecis cornua ferro •

   Fabricat et talpas[b] urbis ad excidium •

Intonat inde minas poenas et bella minatur • 675

   Jurans quod licitum si sibi sit spacium •

Moenia dissolvet turres aequabit harenis •

   Elatam turrem destruet aggerie •

Talibus auditis cives pavor atterit urbis •

   Occupat, exagitat, torquet et excruciat • 680

Intus erat quidam contractus debilitate •

   Renum[c] sicque pedum segnis ab officio •

Vulnera pro patria quoniam numerosa recepit •

   Lectica vehitur mobilitate carens •

[a] An initial *Gu* was pronounced *W* by the Normans and Franks, hence *Guillaume* for William and *Guest* for West.

[b] This is a unique usage of *talpas*, mole, as a method of undermining defensive walls.

[c] *De debilitate renum* appears as a chapter heading in a 13th century medical text by Guilielmus de Saliceto which describes kidney failure. A humorous implication, appropriate perhaps to the context and the unusual personal detail, is that the man was among those within wetting themselves in terror.

In the king's demesne[94] half a league distant from the city is a royal palace of surpassing beauty, reputed to have been called West by ancient settlers, afterwards taking a name from Peter's minster.[95]

The provident king chose this seat for his household, which rightly pleased him, and not undeservedly, for as the histories of earlier fathers bear witness, by tradition kings wear their crowns here.[96]

King William built a monster siege-engine, ram-horned with iron, and dug mines for the destruction of the city.

He then bellowed threats, menacing vengeance and battles, swearing that, if given enough time, he would raze the walls, he would level the towers to the strand, he would demolish the proud keep to rubble.

Having heard such things, fear ravaged the citizens of the city; it possessed, tossed, twisted and tormented them.

There was within a certain man withered by weak loins, and thus slow-footed from duty because he had received many wounds for his homeland. Lacking mobility, he is borne on a litter.[97]

---

[94] The city of London was not royal demesne but Westminster was. King William stopped in the royal seat where he had a right to settle as king.

[95] Ancient emporia like London customarily had separate visitor settlements with hostels near the port, often identifiable by *Guest* or *Thorn* in local names. Separation kept unruly seamen from prosperous merchants and burgesses in the emporium.

[96] Westminster was not a place of coronation before 1066. The line references the Anglo-Saxon tradition of crown-wearing ceremonies: Easter in Winchester, Pentecost in Westminster and Midwinter in Glocester, a tradition King William continued.

[97] More lines describe this man than any other character, enough to identify him to listeners familiar with recent events in 1067.

Omnibus ille carens[a] primatibus imperat urbis •   685

  Ejus et auxilio publica res agitur •

Huic per legatum clam rex pociora revelat •

  Secreti[b] • poscens quatinus his faveat •

[a] *Tamen* is substituted for *carens* in the manuscript.

[b] Amended to *secretim* by earlier editors, but the genitive case is correct if *secreti* modifies *pociora* – 'a better means of separation'. Such an interpretation is consistent with London's commonwealth mandated status from the papacy of Gregory the Great until 1693, when James II revoked the London Charter of Liberties. *The Chronicle of Battle Abbey* describes the eventual deal with London as a *'rationisque ac pacis confederatione'* – 'a prudent and peaceful confederation' – in essence a Dacian truce. The king recognised London as distinct from hinterland England, but both jurisdictions owed loyalty and service to the king.

That man nonetheless rules over all the principal men of the city, and public affairs are administered by his aid.[98]

To this man, by envoy, the king secretly proposes better means of separation, asking to what extent he might support this.

---

[98] This appears to identify Godfrey the portreeve. Godfrey de Magnaville had become portreeve in 1051 and was still the royal agent and secular magistrate of London in 1066. Norman by birth, he would be the obvious person for a Norman king to approach for negotiations. Godfrey and his heirs became very wealthy and influential under the name de Mandeville after 1066.

Solum rex vocitetur ait • sed commoda regni •

Ut jubet Ansgardus[a] subdita cuncta regat[b] •   690

Ille quidem cautus caute legata recepit •

Cordis et occulto condidit in thalamo •

[a] The name *Ansgardus* here and at line 726 is taken to identify Edgar the Aethling. Ansgar, a very popular name in 11th century eastern Germanic and Nordic realms, may be the christening name given the boy in the royal court of Hungary, consistent with his sisters' Germanic names, Margaret and Cristina. Ansgar is not attested as a name in England until after the Norman Conquest, so the boy's unfamiliar Germanic name may have been Anglicised to Edgar to promote him as a part-Saxon heir. A Frankish cleric writing for a continental audience would naturally prefer the Germanic name to emphasise the boy's foreign origin.

Both lines using the name make better sense referencing Edgar the Aethling, then the king-elect in London. William offers Londoners himself as an alternative figurehead sovereign here, with mandated self-rule as a commonwealth ceded at line 732. Line 726 says the envoy is 'from Ansgardus', appropriate to an envoy from London's king-elect.

Other editors, following the suggestion accompanying the *Carmen*'s first publication by Augustine Thierry in 1825, have taken *Ansgardus* to refer to Esegar the Staller, an Anglo-Danish manorial constable long allied to King Harold in Essex. Arrogant, prosperous, multi-cultural London, with a veteran Norman magistrate, would be unlikely to cede control in a crisis to an aged Anglo-Danish provincial retainer. If Esegar lived so long, it is more likely Harold required him at the battles at Stamford Bridge and Hastingas where he likely died.

[b] William of Poitiers, *Gesta Guillelmi* II(33): *Multa Lundoniae posteaquam coronatus est prudenter, iuste, clementerque disposuit, quaedam ad ipsius ciuitatis commoda siue dignitatem, alia quae genti proficerent uniuersae, nonulla quibus ecclesiis terrae consuleretur* – 'At London, after his coronation, [King William] made many wise, just, and merciful provisions; some were for the interests and honour of the city, others to the profit of the whole people, and some to the advantage of the churches of the land.'

Merely call him king, he said, but by the prerogatives of
royal power, as Edgar now commands, he instead
might rule in total submission.[99]

Indeed that cautious man received the offer warily,
and sheathed it in the chamber of his heart.[100]

The London Charter of Liberties

*William the king amicably greets William the bishop and Godfrey the
portreeve and all the burgesses within London, both Frankish and
English. And I declare that I grant you all remain law-worthy as you
were in the days of King Edward. And I grant that every child shall be
his father's heir after his father's days. And I will not suffer that any
person do you any wrong. God keep you.*

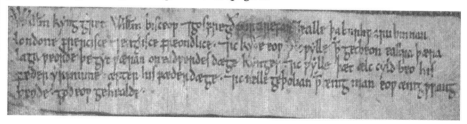

---

[99] The offer was to make London a self-rule commonwealth so long
as Londoners swore loyalty to King William and committed no
treason. The London Charter of Liberties was the original 'civil
rights act', the first document to cede sovereign prerogatives to
citizenry. Its survival proves that the bargain described in the
Carmen was fulfilled. The charter is still preserved securely in the
London Metropolitan Archives, though it was revoked for treason by
Lodoners in 1693 by James II.

[100] Luke 2:19.

Natu majores omni levitate repulsa

    Aggregat • et verbis talibus alloquitur •

Egregii fratres cum vi tum saepius arte •   695

    Est ubi nunc sensus vester • et actus ubi •

Cernitis oppressos valido certamine muros •

    Et circumseptos cladibus innumeris •

Molis et erecte transcendit machina turres •

    Ictibus et lapidum[a] moenia scissa ruunt •   700

Casibus a multis ex omni parte ruina •

    Eminet et nostra corda timore labant •

Atque manus populi nimio percussa pavore •

    Urbis ad auxilium segniter arma movet •

Nosque foris vastat gladius pavor angit et intus •   705

    Et nullum nobis praesidium superest •

[a] *Palidum* in the manuscript; *lapidum* suggested by earlier editors.

He convened all older men having spurned levity,[101] and addressed them in such words:

"Brothers, distinguished not only by power but often by craft, where now is your vision? And where your action?

"Regard the walls besieged in mighty conflict, and surrounded by immense devastation, and the raised monster battering-ram is over-reaching the barbicans, and our walls are being ruined, split by blows of stone.

"After many calamities, collapse on all sides!

"He stands tall and our hearts sink in fear.

"And too the militia of the people is stricken with such great terror that they take up arms half-heartedly for defence of the city.[102]

"The sword lays waste to us without, fear and anguish within,[103] and not one of the garrison has been left to us.[104]

---

[101] Aldermen – 'elder men' in Nordic and Germanic languages – would translate as *senatus*, used in the *Carmen* at lines 741, 789, 809 and 815. Aldermen were long-established in London by 1066, perhaps preserving a Romano-Dacian metropolitan institution.

[102] Following the Roman model, urban citizens were required to covenant to protect the city, attend its councils, and provide services such as wall-building in return for municipal privileges in the city and royal protection in the hinterland. The militia raised during the siege in 1066 was composed of shopkeepers, tradesmen and craftsmen rather than trained warriors. Baudri of Bourgueil's *Letter to Adela* describes old women and children joining the militia on the walls with brooms and sticks.

[103] Deuteronomy 32:25.

[104] Line 176 indicates that King Harold took London's garrison with him to Stamford Bridge, and then presumably to Hastingas, leaving London with only its citizen militia for defence.

Ergo precor vobis si spes est ulla salutis •

   Quatinus addatis viribus ingenium •

Est quia praecipuum si vis succumbat in actu •

   Quod virtute nequit fiat ut ingenio •   710

Est igitur nobis super hoc prudenter agendum •

   Et pariter sanum quaerere consilium •

Censeo qua propter si vobis constat honestum •

   Hostes dum lateant omnia que patimur •

Actutum docilis noster legatus ut hosti •   715

   Mittatur • verbis fallere qui satagat •

Servitium simulet necnon et foedera pacis •

   Et dextris dextrae[a] subdere si jubeat •

Omnibus hoc placuit dicto velocius implent •

   Mittitur ad regnum • vir racione capax •   720

Ordine qui retulit decorans sermone faceto •

   Utile fraternum non secus ac propium •

a   *Dextras dextre* in the manuscript.

"Therefore I beseech you, if there is any hope of salvation, that you supplement our forces with cunning, because it is preferable, if the city's might is about to succumb, that what cannot be done by our strength might be accomplished by stratagem.

"Accordingly, it is up to us to deal with this matter prudently, and to seek a sensible resolution together.

"On which account, I recommend, if agreed proper by you, while all we suffer lies hidden from the enemy, our envoy might immediately be sent as if biddable to the enemy.

"He might exert himself to beguile by words.

"Let him feign servitude and promises of peace, and indeed, if King William so commands, pledge our right hands."

This pleased everyone.

They accomplish it more swiftly than it is said.

A man deft in reasoning was sent to the king who duly delivered, embellished by clever speech, what was useful to his brothers no less than to himself.

Set quia vix patula teneatur compede vulpes •

    Fallitur a rege fallere quem voluit.

Namque palam laudat rex atque latenter ineptat •   725

    Quicquid ab Ansgardo nuncius attulerat •

Obcaecat[a] donis stolidum verbisque fefellit •

    Praemia promitens innumerosa sibi •

Ille retro rutilo gradiens honeratus ab auro •

    A quibus est missus talia dicta refert •   730

"Rex vobis pacem dicit profertque salutem •

    "Vestris mandatis paret et absque dolis •

Sed Dominum testor, cui rerum servit imago •

    Post David regem nescit habere parem •

Pulchrior est sole sapientior et Salemone •   735

    Promptior est Magno largior et Carolo •

[a] Corrected from *obcecat.*

But since a fox is scarcely taken by a wide-spread snare, he was beguiled by the king whom he wished to beguile.

For while the king openly praised, yet too he privately derided, whatever the envoy from Edgar conveyed.

The king dazzled the fool with gifts and duped him with words promising countless rewards to him.

That man, staggering back laden with reddish gold to those who had sent him, reported such words:

"The king says peace be with you and offers greetings.

"He yields your mandates[105] and without deceit.

"Yet God as witness, to whom creation of all things is beholden, He knows no king to deem his equal since David.

"He is more beautiful than the sun, and wiser than Solomon!

"He is braver than Alexander the Great, more generous than Charlemagne!

---

[105] 'Mandated territory' in international law is land assigned by treaty to another authority, usually for a religious foundation, port canton, free trade zone, embassy or international organisation. The use of *mandatis* in the *Carmen* is consistent with both the London Charter of Liberties confirming a commonwealth run by citizenry and the historic sanctuary for fugitives at line 642. A self-defended, self-governing mercantile canton with indulgence and protection of both pope and king could attract skilled and wealthy foreign immigrants, artisans and merchants who might otherwise fear discrimination, violence, oppression or religious persecution from hinterland natives and nobles. Interestingly, *ghet* in ancient Hebrew also meant 'land ceded by deed for settlement' and gave rise to the word ghetto.

Contulit Eguardus • quod rex donum sibi regni •
   Monstrat et adfirmat vosque probasse refert •
Hoc igitur super est ultra si vivere vultis •
   Debita cum manibus reddere jura sibi •   740
Annuit hoc vulgus justum probat esse senatus •
   Et puerem regem coetus uterque negat •
Vultibus in terra deflexis regis ad aulam •
   Cum puero pergunt agmine composito •
Reddere per claves urbem sedare furorem •   745
   Oblato quaerunt munere cum manibus.

"That King Edward had conferred the gift of the realm on him he has shown and affirmed. He reports you also assented.[106]

"Therefore this is up to you if you wish to live longer: render to him the oaths he is owed with your hands."

The citizens assented to this, the aldermen confirmed it to be proper, and each side renounced the boy-king.[107]

With downcast faces they proceeded with the boy in an orderly column to the palace of the king[108] to surrender the city by its keys, to settle the rebellion.

They sought binding in service by oaths of their hands.

---

[106] There is no English record of a Witenagemot approving Duke William as heir, but it is not unlikely for 1051 or 1052. King Edward was nearing 50 and unlikely to produce an heir. Queen Emma was still living and influential in all of England, and she and Edward had placed many Norman prelates and nobles among the Witans since her arrival in 1002. Duke William might have been urged as a kinsman of Queen Emma, kinsman of King Edward, and a capable general and ruler. Duke William had the strength, wealth, allies and command to keep England safe from Nordic kings who still pressed their claims and might preserve reforms like repeal of Heregeld.

[107] This description of London's municipal government echoes Roman municipal governance: the citizen assembly and senate/aldermen jointly determine public affairs.

[108] Version D of the Anglo-Saxon Chronicle has the surrender of Edgar the Aethling, archbishop Ealdred of York, earls Edwin and Morcar and others at *Beorh-hamstede*. As the name means 'noble-home-place' in Old English, it probably meant the 'royal-palace-place' at Westminster rather than the village at remote rural Berkhamsted in the Chiltern Hills, notable only for its abundant swine in Domesday Book. The Worcester Chronicle says *Beorcham*, again consistent with 'noble-home' or 'royal settlement', and omits Berkshire from its account of the Norman line of march on London. Version E of the Anglo-Saxon Chronicle says that William 'came to *Westmynstre* where Aeldred consecrated him king', agreeing with the account in the *Carmen*.

Novit ut adventum factus rex obvius illis •

   Cum puero reliquit oscula grata dedit •

Culpas indulsit gratanter dona recepit •

   Et sic susceptos tractat honorifice •   750

Per fidiae speciem proprium commendat honorem •

   Et juramentis perfida corda ligat •

Christi natalis nostrae spes una salutis •

   Quam mundus celebrat proxima lux aderat •

In quam promeritam disponit ferre coronam •   755

   Et ducis abjecto nomine rex fieri •

Auro vel gemmis jubet ut sibi nobile stemma •

   Illud quo deceat fiat ab artifice •

Misit Arabs aurum • gemmas a flumine Nilus •

   Grecia prudentem • dirigit arte fabrum •   760

Qui Salomoniacum vix deterior Salomone •

   Mirificum fecit et diadema decens •

As he knew of their approach, the king went to meet
them.

He gave a kindly kiss to the boy Edgar along with the
rest.

He graciously forgave their offenses and accepted their
gifts, and having received them thus, he treated them
honourably.

By his own show of good faith he commended honour,
and in oaths he bound their faithless hearts.

The day of Christ's birth, our only hope of salvation,
which the world celebrates, would arrive the next day.

The king appointed upon such day to take up the well-
merited crown, and cast aside the title duke to become
a king.[109]

He ordered a noble diadem of gold and jewels, such as
would become him, be made by an artisan.

An Arab had sent gold and gems from the River Nile.

A Greek ingenious in his craft guided the artisan, who
Solomon-like – scarcely less worthy than Solomon –
had made a magnificent and handsome crown.

---

[109] Christmas Day was a preferred consecration date for kings
succeeding by conquest to emphasise their divine legitimacy. It was
the date Charlemagne was consecrated emperor in Rome in 800 and
also the date of King Cnut's consecration as king of England in
1016.

Principio • frontis medium carbunculus ornat •
    Posthinc • jacinctus lucifer insequitur •
Et tunc aurifico resplendet in orbe topazon;   765
    Saphirus quartum ditat honore gradum •
Sardonicus quintus regales obsidet aures •
    Cui calcedonius ordine sextus adit •
Septimus est jaspis, procul a quo pellitur hostis •
    Sardius octavus ignivomus rutilat •   770
Figitur in nona cella lux chrysolithana •
    Tuque, berylle, locum clarificas decimum •
Undecimum viridis numerum smaragdus adimplet •
    Huic quoque chrysoprasus fert duodenus opem •
Verticis in summo stat margarita suprema •   775
    Quae sibi subposito[a] luce replet lapides •
In cujus dextra levaquae parte locata •
    Est amethisti lux, cui color est geminus •
Ethereus veluti propulsis nubibus axis •
    Insitus ignitis syderibus rutilat •   780
Aurea lucifluis distincta corona lapillis •
    Undique sic renitet lumine clarifico •

[a] Corrected from *suposita.*

First, in the middle of the front a ruby was set;

   Next a jacinth gleaming like the rising sun;

Then a topaz shone from a golden ring;

   Fourth, a sapphire enriched the honoured rank;

Sardonyx was fifth, in a royal setting of gold;

   Then Chalcedony ranked in sixth place;

Seventh was jasper, which routs foes from afar;

   Carnelian was eighth, glowing red;

In the ninth setting a gleaming chrysolite;

   Then a beryl seated lustrous in tenth;

Eleventh a green emerald was mounted;

   To this a chrysoprase added in twelfth place.

Atop the crown is set the most perfect pearl

   Which itself filled with light the stones set below.

On either side of this were placed

   Gleaming amethysts, matched in colour.

Like a cloudless heaven

   Studded with fiery stars,

The gleaming golden crown was adorned with precious stones.

   Thus it gleams on all sides with light made glorious.

Sceptrum cum virga componit post diadema •

    Commoda quae pariter significant patriae •

Nam sceptro tumide regni moderantur habene •   785

    Dispersos virga colligit ac revocat •

Tempore disposito quo rex sacrandus habetur •

    Terrae magnates et populosi manus •

Pontificale decus venerabilis atque senatus •

    Undique conveniunt regis ad officium •   790

Ex his eligitur praesul celeberrimus unus •

    Moribus insignis et probitate cluens •

Qui regem sacret simul et sacrando coronet •

    Et regale caput stemmate nobilitet •

Illius imperio solito de more priorum •   795

    Bini ponuntur magnificare Deum •

Ordo cucullatus • clerus cum pontificali •

    Nobilitate petunt templa beata Petri •

Following the crown, he made a sceptre and a rod which together signify the welfare of the kingdom.

For by the sceptre the arrogance of royal power is held in check; the rod recalls and also herds the disunited.[110]

The time for the king's consecration having been appointed, the great men of the land and a crowd of the people, the distinguished prelates, and also the venerable aldermen, gathered from every direction to take service of the king.

From these one distinguished prelate was chosen, notable for his morals and famed for his integrity,[111] who might consecrate the king, and likewise crown him with a blessing, and ennoble the royal head with the coronet.

By that prelate's command, following the custom of former times, his men were placed two by two to glorify God.

A hooded column of monks with with high-ranking priests made for the blessed shrine of Saint Peter.[112]

---

[110] The sword and ring, the remaining two royal regalia, were not fabricated for the consecration as line 295 states that King Edward had sent these earlier to King William in token of succession.

[111] Archbishop Ealdred of York officiated at the consecration. The emphasis on his morals and probity distinguishes him from the corrupt, uncanonical and excommunicated Stigand of Winchester and Canterbury.

[112] King Edward had been buried by the shrine of Saint Peter in the church of Westminster Abbey. Having the rite of consecration for King William beside the tomb of his predecessor and kinsman emphasised William's legitimacy as his heir and promoted dynastic continuity.

Ante ferendo cruces sequitur processio cleri •

   Post clerum pergit pontificale decus •   800

Rex multa comitumque ducum vallante caterva •

   Ultimus incedit cum strepitu populi •

Illius et dextram sustentat metropolita •

   Ad laevam graditur alter honore pari •

Taliter aecclesiam[a] laudes modulando requirit •   805

   Rex et regalem ducitur ad cathedram •

---

[a] *Aecclesia* seems used in this context to distinguish the Universal
Church under Holy Apostolic See authority, as distinct from
ecclesia which is used for a single church or its building.

A procession of clergy follows, bearing crosses before them. After the clergy comes the pontifical splendour of the bishops.

The king with many companions and commanders in an honour guard marched in last place to the cheers of the people.

The metropolitan archbishop supported his right hand, to the left walked another equal in rank.[113]

In such manner, to the chanting of the *Laudes Regiae*,[114] King William petitioned for communion with the Universal Church[115] and the king was led to the royal throne.

---

[113] The metropolitan archbishop was Ealdred of York and the metropolitan of equal rank was William the Norman, bishop of London. Pope Gregory the Great had laid down in a letter to Saint Augustine recorded by Bede that the metropolitans of York and London should hold equal status, confirmed by an Anglian council convened by Archbishop Lanfranc in 1075.

[114] The *Laudes Regiae* derived from the tradition of chanting to triumphant Roman generals or emperors entering Rome after great battles. Charlemagne adapted the tradition, adopting *Christus vincit, Christus regnat, Christus imperat* for his personal motto. By 1066 chanting of the *Laudes Regiae* had become an accompaniment to all Frankish royal consecrations. The oldest manuscript of the *Laudes Regiae* in England is for Queen Mathilda's 1068 consecration.

[115] The purpose of ritual consecration is binding communion of the monarch with the Universal Church of Rome so the king can rule as God's instrument under dominion of the pope rather than as an uncanonical tyrant. The Frankish *ordo* prescribed petition for communion, response, oath, consecration, blessing and investment. The king begins the rite with a petition for communion. Bishops respond, asking the king to swear four undertakings: protect the church, maintain justice, uphold the orders of society, and fight any who threaten his charges. The king so swears. Only after this ritual exchange can the king be anointed, blessed, and invested with sword, crown, ring, sceptre and staff. The English *ordo* added public election and affirmation from the Nordic and Anglo-Saxon tradition.

Laudibus expletis turba reticente canora •
　Indixit pacem cantor et ut sileant.
Conticuit clerus • compescuit ora senatus.
　Non est auditus ullus ab ore sonus •　　　　　　810
Normannus quidam praesul mox pulpita scandens •
　Famosis Gallis talia verba dedit •
Oblatus vobis si rex placet • edite nobis •
　Arbitrio vestri nam decet hoc fieri •
Concessit populus, clerus favet atque senatus •　　815
　Quod sermone nequit innuit et manibus •
Sermo peroratur • post illum metropolite •
　Haec eadem lingua protulit Angligena •

The *Laudes* came to a finish; the melodious choir kept
   silent.

The precentor declared peace and enjoined silence.

The clergy fell silent and the aldermen shut their
   mouths.

Not a sound was heard from any mouth.

A Norman prelate next ascended the pulpit.[116]

He addressed such words to the famous Gauls:

   "If the offered king is pleasing to you, declare it to us.

   "For it is fitting this be done by your judgement."

The people consented, clergy and aldermen together
   affirmed it.[117]

What they could not express in words they approved by
   their hands.

The responses delivered, next the English archbishop
   presented the same thing in the Englishmen's tongue.

---

[116] Geoffrey, bishop of Coutances, was present to jointly officiate.
The English church had been alienated by the excommunication of
Stigand and his rebellion against canonical authority of popes, so it
was prudent to have a Norman bishop of unquestioned legitimacy
co-officiate.

[117] The aldermen of London affirm the king in response to the Old
French speech, not the later English speech, perhaps confirming the
multi-cultural nature of 11th century London as *Franci et Angli*, as
addressed in the London Charter of Liberties.

Spirat utraque manus • laudat • spondet famulari •

    Annuit ex toto corde subesse sibi •   820

Convertens sanctam se summus praesul ad aram •

    Ante suam regem consituit faciem •

Ad se pontifices accitos congregat omnes •

    Et cum rege simul membra dedere solo •

Inchoat incentor stans rectus kyrieleison •   825

    Sanctorum pariter poscit habere preces •

Postquam sanctorum fit lytania peracta •

    Praesule cum summo pontificalis honor •

Erigitur solo prostrato rege relicto •

    Incentor siluit • omnis et ordo tacet •   830

Summus et antistes populo praecepit ut oret •

    Incipit et proprium protinus officium •

Collectam dixit • Regem de pulvere tollit •

    Crismate diffuso regis et ipse caput •

Unxit et in regem regali more sacravit[a] •   835

[a] At least a pentameter may be missing according to the metre.

Each oath-taker whistled, he cheered, he pledged his
service; each assented with a whole heart to submit to
him.[118]

Turning himself toward the holy altar, the archbishop
took his station facing the king.

He gathered all the assembled bishops to him, and with
the king all knelt together on the floor.

Remaining standing, the precentor began the *Kyrie
Eleison.*

He invoked the intercession of the saints as well.

After the Litany of the Saints came to an end, the
archbishop with the other bishops rose.

The king remained kneeling on the ground.

The precentor fell silent, and all the clergy kept still.

The archbishop ordered the people to pray, and
immediately led them himself in this observance.

He said the Collect. He lifted the king from the dust.

He himself annointed the head of the king by spreading
the chrism and consecrated the king in the royal
manner.[119]

---

[118] From this moment each person who affirmed William as king was
bound to him in duty, and each of them and all their own retainers,
heirs and successors became vassals of the king.

[119] The *ordo* or ritual of English coronation has remained the same
for more than 1300 years. It is still a service of public election by
the military, church and mercantile elites, affirmation of the people's
choice, dedication of the sovereign to the service of God and his or
her subjects, and holy consecration. The sign of the cross is
annointed in sacred oil on head, heart and hands.

Boats in the Rye Camber in the 1930s still had the design of Norman ships pictured in the Bayeux Tapestry: shallow rounded hulls for beaching, single mast and sail amidships, hinged rudder, and pole for navigating shallows. Source: Ann Newman via Rye Castle Museum

APPENDIX I

IMPERIUM IN BRITAIN TO 966

Competing claims to imperium in Britain among Britons, Angles, Saxons, Danes, Norwegians, Franks and Normans are the backstory to 1066, as are centuries of trading, raiding, tribute, migration, religious conflict, alliance, intermarriage, fostering, family rivalry, looting, and slaving that precede the 11th century. The challenge for medieval historians is that the original sources provide a kaleidoscope of fragmentary records in a variety of languages and media only imperfectly understood by contemporary scholars. Each source must be weighed with an appreciation of its authorship, purpose and biased perspective. Scribes and bards who compiled histories were usually clerical foreigners paid to take sides and flatter their royal or ecclesiastical patrons in a written language unfamiliar to natives. They selectively compiled memories, hearsay and oral traditions which were often misconstrued and distorted when recorded. Often foreign clerics were sought out and paid to deliberately exaggerate local prestige and reputations with fantastical tales of miracles or outright fabrications. Each generation of modern historians also brings contemporary parochial, ethnic, religionist and nationalist filters to selective sourcing and interpretation of the partial record. Modern historians too have been paid to take sides and flatter their royal patrons, especially during the Elizabethan and Victorian eras of global empire when most modern English histories were compiled. The 19th century produced many romantic histories with little factual basis, for example Arthurian legends and myths of Saxon nobility and independence. The following summary of the first three thousand years of English history may not be accepted by any reader as truth in its entirety, and it certainly invites continuing research, but the summary attempts to be rational in integrating the currently available documentary, geographic, archaeological and scientific evidence. Each assertion about individuals or events can be substantiated by at least one original source.

The novelty of this history is the suggestion that the Norman Conquest was the last great battle between sea-army tribes of the north – Anglians and Nordic Dacians – and sea-army tribes of the south – Romano-Gallic Normans – for imperium in the lands that became England. This history is deliberately about imperium, not about nations or kings, as it was sea-army imperium from coastal cantons that exploited native client kings, hinterland labour, agricultural surplus, mineral resources, slaves, mints and trade. It was sea-army imperium that compelled client kings and chieftains to extract taxes and levies of slaves and labourers, to provide rich provisions to sea-army cantons, and to pay tribute in gold and silver for protection from brutal hinterland raids and urban attacks.

In 1016 imperium over southern England was won by the the Danes from Nordic Dacia supported by the Anglians from the Danelaw. The Saxon kings and chieftains of southern England were defeated and slaughtered, with few survivors according to the Anglo-Saxon Chronicle. Despite the wishes of romantic Victorians who fictionalised the reigns of Danish kings, it is irrational to think Saxons rose again to any military rank or authority after 1016. Saxons between 1016 and 1066 were a subjugated tribe, reduced to working lands and mines for the profit of their Danish and Anglian masters. In 1066 the earls, huscarls and thegns (all Danish titles) that were loyal to King Harold (a Danish royal name) were Anglians and Danes – *Angli et Daci* in contemporary sources. Resenting King Harold's encroachment on Gallic cantons and trade, and his spurning of communion with the Roman Church, the Romano-Gallic Normans of the continent and Mediterranean rallied behind Duke William of Normandy and his papal banner to restore Romano-Gallic imperium to the south and impose Romano-Gallic imperium on the Anglian north. The Normans then had the wealth of England to export via their Mediterranean trade routes at vast profit.

The fabrication of Bronze Age metal weapons and tools, and the crafting of stronger sailing ships, gave rise to the most basic and persistent division of early man. Before languages, borders, nations, kings and religions were conceived to divide humankind, the most basic divide was between the *nauta* – 'sailor' – and the *agricola* – 'farmer'. Whether a child was born a sailor or a farmer influenced early language, culture, education, technology and ambition. From the first Bronze Age sea-armies, farmers have laboured to produce surpluses seized or delivered voluntarily to sea-armies. The sailor and the farmer have few interests in common.

> *Mores et studia nautae et agricolae dissimiles sunt. Nauta locum mutat, agricola stabilem habet sedem. Ita unus mores antqui servat, alter mores alienos amat. Nauta linguas diversarum gentium cognoscit, eum flumina celeria et maria alta delectant, vitam plenam periculorum omnium habet. Agricola sermonem tantum patriae scit, eum agri, horti et prata delectant, vitam tranquillam habet.* – Anon.

The customs and pursuits of sailors and farmers are unalike. The sailor changes place, the farmer holds to a stable home. The sailor understands the varied languages of nations; fast rivers and deep seas delight him; he has a life full of every peril. The farmer knows only the speech of his homeland; his fields, gardens and meadows delight him; he has a tranquil life.

Mariners lived in coastal cantons, the first city-states. Mariners valued salt for currency, salt-food and leather preservation. They valued metals for currency, weapons, tools and chandlery. They valued coins, rings, torcs and jewels for portable and tradeable mercantile wealth. Mariners also valued slaves for sex, household servants, mining, ship-building, weaving, construction, agriculture and industry. Status was won through conquest, commerce, wealth and slaves. Weapons, tools and ships required complex assembly, quality materials, and skilled artisans, so urbanisation, specialised craft guilds, and industrialisation all started at mariner cantons. Trade required recorded accounts and contracts, so written language and mathematics too started in mariner cantons.

Hinterland farmers, by contrast, remained more dispersed and disorganised. They presented soft targets for raiding agricultural provisions and slaving into the modern era. Though physically strong, farmers were kept poorly educated, poorly armed, poorly organised and poorly trained by their own chieftains to forestall local rebellions against oppressive taxation. Mariners and farmers were never allies in the thousands of years when conquest, raiding, extortion, exploitation and slaving expressed sea-army imperium.

Science, archaeology and DNA are revealing a truth that makes many parochial historians uncomfortable: international affairs were much the same for the past four thousand years. Mass migrations were not uncommon. Superior militaries with superior mobility and weaponry seized control of land, mineral resources, ports, trade routes and monetary policy, slaughtered indigenous warriors, and demanded exploitation of indigenous people by client kings and tribal chieftains. Imperial armies forced native leaders to exploit native labour, agriculture and mineral industries for the profit of sea-armies. Else the sea-armies laid waste the lands and slaughtered indigenous people without mercy. Native chieftains that collaborated in local exploitation gained imperial approval, prestige, wealth and security. The stability of imperium was ensured by the strength and cohesiveness of military and mercantile elites and the complicity of native chieftains who profited hugely from enslaving, oppressing and taxing indigenous peasantry.

It is an uncomfortable truth that ancient British kings were often tributary or client kings, both tributary to sea-armies in coastal cantons and distant empires. It was simply more efficient 4000 years ago, 3000 years ago, 2000 years ago, 1000 years ago, as it remains today, to exploit local resources and local labour through local chieftains, local military auxiliaries, and local tax collectors. Local chieftains are more acceptable inflicting violence, oppressive taxation and labour exploitation, and are better too at detecting and supressing local dissent. Early Roman exploitation of Britannia under truce with Briton and Gallic client kings was so massively profitable that Strabo observed in the early 1st century that Britannia already paid more to Rome in tribute and levies than could be gained by invasion and occupation.[120]

Most early English histories, like those of Gildas, Bede or the Anglo-Saxon Chronicle, start with the conquest of Britannia by Julius Caesar and the birth of Christ. These are Roman-centred histories that were written by Romanised clerics to engender a Roman-centric allegiance to popes and papally-approved and church-consecrated local kings. Tribes and priests that rejected communion with the Holy Apostolic See are cast as uncivilised heretics and pagans; kings and chieftains that rejected the primacy of popes and ruled without episcopal consecration are cast as tyrants.[121]

---

[120] Strabo, *Geographica* 4:5.

[121] Gildas explicitly rejects earlier native histories, noting 'Britain is

The truer history will prove subtler and more exciting. The Phoenician empire extended to Britannia long before the Romans. Sea-armies exerted imperium over British tribes before Julius Caesar and after Rome fell as Phoenicians, Hellenes and Nordic tribes struggled for supremacy. Sea-armies that held imperium both before and after the Roman Empire resisted Roman religion, Roman imperium, and later Roman papal authority. Nordic tribes maintained the city-state democratic law of the Hellenes in choosing rulers and affirming laws, laying the basis for the constitutional principles of Magna Carta and common law in England. Britannic Christians whose monotheistic faith antedated the founding of the Roman Church and the reforms of Constantine resisted Roman papal authority and the orthodoxy brought west by Saint Augustine long before King Henry VIII divided the English church from Rome, again, and dissolved more than 800 monasteries with the Reformation.

The history of the Norman Conquest starts before the Romans and before Christianity because far-ranging sea-army tribes originating in the Bronze Age from the Pontic Steppe were already exploiting Britannia long before Rome was founded. The Norman Conquest was the culmination of a thousand-year contest for Britannic imperium and religious orthodoxy. Some of the earlier sea-armies allied with Rome while others remained aloof from Rome. Some early Christian kings bowed to papal authority while others resisted Roman religious orthodoxy. Some of the tribes that resisted Rome became British indigenous non-conformist Christians and pagans. The schisms persisted to 1066, after King Harold having spurned communion with Rome from his earliest days as earl and certainly after the 1052 rebellion. When King Harold marched to battle with *innumera multitudine Anglorum et Dacorum*[122] – 'an innumerable multitude of Anglians and Dacians' - he carried the Dacian wolfskin battle standard in defiance of Rome; Duke William brought a papal banner sent from Rome.

---

a land fertile in tyrants', meaning chieftains who resisted Roman and papal authority. *De Excidio et Conquestu Britanniae*, II:4.

[122] *Quedam Exceptiones de Historia Normannorum et Anglorum.*

Dacian wolfskin standard on Trajan's column in Rome, Dacian wolfskin standard by King Harald Fairhair in the Icelandic Flateyarbok ('book of sea-armies'), and Dacian wolfskin standard at the death of King Harold in Scene 57 of the Bayeux Tapestry. Side by side the similarity is obvious from the gaping wolf's head to the curling tail.

The confusion of tribal names before the Romans necessitates the coining of the term 'Pontic imperium' for earlier Bronze Age, Iron Age, Phoenician, Hellenic and Dacian sea-army imperium that spread from the Pontic Steppe to coastal cantons as far as the Baltic, the Britannic Sea, the Celtic Sea and the Irish Sea. The distinguishing features of Pontic imperium may be fortified Pontic maritime cantons or city-states, tributary realms secured by conquest and truce with native client kings, and sea-army monopoly of industrialised salt production, mines, metallurgy and sailing ships. Pontic cantons often preserved secure separation from exploited hinterlands on fortified islands or promontories. Pontic ships were constructed with bronze or brass nails. Pontic bronze, brass, iron and steel tools and weapons shared superior metallurgy, workmanship and quality. Tributary realms and hinterlands were governed by client kings who paid tribute and provided provisions and slaves to their imperial Pontic masters in return for protection and the profits of trade.

The earliest narrative history to be deciphered is a 3,200-year-old Luwian hieroglyphic stone inscription that tells how Muksus, a Pontic Steppe prince of the Mira, a confederated 'sea-people', led a sea-army to conquer Troy, then re-instated the king of Troy as a client-king paying tribute. The translated text was published for the first time in late 2017. I had coined 'Pontic imperium' before the Mira translation was announced, but Mira text elegantly confirms the elements of sea-army imperium as conquest, truce and tributary subjugation of a client king.

'Pontic imperium' seems a fitting coinage as *Pontos* was the ancient name for the Black Sea. The DNA record tells us mariners from the Black Sea spread Pontic Steppe DNA, grains, cattle, cats, metallurgy, and Pontic mercantile imperium together to the coasts and rivers of Europe and North Africa. Pontic mariners also spread the rule of law: the earliest international law may be an edict requiring cats to be carried in grain ships to control the spread of rats port to port. A recent archaeological survey of the deepest recesses of the Black Sea has discovered near-perfectly preserved cargo and war ships which will greatly contribute to our future understanding of Pontic maritime technology and trade. Some are thought to be more than 4,000 years old. Their cargo is likely to confirm the scope of early trading routes extending to Britannia, as British tin was the critical component for the bronze and brass metallurgy that gave Bronze Age sea-armies superior mobility, weaponry and influence.

Pontic is also appropriate for sea-army imperium as the Indo-European word *pons* means connecting waterway, causeway, ford, road or bridge – places where thelony (tolls for passage) and levies on trade goods could be collected by sea-armies controlling mercantile traffic. Thelony, *portoria* and *vectigalia* – passage, port and market tolls – were the principal imperial revenues of all early empires. *Tributa* – imperial tribute – was collected additionally as protection money or provisions from hinterland chieftains, tribes and mercantile elites. The privileges granted to Winchester and London in the *Carmen* prove imperial privileges of the earliest Pontic cantons endured to 1066. Winchester was allowed to retain *tributa*, only paying *vectigalia*, and London was ceded self-rule as a semi-autonomous mercantile canton where *Frencisce et Anglisce* – Franks and Anglians – could be equally law-worthy under the protection of King William.

Pontic mariners who settled cantons on coasts and estuaries used their superior mobility and weaponry to assert imperium over hinterland tribes and chieftains. Pontic imperium as reflected in the Mira, Sumerian, Phoenician, Hellenic, Dacian and Roman empires seems to have encompassed sea-army demands for tribute and provisions, thelony charged on mercantile traffic, and levies of slaves to labour in mines, salt-works, industries, ports, and emporia. The same pattern of sea-army exploitation of hinterlands would endure in Nordic Dacia, Britannia and Eire into the 12th century.

As little written history exists before the first millennium BC, we must look to science and use DNA, archaeology, artefacts and contested landscape and seascape to fill in more of the record. Modern science is greatly improving our grasp of ancient history, challenging many long-held assumptions as entirely misguided or overly simplistic. Geneographic DNA mapping can trace mass migrations through haplogroup DNA markers and mutations across borders and time, revealing mass migrations and sometimes the genocide of indigenous tribes. Spectroscopic analysis can trace the geographic origins of metals and stone back to distant mines and quarries. Geomorphology now reveals the long evolution of boundary changes in liminal regions where landscape and seascape have been transmuted. Geologic data reveals climate variations, periods of intense volcanic activity, earthquakes, siltation and floods. Archaeology is raising megalith temples much like Stonehenge from the grounds of distant Gobekli Tepe in the Pontic Steppe, and ships laden with British trade goods might yet rise from the depths of the Black Sea, *Pontus* to the Phoencians and Hellenes. Even without written records, by tracing which sea-armies established which trading cantons, by analysing which mines produced which tools and weapons, and mapping shipping routes in contested landscape and seascape, we can make better sense of Pontic imperium up to the 1st century BC. From the 1st century BC we have written histories and compilations of oral traditions to guide us in interpreting the past, but better science will still improve our understanding of events, migrations, conquests, and the written record.

The Bronze Age spurred a contest for imperium in Britannia 3500 to 2500 years ago, corresponding to the Mira conquest of Troy, as descendants of Pontic Steppe mariners became confederated sea-armies exercising Pontic imperium over client kings and hinterland tribes from Egypt to Eire. Mariners from the Pontic Steppe, later Phoenicians and Hellenes, industrialised mining of British tin in Cornwall and Devon, and shipped refined tin along secure sea lanes to their kindred in the east. These mercantile mariners, and the valuable metal weapons and tools they carried with them, did not spread so widely into hinterlands. Liminal Bronze and Iron Age sea-armies stayed close to their mines, ships and hill-forts. Sea-armies armed with metal weapons and sailing stronger ships settled in cantons, married their own kind, and preferred their wives' educated, literate, numerate, and multi-lingual children to children of inferior, uneducated hinterland women.[123] Inbreeding is notable among pharaonic and royal families throughout the ancient world. Archaeologists can also trace common Pontic heritage by the shared features of Pontic cantons: raised coastal or estuarine fortifications, salt-works, mines, ships, and metal tools, ornaments, coins, and weapons. In describing the Britons in the first century BC *Commentaries on the Gallic Wars*, Julius Caesar noted the difference between coastal and hinterland tribes, and that the coastal tribes were organised as *civitates*- city-states - affiliated with the coastal tribes across the Britannic Sea.

Detailed geneographic DNA analysis published in the 2015 *People of the British Isles* report has confirmed Caesar's observations and overthrown Victorian assumptions about British ethnicity as Celtic and Germanic.[124] British Celts are not a distinct ethnic group. Cornish, Welsh, Irish and Scots have little DNA commonality with each other or continental so-called Celts. The DNA record suggests 'Celtic' was a convenient designation adopted by the Victorian English elites to distinguish 'subjugated inferiors' across their borders in Scotland, Eire, Wales and Cornwall, not an accurate ethnic identification. In particular, Cornish DNA has more commonality with English DNA than it does with other so-called Celtic tribes.

The same study found scant trace of 'Roman' DNA in the British population if Roman means from Rome, or even Italy. Roman imperial citizenship embraced the warriors and urban elites of British, Gallic, Frisian, Iberian and Germanic provinces. The 'Romans' who oversaw the building of ancient fortresses, ports, roads and causeways

---

[123] A high proportion of unceremonial infant burials have been found at early trade settlements and on borders between liminal and hinterland regions, implying many children of indigenous women or slaves were killed at birth or when women were captured in hinterland slave raids.

[124] Winney, B. J., Boumertit, A., Day, T., Davison, D., Echeta, C., Evseeva, I., et al. (2012). 'People of the British Isles: preliminary analysis of genotypes and surnames in a UK-control population', *European Journal of Human Genetics*: EJHG, 20(2), 203–210.

to industrialise, colonise and exploit Roman Britannia were Romano-Britons, Romano-Belgae, Romano-Frisii and Romano-Germani. Common DNA haplogroups with continental populations prove these 'Romans' did contribute their DNA to the English. White, indigenous southern and central English share about 40 per cent of their DNA with the French, about 30 per cent with the Germans, 11 per cent with the Danes and nine per cent with the Belgians. There was a later Saxon migration into an unsettled and vulnerable Britain in the fifth century after a super volcano eruption in Central America spread crop failure, famine and disease widely through Europe. Contrary to early histories by Gildas and Bede, however, indigenous Britons were not forced into Wales or Scotland when the Saxons came. The Saxons integrated with the indigenous Britons. In short, Britannia was peopled by coastal seafaring tribes of Western Europe in the three thousand years when liminal lands and sea-lanes were commons for sea-army imperium, fishing, raiding, trading, tribute, fostering and marriage.

An earlier ancient migration of Pontic Steppe mariners has also been revealed in British DNA. In the Neolithic period about 3500 years ago – the dawn of the Bronze Age – Near East mariners from the eastern Mediterranean or Black Sea brought cereals and cattle into England and introduced settled agriculture and maritime trade. The DNA record shows these Pontic Steppe mariners started farming, growing grains and breeding livestock, and also interbred with indigenous women. Near East DNA grew dominant and spread north in Britain and Eire until indigenous hunter-gatherer men disappeared from the genetic record almost entirely. Only female indigenous DNA was perpetuated. British women were by no means unique in preferring mariners and farmers to hunter-gatherers, assuming they were given any choice. 80 per cent of European men have DNA from Neolithic Pontic Steppe migrants. The eradication of indigenous males in Britain and Eire is unusual, but perhaps easier to accomplish on islands.

The ancient Pontic sea-warrior tribes who rose to power with bronze and brass gave the British archipelago its first written name: *Cassiterides* – the 'tin islands'.[125] Without British tin there would have been no Bronze Age and no spread of writing or early urban

---

[125] Herodotus (c. 430 BC).

civilisations. The alloy bronze is 2 per cent tin; naval brass is 1 per cent tin. Each shipload of refined tin from Britain massively enhanced the military superiority of sea-armies fabricating and trading bronze weapons for conquest, brass chandlery for ships, and bronze or brass tools for industry along ancient maritime trade routes as far as the Danube, Levant and Nile. Recent isotopic and spectroscopic studies of metal origins prove British tin in metal artefacts owned by elites in ancient tombs found in these far-distant places.

Tin was so crucial to sea-army military, mercantile and monetary imperium its British origins were jealously shrouded in secrecy by the Phoenicians and Hellenes. Phoenician tribes at Cadiz prevented any Mediterranean or African ships venturing further north. Strabo tells of a Phoenician captain followed by a Roman ship who steered both vessels to destruction rather than reveal the port from which tin was shipped to the Romans. The ignorance of Gallic *mercatores* interviewed by Julius Caesar for intelligence of Britannia in 55 BC confirms similar precautions against spying were still being enforced.[126]

Pontic imperium was a 'protection racket' that should be familiar to military historians of any empire, ancient or modern. While raiding and slaving were quite profitable and good sport for warlike young men, they were also a technique by which sea-armies could force vulnerable chieftains and elites to compact truces for provisions, slaves and tribute. Reading the Anglo-Saxon Chronicle as a record of Pontic imperium, we can identify a recurring pattern of raiding, truce and subjugation that makes sense of conflicts between hinterland kings and liminal sea-armies during the Migration Age after the fall of Rome. Sea-armies raided 'causing every kind of harm' until they compelled kings, ealdormen, church prelates and urban elites to truce. Under truce sea-armies received gold and silver tribute, stipendiary provisions, levies of slaves, and self-ruled, privileged coastal commonwealths for settlement.

All boys and men in Pontic cantons trained for combat constantly, and all gained wide experience of war through raiding hinterlands, supressing rebellions, attacking unconfederated tribes, and defence against pirates. Pontic mariners were schooled to fight as a

---

[126] *Commentaries on the Gallic Wars* IV:20.

ship, and Pontic sea-armies were schooled to fight as a fleet, ensuring effective Pontic military leadership, lines of command, and strategic cooperation. Pontic children, both sons and daughters, were fostered after infancy away from their birth homes to promote literacy, numeracy, inter-cantonal cohesion and multi-lingual communication. Pontic mariners fought and traded widely abroad before marrying and settling in cantons, so cantonal garrisons had more effective weaponry and experienced civil militias for cantonal defence.

Pontic political hierarchies were more democratic and meritocratic, rewarding more able leaders with election to command. Raiding seasons were spring and fall, and convening at neutral muster ports put all free men on an equal footing. Mariners and ships were widely distributed to varied home settlements and harbours in winter and summer. Freemen warriors coming to the spring or fall muster chose service with competent skippers, and skippers chose to join fleets of competent sea-lords for raiding and trading. Losing a skipper or sea-lord rarely impaired the effectiveness of a ship or fleet for long. New skippers or sea-lords of similar merit would be elected to take command.

Salt was 'white gold' to Bronze Age sea-armies even as metals became currency. Salt-foods and metals are both force multipliers for early maritime, military and mercantile dominance, but production of salt-foods and metallurgy are hugely labour-intensive and unpleasant. These industries developed in cantons around sea-army fortifications because they needed many resources and slaves. It was slaves who cut firewood and made charcoal in bloomeries. It was slaves who concentrated brine pools and cooked salt, who smoked and salted meats and fish, who churned salt-butter and made salt-cheese, and who salted grain and pickled vegetables for storage. It was slaves who mined ore from the ground, crushed ore, smelted copper, tin, zinc and iron, and who stoked the forges for skilled smiths and moneyers. Part of the status conveyed by elite salt-foods, metal ornaments and coins in ancient civilisations may have derived from the many days, months or years of slave labour required to produce the luxuries enjoyed by sea-army and urban elites.

With salt-foods mariners could travel further, armies could campaign longer, and urban populations could withstand sieges longer.[127] Salt was essential too for sanitation and curing, reducing food wastage, disease and contagion, so an early connection between salt, urbanisation and religious salvation is not surprising. The first stone temples were erected at salt-works, probably for secure storage of salt blocks away from moisture degradation, rodents and thieves. Early priests in these temples held a monopoly on the salt trade, and oversaw the markets and industries that converged on port cantons, a monopoly continued by the early Roman church through royal foundation churches and abbeys. Salt was involved in the earliest sacrifice and religious rites too. The Old Testament enjoins the faithful not to bring grain to the temple without salt.[128] Unsalted grain would moulder in the storehouse, spreading rot and wastage. The early Roman church salted communion wafers and baptismal fonts, practices preserved in the Orthodox church today. Many miracle stories from early Christian annals attesting to the corporeal preservation of saints suggest salt-curing of the dead prior to entombing, much like Egyptian sacred mummification.[129] Salt was also required for industrial dying, leather tanning and metallurgy, so was essential for leather body armour, weaponry, tools, trade goods and coinage.

Southern Britain offered many coastal estuaries ideal for tidal brine evaporation pools and nearby woods or peat bogs to fuel salt cooking, as well as offering plentiful tin and iron. The Domesday Book records Sussex the richest source of marine salt. Fully 30 per cent of English salt-pans were in Sussex, and almost 10 per cent were in Rameslege – the greatest estuarine port of the Sussex coast. It is not accident or coincidence that King Harold and Duke William battled for imperium of England near the port of Hastingas, rich in both salt and iron, dispossessed from the Normans by King Harold since 1052. The loss of salt and iron had impoverished and weakened the Normans.

---

[127] King William's army of Normans in 1066 did not get ill until they first ate fresh meat in Dover according to William of Poitiers.

[128] Leviticus 2:13.

[129] Before Christianity encouraged churchyard burials, bodies were never entombed within populated settlements, but buried outside towns and villages. Salt-curing was a sensible precaution for emtombment or burial to prevent smell and disease.

Refined metals were even more valuable than salt and much scarcer. Pontic sea-armies would monopolise mining, refining, metallurgy and mints from the Bronze Age to reinforce military, mercantile and monetary imperium. Bronze and naval brass in the Bronze Age and iron and steel in the Iron Age provided harder chandlery for far-ranging ships, sharper and heavier weapons for warriors, and better tools for exploiting agricultural and mineral resources. Metals first traded as rings and ornaments, then as coins, standardised for purity. Parting gold and silver started with salt-cementation processing of electrum from the 7th century BC.[130] Gold, silver, bronze and copper coins were more valuable than salt blocks or salt-fish, more durable, more easily assayable and divisible, and much more portable. Soon metal coins bore an image of imperium. The first coins to display images bore the impress of a ship and sea-army.

Bronze Age Pontic tribes shared sea-army culture and language, but lived by self-rule as independent loosely confederated cantons or city-states, like the familiar Hellenic model of city-states. The earliest Pontic tribes controlled the Black Sea and Sea of Marmara below the Hellespont – 'strait-pound' in ancient Greek. The region of Europe bordering the western Black Sea would become known in the Hellenic age as Dacia. In this history it is called Illyrian Dacia to distinguish it from Nordic Dacia, founded by later diaspora sea-armies. When Pontic sea-armies spread further from the Hellespont they similarly settled Pontic cantons at strategic islands, straits, estuaries and promontories to extract thelony and tolls from merchant traffic while demanding tribute money, provisions and slaves from protected hinterlands and controlling trade.

Spectroscopic analysis of artefacts and DNA testing of remains from the mid-2nd millennium BC in central Europe, the Levant and Egypt proves British origin of gold and tin and Near East heritage of ruling elites in all these places. Local historians have for centuries patriotically assumed local craftsmanship of finer artefacts and local ethnicity of ruling elites, but science is forcing a new internationalist and realist perspective. Royally entombed Egyptian mummies along

---

[130] The earliest manuscript instructions for salt-process separation of gold and silver require both rock salt and sea salt, which may be why ancient empires sought to control both sources.

the Nile had Near East DNA and British tin burial goods. These
Pontic Pharaohs ruled over and exploited native North Africans
working the plantations of the Nile and quarrying stone for their
temples whose bodies were thrown without ceremony into anonymous
mass graves. Prosperous Phoenician merchants in Tyre had Near East
DNA and British tin trade goods. Pontic Phoenicians exploited the
native tribes of the caravan routes that brought spices, silks and other
luxuries from the east to trade with the west. Fierce Danube war-lords
in the north of Europe had Near East DNA and British tin in their
bronze weapons and British gold on their ornamented shields. These
Pontic war-lords exploited native Illyrian and Slavic tribes to slave in
their mines and on farms. The English, Bretons and Irish too have
Near East DNA, with the insular Irish retaining much more than the
English. Near East migrants once ruled these islands too, and
exploited the natives just as ruthlessly as elsewhere along trade routes.

Pontic imperium can be traced through the tribes that began
recording their history in writing as well. Sumerians were the first
Pontic empire to spread writing through trade. They were superseded
by Minoans, who were better sailors and based at Crete. Crete
controlled the strait for navigation between the Hellespont, Troy and
the Levant trading cantons. The Minoans were then superseded by
Macedonians who possessed bronze – an alloy of copper and tin –
which built stronger ships and sharper weapons, then naval brass – an
alloy of copper, zinc and tin – which was more resistant to corrosion.
Minoan DNA from skeletons at Knossos confirms Minoans were
descended from Neolithic natives and European mariners. No North
African DNA has been found at Knossos, confirming the absolute
supremacy of the migrant sea-army.

The Minoans were eventually conquered by the Hellenes. *Hellas*
means 'strait' in ancient Greek, so the very name Hellenes implied
confederated sea-armies controlling straits or pounds along navigable
waterways. Recent DNA analysis has confirmed that Hellenic myths
are factually correct tracing Macedonian descent from north European
migrants and distinguishing the Macedonians as ethnically distinct from
Minoans. Macedonian DNA includes DNA from Illyrian Dacia and
the Pontic Steppe tribes who controlled early metallurgy of bronze and
brass. This Dacian DNA better explains Hellenic conquest of the
more cultured Minoans. Troy is an excellent example of a Pontic city-
state controlling mercantile traffic by sea while exploiting the hinterland

for provisions and slaves. When Troy fell to Mira imperium, as explained in the Luwian hieroglyphic, its king retained his city-state but paid tribute for protection and tolls for trade to the Mira sea-army.

The dominant tribe during the Trojan Wars at the end of the Bronze Age, approximately 1200 BC, is named by Homer as the Achaeans (Ἀχαιοί). If the ethnonym derives from ancient Greek then it means *ax-cynn* or *ex-cynn*, 'foreigner or outsider tribe'.[131] The name is apt for a Dacian-derived tribe that settled in liminal Pontic cantons and kept itself distinct and separate from hinterland tribes. If we trace homonym names along the southern English cantons we find many incorporate *ax-* or *ex-*, from tin-rich Exeter, to Exmouth, to Axmouth, to Exceat, to Icklesham, to *Portus Iccius* on the Gallic coast, advancing tide by tide, pound by pound, as the ancient Pontic mariners carrying tin toward the ancient Achaeans in the east would have navigated.

When the smelting of iron and forging of steel spread through Europe, Pontic military and maritime superiority based on a tin monopoly and control of sea-routes was undermined. It is unlikely to be coincidence that the Iron Age dates from about the fall of Troy. The fall of Troy was a critical event in Hellenic oral histories because it marked the end of uncontested and widely collaborative Hellenic imperium. Iron smelting and forging require much higher temperatures than copper, zinc or tin metallurgy, but iron can be smelted and forged anywhere with enough ore, fuel and labour. Hinterland chieftains with iron and steel raised well-armed land-armies and became military rivals to Pontic sea-armies. Hinterland chieftains retained slaves for their own mines and iron works, fortifications and road-building, rather than cede slaves to Pontic sea-armies. With iron and steel hinterland chieftains could protect their own lands, emporia and trade routes, spurning sea-army protection and imperium.

The rise and fall of Pontic imperium has perhaps been unsuspected because it offends against the ethno-centric nationalism of

_____

[131] *Graeci* or Greek was an ethnonym innovated by Romans which spread through Latin texts of history to European languages, but Greek confuses rather than clarifies the Pontic history of imperium before the Roman Empire. It is more useful to think of Hellenic or Pontic tribes – sea-armies on straits and navigable pounds.

modern histories. Pontic imperium could not be suspected by patriotic historians keen to celebrate early armies as indigenous warriors rather than foreign invaders, early kings as enlightened natives rather than foreign tyrants or subservient clients. Early fortresses and temples were ascribed to the industry and genius of local chieftains and craftsmen, not oppression forced by foreign overlords. Quality grave goods were attributed to local craftsmen rather than foreign artisans. Scientific analysis of metal artefacts and DNA tell a less patriotic but more rational story. Technology and imperium spread together with Pontic sea-armies along navigable waterways everywhere in Europe, the Levant and north Africa. Coastal hill forts, brass ship chandlery and bronze weapons all likely belonged to confederated Pontic sea-armies exploiting native tribes under truce with local chieftains. Iron changed the balance, creating more lasting geographic and tribal divisions by undermining trade networks and military confederation.

The origin myths of Romans, Franks and Britons as deriving from Trojan sea-armies seem to confirm that Pontic imperium long continued in Gallia and Britannia. Clerics of the Roman Church preserved and recorded these Trojan myths, suggesting that a legend of Trojan heritage was important to royal legitimacy. After the fall of Troy some sea-warriors migrated to Rome with Aeneas and founded the Roman Republic, still targeting control of salt, metals, trade, and tributary provinces. Other armies fleeing Troy sailed north to the Black Sea and spread along rivers as the Slavo-Dacian diaspora, extending Dacian cantons up fluvial and maritime routes into Gallia and the Baltic.

One Pontic sea-lord, said to be descended from Aeneas, sailed from Troy as far as the Britannic Sea. According to Gallic and Britannic legends, Brutus of Troy gained imperium over Brittany, Belgica and Britannia, uniting the three realms into one empire. Brittany and Britannia are eponymously named for Brutus, as is the Britannic Sea (the Channel and North Sea together) that untied Britain's coasts with coasts from the continent. The three sons of Brutus preserved his imperium in Britannia as kings: Albanactus as king of Scotia in the north; Camber as king of eponymous Cumbria and Wales (Cymru) in the west; and Locrinus as king of the southern realm on the Britannic Sea. Scotland and Wales were tributary to the Britons of the south, as they have remained for much of history. Each king controlled a sea route too: Albanactus controlled the trade route to the

Baltic, Camber controlled the Irish Sea and Celtic Sea trade routes to Eire and Iberia, and Locrinus controlled the Britannic Sea trade routes to Belgica and Brittany. Britannia became famous for its wealth, eventually drawing the covetous gaze of both Roman and Dacian adventurers.

Brutus of Troy and his sons as drawn by Matthew Paris for his *Abbreviated Chronicle of England*, Cotton MS Claudius D VI, f. 6r. From top left proceeding clockwise: Brutus of Troy conquers Brittany, Belgica and Britannia with his sea-army, gaining imperium over the native tribes; Albanactus became ruler of the Scots, Camber became ruler of the Welsh, and Locrinus, succeeding to his father's staff of imperium, became king of Britannia.

In the *Commentaries on the Gallic Wars* Julius Caesar describes Pontic imperium for controlling trade between Gallia and Britannia across the Britannic Sea. He says the Veneti had control of the most eligible Morini ('mariner') ports on the British and Gallic coasts, and were the most expert mariners, and 'so extracted market tolls from all who traffic in that sea' – evident Pontic imperium.[132] The Veneti may have been the Pontic tribe who established the emporium at Winchester, *Venta Belgarum* – 'Belgic-Veneti emporium'. There are Celtic, Belgic and Baltic Veneti and Slavic Wends (a cognate of Veneti), and all may relate to the Veneti founders of ancient Venice in pre-Hellenic times – the Ἐνετοί. Caesar also refers to the Veneti as a *civitatis* – city-state – of great influence, and he makes explicit that only the sea-army tribes confederated with the Veneti in 56BC to rebel against Roman rule. The Veneti chieftain invoked a legacy of independence and imperium over tributary hinterlands in Gallia and Britannia in urging resistance to Caesar.

Morini may likewise derive from the pre-Hellenic *Mira* 'sea-people' and have named the later Mercians, tribes forced north of the Thames by the Romans. Caesar notes that the Morini ports were the most eligible ports for trade on a coast exposed to the violence of the open sea. The three ports Caesar describes are now thought to be the estuarine ports of Le Touquet, Quend (*Quentovic*) and Saint-Valery sur Somme, the same coast used to muster the Norman invasion fleet in the *Carmen*.

The image of disciplined and long-standing Pontic imperium is reinforced when Caesar interrogates the *mercatores* or merchant mariners who regularly cross the Britannic Sea to trade in Britannia. They report they know nothing of the hinterland as they are never allowed to travel further than the canton where they land and trade. Isolating free ports and cantonal emporia protected hinterland tribes from attack and prevented any collaboration against cantonal supremacy. Charging thelony and market tolls earned rich revenues for Pontic cantons as taxes on both the hinterland and foreign merchants.

The Veneti and other allied Pontic tribes contested Caesar's imperium in 56 BC and were defeated in a grand naval battle that saw

---

[132] *Commentaries on the Gallic Wars* III:8.

hundreds of ships from Britannia and Gallia go down to defeat. Caesar and his Gallic allies secured control of Gallia and Britannia was left vulnerable to Caesar's expeditions of the two following years.

When viewed as Romano-Dacian sea-army conflict and alliance, we can re-evaluate the Roman Empire in a new light. The Roman Republic had been suffering low revenues after repeal of local port taxes in protest at port officials' corruption. Rich tributes won by Caesar in Gallia and Britannia bought easy popularity and municipal celebrations back in impoverished Rome. Provincial revenues from tribute and wider trade organised on Pontic principles funded vast new imperial building projects, including the ports at Portus and Ostia. The truces Caesar struck with sea-army tribes who confederated with Rome would become models for Romano-Pontic cooperation at the margins of a growing Roman Empire as imperium spread to Greece, the Levant and Egypt and northward along the Rhine and Danube into Illyrian Dacia. Romano-Pontic auxiliaries ruled, exploited and defended the lands using sea-armies as their merchantmen, tribute collectors, and federated warriors.

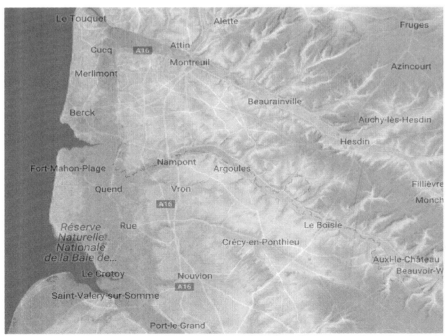

Julius Caesar in the *Gallic Wars* for 55 and 54 BC describes three ports, aligned with and communicating with each other for fleet musters, just as the three sheltered estuarine ports of the Pas de Calais must have done 2000 years ago at then-prevailing sea levels.

It was Pontic imperium that spread Roman sea-armies and city-states. Pontic imperium under Roman direction re-established mercantile traffic from Antioch to Alexandria to Exeter to Eire, excelling the Phoenician and Hellenic empires. The legend of the tin-trading maternal uncle of Jesus Christ, Joseph of Arimathea, has a more rational historical basis when viewed with this Pontic perspective. Joseph is said to have brought some of the 70 original apostles of Christ to Britannia even before Saint Peter reached Rome. Joseph is also celebrated in Arthurian legends for bringing the Holy Grail to the west, perhaps a simple cup of brass using British tin and Hellenic copper rather than something more sparkling and bejewelled.[133]

The persistence of Pontic sea-army city-states, self-rule, trading and tribute collection under Roman imperial contracts is evidenced by some later written records. In the *Notitia Dignitatum*, compiled toward the end of the Roman Empire in the early 5th century as a record of military and exchequer offices, the *Comes Sacrarum Largitionum* collected taxes for trade, ports, mines and mints – the same scope Pontic city-states controlled before the Roman Empire. The office dates to the reign of Constantine the Great, son of a Thracian father and Anglo-Dacian mother, a Pontic heritage spanning the empire he ruled and unified.

The chequerboard cloth or table featured in the *Notitia Dignitatum* as a badge of office was the tool of imperial accounting. Its form gave rise to the games of conquest chequers and chess, and its administrative disciplines were emulated by the exchequers of early kings. Fécamp (*fisc-campus*) was the ducal seat of early Norman dukes but it had earlier served as the Romano-Gallic imperial exchequer. It may have been a Belgae regional treasury before Caesar came to Gallia.

Naturally some sea-armies and cantons continued to resist Roman imperium as the Roman Empire spread its reach. The most important confederation to resist Rome were the Dacians. Dacian imperium has been neglected by historians relative to the Hellenes, the

---

[133] Brass is anti-microbial so much healthier for use in cooking and eating utensils before modern sanitation, a property appreciated by ancient metallurgists.

Roman Republic, the Roman Empire and later Germanic empires, but understanding ancient Dacian confederation, culture, navigation, migration, warfare, truce and rule of law will more fully explain early Western European history in general and British history in particular. As Rome encroached on Dacian lands and waterways, Dacians spread north up rivers from their native Black Sea to the Baltic. Nordic Dacians then settled the seacoasts at cantons and commonwealths in Western Scotland, Cumbria and Wales, controlling the Irish Sea, and also settled in Northumbria, Freesia and East Anglia, controlling the North Sea. When the Britons and Gallic sea-armies of the south allied with Caesar and Rome, the Nordic Dacians remained aloof, warily trading with the Romanised regions at ports designated by Rome as free ports for border trade: York, London and Utrecht in Freesia. The Morini of Caesar's day may have retired beyond the Romanised south to create Mercia in the midlands of Britannia.

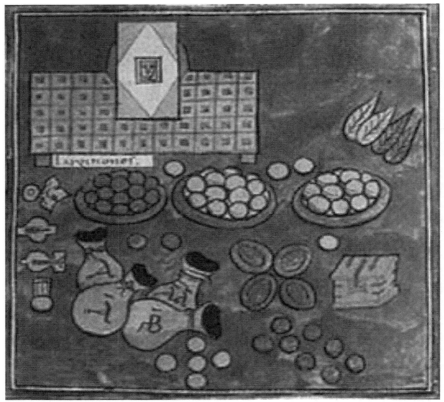

Insignia of the *comes sacrorum largitionem* with exchequer table, codicil of appointment, and money bags of gold and silver as reproduced by Peronet Lamy (died 1453) based on 5th century original of the *Notitia Dignitatum*.

The Dacians, sometimes Geto-Dacians, were an Indo-European people closely related to the Thracians. Herodotus describes the Illyrian Dacians of the Black Sea as 'the noblest as well as the most just of all the Thracian tribes',[134] and Thucydides adds they fought on horseback as mounted archers, confirming early military superiority.[135] The names *Getae* and *Daci* have been thought interchangeable, with Romans preferring *Daci* and Greeks preferring *Getae*. A closer analysis of context in original sources may suggest *Daci* is a combined form of Indo-European *dha – 'to put or place' and εκ – 'foreign or outflowing', suggestive of Pontic cantons or 'settled Achaeans'. *Getae* has been suggested as mariners who 'flow forth' or 'spread seed', describing the sea-armies who adventured, raided and traded more widely from their home cantons, spreading settled agriculture with trade as Bronze Age mariners had done. Strabo supports this distinction by saying the *Getae* occupied the region of Dacia toward the Sea of Marmara, controlling access to the Black Sea, while the *Daci* occupied the fluvial and mining region toward Germania, later Romania, controlling mining, metallurgy and fluvial trade.

An alternative Indo-European derivation may relate *Getae* to the ancient Hebrew *ghet*. A *ghet* was a region ceded by royal or imperial deed for settlement by a distinct tribe, later Romanised as *ghetto*. This derivation fits the diverse settlement of mariner Getae in coastal cantons under truce with hinterland chieftains or kings. Getae as 'tribes of the ghettoes' elegantly aligns with observed archaeology of Hellenic and Dacian coastal and fluvial settlements and the pattern of truce-agreed cantons in Roman accounts and histories like the Anglo-Saxon Chronicle.

Wherever they settled, all sources agree the Dacians shared a common Hellenic language and culture, maintained by military alliances, trade, marriage and fostering. The commonality of language among Dacian diaspora may allow us to further trace Dacian settlement and solve riddles of coastal place names that have long frustrated native toponymists in the west. Many coastal names in England and elsewhere may follow wider Dacian nautical or fluvial

---

[134] *Histories* IV:XCIII.

[135] *Peloponnesian Wars*, Book II.

naming conventions. For example, the early medieval Dacians named the region around the Danish and Swedish strait connecting the North Sea to the Baltic as Dacia, repeating the name of their ancient homeland, and the strait itself was Hellespont, repeating the name of the Hellenic strait they originally controlled from the Black Sea for their earliest wealth and power. Helsinki, Helsingor (Elsinor), and *Helsingiaport* (the port of Hastings as named by Icelandic bard Snorri Sturluson) all appear to have the same Dacian topographical derivation from *hels* – 'strait'. Exeter, Exmouth, Axmouth, Exceat and Icklesham may likewise derive from *ax-* or *ex-*, as 'outsider' or Achaean estuarine cantons. Other coastal place name patterns may be discovered on further reconsideration.

Another challenge for historians may be that Dacian imperium was a distributed system rather than centralised. Romans were centralised with all imperial authority emanating from Rome; Dacians were decentralised with sea-army authority dispersed among confederated cantonal city-states with more fluid leadership. Rome preserved written language and uniform systems of imperial administration and accounting, although the Roman senate sub-contracted administration and taxation to provinces. There was one Roman law and one Roman senate and one Roman citizenry. All public affairs were structured and systematic. All public commerce was transacted in the senate and forum. Tribute collection and trade tolls were uniformly collected and reported. All Roman geography was described relative to Rome at the centre of empire. The *Carmen* preserves this Roman-centric geography at line 639, describing London as having walls to the left and river to the right as if the bard is facing Rome. The Roman *hasta* or short spear was the symbol of Roman imperial authority everywhere. Imperial contracts were signed under the *hasta*; solemn oaths were sworn under the *hasta*; and imperial justice was dealt to offenders under the *hasta*. The *hasta* features in the *Carmen* at lines 310 and 447 when Duke William convenes his men and compels them to his service.

By contrast Dacian diaspora tribes preserved Pontic or Hellenic republican city-state governance as they spread up rivers to the Baltic and then to Eire, Freesia, Gallia and northern Britannia. Dacians did not seek to rule hinterlands, but to achieve profit from truce with hinterland chieftains. Dacians sought direct control only of salt, metals, mints, and waterways. Dacian sea-lords and cantonal magistrates were elected locally and democratically, and each city-state was self-ruled as a republic by its citizenry. Cantons were always vulnerable to uprisings from hostile hinterlands or attack from abroad, so cantons were fortified and secured with local militias. Dacian tribes confederated as sea-armies for seasonal raiding and trading campaigns. The weapon of choice for Dacian warriors was the more democratic bow, and Dacians were famed for sending flights of flaming arrows from either ships or horses to waste fields and raze settlements.[136] Dacians raided by ship and on horseback where no truce bound them, and made local truces for self-rule cantons, slaves, provisions and tribute wherever profitable. The symbol of all Dacian sea-armies was the wolf, an animal that hunts and attacks in packs. Wolf heads were carved into the stems of Dacian ships, wolf heads of brass were the trumpets of their battle horns, and dyed wolfskins were carried as Dacian standards to battle.

Another rough gauge of Dacian and Roman settlement owes inspiration to Professor George Kish, a great geographic historian of the 20th century. Where Dacians settled there was beer and later distilled grain spirits; where Romans settled there was also wine and later distilled fruit brandies. Making beer required only barley looted from the hinterland or delivered as stipendiary provisions by tributary tribes to coastal cantons. Making wines, ciders and brandies required a longer-term stewardship of the land, the vineyards and the orchards, and settled habits of cultivation and distillation. Wine has the advantage of lasting longer than beer, but beer can be distilled anytime throughout the year. The Indo-European derivation of *Getae* for Geto-Dacians as 'spreading seed' may thus be more than metaphor. Illyrian Dacians may have brought barley seed and beer brewing together as they advanced their cantonal settlements from the Pontic Steppe to the north, south and west. The oldest wine vessels are also from the Pontic Steppe, but wine was too valuable as an elite trade good to be widely shared with peasantry. Like preserved salt-foods, beer and wine kept sea-armies healthier as they campaigned and travelled abroad, or lived together in crowded camps and urban settlements.

---

[136] The Romanised tribes of Frisian Toxandria were similarly famed for their skills as shipmen, horsed warriors and archers.

The drinking cult of Dionysos may have served to unite diverse Geto-Dacian sea-armies in ancient times, endowing common religion and rituals to wide-spread trading cantons. The cult was important enough to be suppressed by the Roman senate in 186BC as a threat to state authority. The Dionysian cult may even have given rise to traditions of monotheistic Christianity: Dionysos had a divine father and a mortal mother; he was resurrected to eternal life as a god after being killed by the Titans; communion among diverse communities and with the spirit world was achieved through ritual drinking of wine from a common vessel. As with communion wine, bread was likewise ritually shared at feasts by each man taking only what he needed, not what he wanted, with the aim of the loaf lasting to the last man or boy. Dionysos would be honoured as a saint from the 3rd century, corresponding to the rise of Dacians to military and political supremacy within the Roman Empire, and despite the doubtful historicity of any bishop or martyr of that name. Saint Constantine, of a Thracian father and Dacian mother, imposed an orthodoxy on Christian practice that included the communion ritual. The Merovingian kings of France imposed similar imperial Christianity and promoted trade throughout western Europe through the abbey dedicated to Saint Dionysus, later Saint Denis, near Paris. Clerical cells of Saint Denis would collect taxes and tolls at ports and border crossings throughout the Frankish empire for over a thousand years, including centuries of control of Hastingas from the reign of King Offa and his Frankish queen. Eleutherus, a companion martyr of Saint Dionysus according to legend, was also an epithet of the god Dionysos meaning 'liberator', while Rusticus, the other martyred companion, may evoke the more earthy, playful, clownish character of Dionysos, better known as Bacchus.

Dacian tribes also transmitted their ancient culture and institutions through trade, oral tradition, hereditary privilege, marriage, fostering, and rule of law. Remote fostering of children and inter-marriage were critical to the preservation of diaspora Dacian identity, as they would be critical to preservation of British identity in the global British Empire. The British Empire founded mercantile port cantons secured by the East India Company or the Royal Navy to exploit and trade with subjugated hinterland tribes under truce with chieftains in the Near East, Africa, North America and Asia. British merchants, craftsmen, and other skilled emigrants settled in these cantons under English rule of law to promote hinterland exploitation and trade. British men preferred British wives because natives were deemed ethnically inferior, and because a British mother conveyed her language, education, culture and religion to British children, even if they spent their whole lives abroad. British children were often fostered away from home in remote British schools with British teachers to give them British identity, literacy, religion, and values. Ancient Dacian mariners and merchantmen likewise founded Dacian cantons in Romania, Germania, Freesia, Iberia, Gaul, Eire and Britannia on similar principles, and married, schooled, and fostered children on similar principles. Settled Dacians married Dacian wives to preserve ethnic, linguistic, religious and cultural superiority for their Dacian children. Dacian children were fostered or schooled away from home to promote Dacian literacy, community, religion and values.

Fostering or schooling both sons and daughters away from home cemented inter-cantonal loyalty, cohesion and shared culture, and helped ensure effective collaboration for trading, raiding and defence. Fostered children might be initially given as hostages, a common custom to secure loyalty and performance of oaths and truces, but fostered children were generally educated and treated with respect as a means of cementing long-term military confederation and mercantile collaboration. When foster-sons returned home as freemen they became diplomats and negotiators for the common military and mercantile interests of both home and foster cantons, promoting prosperity of both home and foster families. Foster-sons often married daughters of their foster-families to replace the security of an oath or truce with the greater security of shared progeny. Wherever they married, fostered daughters brought the domestic, religious, and financial management skills that could promote their families' prosperity and reputation.

Marriage of Dacian women secured more enduring Dacian imperium than raiding by Dacian men. What Dacian men won by terror and truce with their swords, Dacian women secured more permanently with their intellects and their wombs. The royalty of a target realm could be co-opted in one or two generations by intermarriage with powerful Dacian women. An educated and proud Dacian noblewoman would accept marriage to an ethnically and educationally inferior hinterland king or ealdorman to secure effective mercantile imperium as consort during her lifetime and a realm for half-Dacian royal sons and daughters after her husband's death. Dacians insisted on hereditary property rights for their children. We see this pattern in Britain repeats through early history up to the Norman Conquest. A native king would gladly seek marriage to a Dacian wife as she was literate, multi-lingual, mercantile and financially astute. A Dacian queen would enhance a king's prestige abroad, his standing with the church, and his prosperity at home. If we look at the English kings who promoted early military, mercantile, religious and monetary reforms, we find many of them – King Aethelberht, King Offa, King Edgar, King Aethelred – married powerful foreign wives who may have been Dacian noblewomen. The charter of London's liberties, indirectly referenced in the *Carmen*, assured the burgesses of London hereditary property rights for their children.

Marrying Dacian women conferred enormous advantages. Dacian wives and daughters were educated, literate, numerate, commercially astute, religious and respectable. Dacian wives were a source of status and prestige. Dacian wives administered royal household treasuries and domestic affairs in their lords' frequent and lengthy absences. Wives wore the key to the family treasury at their waist as a symbol of their trust and authority. They promoted schools, communal loyalty, religious observance, social cohesion and inter-tribal diplomacy. Wives had responsibility for rituals, celebrations, reciprocal gift giving, stipends to the needy, and religious endowments for the public good. Dacian women often succeeded to their father or husband's authority and property, providing continuity until their sons were of an age to command, and sometimes they even led men into battle.

Oral traditions, archaeology and modern DNA analysis agree Dacian populations migrated further north from Illyrian Dacia, establishing riparian settlements at salt springs in Poland in the Bronze Age, in iron-rich Romania and Germania in the Iron Age, and then spread east into central Gallia and north to the Baltic in the Hellenic Era. Migrating Dacians continued to target control of salt and metals as well as control of watercourses and straits. Baltic Dacians colonised the strait between Helsinki ('strait-people') and Estonia ('sea strand settlement' or 'Achaen settlement') for sale of Slavo-Dacian salt to Baltic fishing fleets. Dacians then colonised the Danish Hellespont ('strait-pound'), the narrow route between the North Sea and the Baltic, taking control of the Jutland peninsula, Swedish coastal regions and Scandia Islands, just as they had once controlled the Hellespont below the Black Sea. Dacia remained the name of the Danish Hellespont region until the late medieval era created separate nations in Sweden, Denmark and Norway. In 11th and 12th century annals King Cnut's forces and even King Harold's elite troops at the Battle of Hastings are all recorded as *Daci* or *gens Dacorum* – Dacians.

A DNA mutation, the H1A haplogroup, suggests Dacians expanded from Nordic Dacia or central Gallia to confederated cantons on coastal islands, promontories and estuaries, gradually controlling fluvial and maritime trade in the Baltic, the North Sea, the Irish Sea, the Celtic Sea and the Britannic Sea. The principal migrations may have coincided with the Fall of Troy, as in legends. Medieval histories of the Britons, Franks and Normans all trace tribal descent to Trojan warriors. Nordic Dacian trade routes persisted for centuries, secured by control of salt, tin and iron, but lacking written records we can only guess at some of the details based on patterns of mercantile imperium that persisted into the medieval era when histories were compiled.

Later confederations controlling trade attest to the stability of sea-army imperium. The Confederation of the Cinque Ports appears to be a Dacian-inspired confederation of cantons and mercantile sea-armies to provide coastal defence and promote control of profitable trade and fisheries. Dacian imperium finds its strongest echo in the Hanseatic League, which was a distributed network of maritime cantons for controlling salt, fisheries metals and trade from the North Sea through the Baltic to the rivers of Central Europe. The same principles are also evident in the Dutch East India Company and the British East India Company which used sea-armies and cantons to control the global spice and salt-fish trade.

Dacian tribes collaborated with each other for raiding, conquest, defence and trade, but also developed distinctive identities as Getae, Illyrian Daci, Germanic Daci, Rus, Goths, Suevi, Nordic Daci, Frisii, York Parisii, Gallic Parisii and Belgae, and following the Gregorian Mission, the Anglians of Northumbria and the Danelaw. Common DNA now links these tribes long linked by common nautical culture and oral traditions.

Original medieval sources use *Daci* or *gens Dacorum* for sea-armies from Nordic Dacia, carelessly translated as Danes by modern historians. *Dani* was rarely used to mean people from what we now call Denmark in these texts. *Dene* simply meant lowland, so *Dani* might be any liminal people occupying coastal strands, fens or watercourses, rather than referencing a specific or foreign origin. *Dengang* meant a raiding army or sea-army regardless of ethnicity. It is even possible *Dani* derived from the Hellenic language of the ancient Dacians because the sea-armies demanded provisions and tribute. Δανε – pronounced danae – means 'taxes' in Greek, consistent with Danish sea-armies extracting tribute and provisions from tributary tribes, and thelony and tolls on waterways from mercantile traffic.

Vikings as a wider ethnonym for sea-armies may also have Greek roots. The ancient Greek *vīkη* (genitive *vīkης*) meant 'conquest'. *Vīkη* may be the source of cantonal -wich or -vic place-names, often associated with salt production or markets, and may even give a Greek word origin for Vikings – 'tribes of conquest' or 'tribes of imperium'.

Medieval sea-army raids are characterised in early histories as a contest between pagans and Christians, and in modern histories as Vikings against English, but early medieval sea-armies may have been more ethnically diverse, politically astute, and tactically sophisticated. Gold and silver were looted and settlements were burned not just for profit and glory, but to deny recruitment of warriors and effective fortifications to rivals or hinterland chieftains. Regular raids, slaving and labour levies kept the hinterland impoverished and elites compliant. Murder, mayhem and trade disruption forced hinterland chieftains, prelates and urban elites to betray each other and seek truce. Once truce was agreed, chieftains, prelates and urban elites shared in the revenues from exploitation, slaving and trade. It is not a patriotic narrative, it does not inspire native pride, and it may not prove popular, but a Dacian imperium narrative of the Anglo-Saxon Chronicle makes much better sense of recorded events. It remains a sad fact that local elites almost everywhere, even in the 21st century, will compact with powerful militaries and mercantile interests, both domestic and foreign, to tax and exploit their own people when it gains incumbent chieftains personal security, prestige and great wealth.

Roman and early medieval history are better understood when reviewed as a series of Dacian alliances, confederations and truces. The pattern of Dacian oath-taking and truce-making can be traced from Roman sources all the way to 1066 and the narrative for oaths in the *Carmen*. All oaths of service among Dacian sea-lords, warriors and magistrates were temporary and based on reciprocity. All Dacian military service on land or sea was for payment in tribute, booty or stipendiary provisions and implied no permanent loyalty. There were no standing armies or navies, and no warrior served a sea-lord or a king for patriotism without profit; only booty, slaves and geld proved honour in military service. Oaths ended when a contracted military campaign was complete, booty and geld were distributed, and the sea-army was sent home. Truce ended with the death of either Dacian or hinterland oath-taker chieftain or king. Oaths and truces were rendered null by a failure of reciprocity or treachery on either side. Treachery against a king or chieftain, if upheld by a peer tribunal, resulted in the oath-breaker forfeiting land, title and protection of the law, rendering the oath-breaker an exile and outlaw. If a king or chieftain refused land and law to a Dacian lord or warrior unjustly, however, for example denying a peer tribunal or breaching a covenant of truce, the outlaw could waste the oathbreaker's lands mercilessly without perjury. We see the patterns of oath and truce repeat themselves for a thousand years if we re-evaluate the Anglo-Saxon Chronicle and Nordic Sagas with these simple rules in mind.

Roman-era Dacians alternately allied and competed with the Roman Empire. The Belgae, perhaps descended from Brutus of Troy and so Aeneas of Rome, allied with Julius Caesar under truce in the 1st century BC as tax farmers, merchantmen, and coastal auxiliaries for defence and exploitation of Gallia and Britannia.[137] Truce between the Roman Republic and liminal Belgae followed the old Dacian pattern. The Belgae provided coastal protection of Roman provinces in exchange for mercantile commerce, ports, mines and mints and self-rule coastal cantons. Caesar records that Commius of the Belgic Atrebates held imperium on both sides of the Channel even before Caesar came to Gallia, as did the Veneti city-state, who they jointly defeated. Caesar gave more power to Commius by giving him joint imperium in Britannia and Gaul over tributary hinterland tribes, imperial tax-farming privileges, and the Morini ports either side as cantons. The Atrebates became sea-army auxiliaries as *foederati* – 'foreign auxiliaries' – or *collegia naviculariorum* – 'associations of skippers' – in alliance with the Republic.

---

[137] The Roman senate auctioned contracts for collecting taxes to *publicani*, leases for iron and salt exploitation to *conductores*, and navigation monopolies to *collegia naviculorum*.

It was revenues, slaves and auxiliaries from Gallia and Britannia that propelled Caesar to power in Rome. It needs much greater exploration, but Dacian imperium in the west may have provided Caesar's model for the Roman Empire. The Roman Republic was by then impoverished and weakened by internal political divisions and suspension of tax collections at Roman ports. Commius collected and shared tribute from British and Gallic tributary tribes and levies from commerce with Caesar. Commius and other client kings, sea-lords, skippers and sea-warriors were then given Roman citizenship and generous mercantile privileges when Caesar became emperor and consolidated his power with the aid of his armies. Tribute and trade in salt, metals, grain, wool, and preserved salt-foods was craved by Roman land-armies and the citizens of Rome itself. Coins commemorating Commius and his sons are plentiful on both sides of the Britannic Sea evidencing a well organised and enduring mercantile traffic.

Despite Strabo's warning that it would prove more costly, the Roman Empire invaded and occupied Britannia in the early 1st century to secure supplies of salt-foods and iron for the continental armies expanding the empire to the north and west. Not content with the iron and salt of the Sussex Weald, Rome needed the iron and salt from the lands around the Severn and the Wash too, if only to deny these resources to Dacian enemies resisting Rome's expansion. Anglo-Dacians had been providing support to continental Dacian tribes threatening the empire from beyond the Rhine. Roman armies and fleets controlled little iron in the west and Roman sea-armies and riparian armies demanded more.

The push for expanded Roman imperium was contested by settled Britons who had held imperium and controlled salt and iron for centuries. Caratacus declared independence for Britons from his iron and salt-rich capital Camulodunum (Maldon or Colchester) in the year 42. Caratacus was killed, southern Britannia was re-conquered, and Colchester became a military colony for Romano-Dacian auxiliaries resettled from the continent. Suppression of that rebellion spurred wider dissatisfaction with Rome among Britons as slavery and taxes spread more widely.

An Iceni rebellion in East Anglia was settled by truce in 47 whereby Romans ceded an Iceni commonwealth to the client-king Prasutagus on condition the king recognise the Roman emperor as co-heir with his royal daughters. When Prasutagus died, the Romans disregarded the truce and looted the prosperous Iceni strongholds, whipping the royal widow Boudica and raping her royal daughters. This treachery justified the brutal uprising that followed under Dacian rules of truce. The widowed Queen Boudica confederated the tribes of Britannia in 61 as land and sea-armies. They raided Roman-occupied provinces, wasted Roman strongholds, destroyed the emporium at Londunium, and slaughtered over 70,000 Romanised settlers.

English historians characterised the Iceni as a domestic Celtic tribe. We now know from DNA there is no distinctive Celtic ethnicity, and certainly none in East Anglia. East Anglian DNA most closely resembles Frisian or Belgic DNA – lowland, liminal sea-army tribes. The truce between Roman authorities and Prasutagus follows the Dacian model of a self-rule commonwealth in exchange for coastal protection, maritime trade and exploitation of salt and iron. Heritable claims of children were a legal concept common to Hellenic city-states. Boudica's insistence on rule of law to enforce her husband's written truce, her exercise of martial authority as a widow, her command of confederated land and sea-armies, the wasting of the settlements of truce-breakers, and her tactics in terrorising urban and mercantile elites, are all perfectly consistent with Dacian traditions. It appears more probable the Iceni were a Dacian or Hellenic tribe.

Where did the Iceni come from? Achaean was the collective name given by Hellenes to themselves for many centuries before the Romans began calling them *Graeci* or Greeks – a Roman-originated exonym for a subjugated race. Iceni and Achaeans are homonyms and likely related sea-army tribes from Hellenic control of British salt, tin and iron. The hills around the Wash are rich in iron and the Wash itself ideal for salt-pans. Iceni mariners may have traded and confederated with their Achaean kinsmen for more than a thousand years before Julius Caesar came into Gaul. The Achaean League – a confederation of city-states – had been particularly powerful in the 3rd and 2nd centuries BC when Roman historians record Gallic imperium in Britannia. The same Achaean city-states contributed to the spread of Roman imperium once their sea-armies allied with the empire in the 2nd century. Caesar names the Gallic port of departure as *portus Iccius* in 54 BC, possibly the 'port of Achaeans', 'port of the Iceni' or 'port of outsiders'.

In Roman times the Wash extended to Peterborough and Cambridge, strongholds of the Iceni. The tidal Ouse was canalised below Denver – 'lowland-crossing' – where a stone causeway extended through the tidal fens to iron and salt-rich Peterborough. Exploitation of the region was heavily indusrtrialised. A fortress at Mildenhall controlled fluvial access to the emporium *Villa Faustini*, later Bury St Edmunds. St Botolph's 7th century Benedictine minster at *Icanho* – 'Iceni fluvial promontory' – may have been sited at Mildenhall, consistent with Botloph's influence founding Benedictine mercantile abbeys at Peterborough, Thorney, Ely, Bury St Edmunds and Waltham which together form an arc controlling hinterland trade with Utrecht. Botolph's brother Adolf was bishop at Utrecht, formerly a Romano-Dacian free port.

The Roman Empire re-conquered Britannia after the Iceni revolt. Successive Roman emperors then industrialised production of grains, wool, meats, salt, salt-foods and metals using Romanised overlords and indigenous slave labour. Romano-Briton, Romano-Frisian and Romano-Gallic auxiliaries provided urban garrisons and fortress-based land armies. Supply chains of salt-foods, weapons, chandlery and tools from Britannia soon strengthened Roman continental armies who extended and secured imperium along the Rhine and Danube in alliance with Gallic and Germanic auxiliaries. The Roman Empire also conquered and colonised iron and salt-rich Illyrian Dacia in 106. Those Illyrian Dacians who did not flee north to Dacian commonwealths in Slavic, Germanic and Baltic regions became Romanised as powerful Roman military and mercantile elites.

An innovation in Roman imperial administration about this time offers an intriguing line for further investigation. *Collegia* had long been permitted to associate, but these associations had to be re-established on the death of any citizen member. They had no permanent, independent legal nature to contract with the Roman state. Like partnerships, they had to be reconstituted when any partner died. Coinciding with the conquest of southern Britannia and Illyrian Dacia, Rome innovated *corpora naviculariorum* – 'corporations of skippers' – which had corporate legal status to contract with the Roman state and create hereditable interests that survived a mariner's death and passed to his heirs. These were the first joint stock corporations, and they came to dominate Roman trade and food supply throughout the Roman Empire. It merits investigation whether these corporations enabled Rome to contract a new form of the Dacian truce: Rome recognised a separate legal identity, ceded heritable interests, and allowed for republican self-rule of city-states and corporate shipping fleets for common profit. Two *corpora naviculariorum* were established to control Britannic and Gallic waterways: the *Classis Britannia* based in the Brede Basin of Sussex and the *Classis Sambrica* based in the Somme estuary in Gaul. These are the same ports the *Carmen* suggests for the Norman navigation in 1066.

Given Roman citizenship, state contracts for shipping and tax-farming, and self-rule port cantons for trade, Dacians from Britannia, Gallia and Illyria quickly gained political influence within the Roman Empire. Romano-Dacians from east and west came to dominate the military, maritime trade and urban commerce from Eire to the Near East as they had in the Hellenic Empire. Latin became the public language on Romano-Dacian coasts and in Romano-Dacian cantons throughout the empire, but Hellenic principles of cantonal autonomy and local election of sea-lords and magistrates were preserved.

Soon ambitious Romano-Dacians sought imperial power even in Rome itself. Perhaps inspired by Julius Caesar's example, the Gallo-Dacian Carausius rose from commander of the *Classis Britannia* – the sea-army fleet providing British defence, tribute collection and trade – to usurp the Roman title emperor in 286. He gained imperium over Britannia and Gallia with his sea-armies, holding the rest of the empire to ransom for the salt-foods and materiel that had once flowed to the Rhine armies and to Rome. He declared a military republic of Romano-Dacian sea-warriors on both sides of the Britannic Sea and a confederation of Dacian city-states. His early silver coins featured partnership with the goddess Salacia – the goddess of salt-seas – and the legend *Expectate Veni* – 'O wait for I come' – a promise of confederated mutual defence among Dacian cantons. Carausius struck a truce with Emperors Maximian and Diocletian to refrain from attacking hinterland Gaul if given imperium over Britannia, northern Gallia, trade, mines and mints. Carausius then issued coins of the three co-emperors as brothers and the legend 'the Peace of the three Augusti'. He was killed by an aide in 293 and the revolt suppressed in 297 by an Illyrian Dacian, the Emperor Constantius.

A silver coin of Carausius shows him holding the hasta or spear of Roman imperial authority in his left hand and shaking right hands with Salacia with her cap and trident. After defeat of the rebels Salacia was replaced with a new mythic spirit, Britannia, as a symbol of British communion with the Roman Empire under Roman imperium.

Constantius Chlorus and fellow Illyrian Dacian Galerius were made imperial caesars in 293 and elected emperors augustus in 305. Clearly identifying as more Dacian than Roman, the Emperor Galerius avenged the Roman conquest of Illyrian Dacia two centuries earlier by looting, burning and starving the people of Rome. Galerius then moved his administrative capital to Illyrian Dacia and officially proposed changing the name of the empire to the Dacian Empire, scandalising a citizenry schooled to Roman citizenship.[138] Diocletian, with co-emperor Maximian, agreed a truce with co-emperors Galerius, and Constantius, with elements of a Dacian truce. The empire was divided into east and west, a Dacian eastern empire and Roman western empire. The eastern empire was to have its capital at the Hellespont, the fount of all Illyrian Dacian sea-faring tradition and

---

[138] Lactanius, *De Mortibus Persecutorum* 23.

power. The western capital was to continue at Rome. The four co-emperors also issued edicts banning Roman citizens from observing the Christian faith and requiring citizens participate in traditional Roman religious rituals. The edicts were enforced most harshly in the Dacian east, and most lightly in Romanised Gaul and Britannia.

A gold medal of Constantius, now in the British Museum, features a Dacian wolf-head warship carrying the imperial sea-army, a mounted Constantius with the Roman *hasta* or imperial spear, and the submission of cantonal emporium London to Roman imperium under the *hasta*. The legend means 'Restorer of the Eternal Light' as Constantius restored Britannia's communion with the Roman Empire.

As he lay dying in Illyrian Dacia in 311, Emperor Galerius's last act was to issue a decree of toleration making Christian worship permissible again. This act of toleration set the scene for the Emperor Constantius' son by a Christian noblewoman to march on Rome as the first Christian Roman caesar.

Emperor Constantius died in York after suppressing the Picts in 306 and his armies immediately elected his son Constantine as caesar, following the Dacian tradition of sea-armies electing their war-lord. Constantine's mother was Saint Helen, by legend a daughter of Coel, king of the Romano-Britons of East Anglia and a Christian. Helen was raised in Colchester, canton of the rebel Caratacus, but long since a Romanised canton for exploiting hinterland Britannia. As Caesar Constantine had the support of Roman imperial armies in Britannia, Gaul and Iberia whose Romano-Dacian equestrian orders, maritime fleets and urban mercantile elites would prosper greatly from his Hellenic-modelled reforms of Roman military, monetary and mercantile administration. The other emperors made truce with Constantine when he and his fearsome armies advanced on Rome. In advance of battle against his last rival co-emperor Constantine ordered the Hellenic symbol for Christ, *chi-rho*, painted on the shields of his warriors, and so claimed God's favour for his victory. After the battle Constantine named his mother Helen as *Helena Augusta*, sharing imperial power with her. Her image then appeared on coins with the legends *Securitas Reipublicae* and *Pax Publica*, both invoking imperial unity. Helen is, of course, derived from Hellene, the ethnonym meaning 'strait people'. The connection would not be lost on Romans, Hellenes or Dacians.

Source: Roma Numismatics. On VCoins

Emperor Constantine and Empress Helena elevated the Christian church within the Roman Empire. Saint Helen began the custom of pilgrimages to the Holy Land, claimed to have found the true cross, and began spreading commerce in sacred relics from the Holy Land that could convey sanctity and protection to remote holy places and kings. Trade in valuable wines, oils and spices expanded with the trade in holy relics. Christian clerics became imperial agents for religious authority, but also for trade, diplomacy, monetary reforms, imperial communications, resource exploitation, tax collection and urban administration. Christian clerics assumed the roles Hellenic priests had held as state agents in the Hellenic empire centuries earlier. Constantine himself endowed the building of Saint Peter's Basilica in the Holy Apostolic See at Rome, and also built the Hagia Sophia in Constantinople, his favoured capital on the Dacian Hellespont.

In 325 the Emperor Constantine convened the Council of Nicaea as the first ecumenical conference of Christian prelates. Until this time Christians had lacked any governing creed or hierarchy. Christians in dispersed geographies self-organised and loosely confederated under locally elected bishops and prelates on Hellenic principles. Constantine gave his imperial approval to Roman Council edicts on a common creed, theological orthodoxy, and canon law, and he promoted the standardised copying of select, ordered books of Christian scripture – the Bible, as it came to be known. Bishops from London and other parts of Britannia attended the council and brought the edicts and scripture back with them to Britannia and Eire. British Christians predictably resented and resisted the assertion of Roman theological authority and doctrinal orthodoxy, as documented by Bede, but Irish clerics embraced and spread the Roman orthodoxy through coastal minsters at trading ports.

A mosaic portrait of Saint Constantine in the Hagia Sophia at Istanbul shows the saint and emperor extending his protection to the Christian church. The stone, palisaded building with crosses on its two doors resembles an urban keep or imperial treasury.

Another innovation of Emperor Constantine was a variation on a Dacian truce with the pope. The Donation of Constantine granted the Holy Apostolic See, through the agency of the pope, independence from imperial imposts, supremacy over all other episcopal sees wherever located, authority over all Christian clerics, and power to impose the orthodox doctrine of the emerging Universal Church. It also exempted Holy Apostolic See landholdings from imperial taxes and tribute so long as Christian clerics cooperated with the empire in secular administration. Genuine or not as a written act of Constantine the Great, the Donation of Constantine was widely accepted as genuine in medieval Europe, and Christian kings were encouraged to emulate Constantine's model of truce by written charters of donation and privileges for local bishops and abbots. Charters generally ceded ecclesiastical jurisdiction, freedom from taxation, and establishment of ports and emporia for mutual prosperity and stability of church and state.

Under Constantine's long rule Britannia prospered, exporting a huge agricultural and mineral surplus to continental armies and markets. Peace finally ended in 367 when jealous indigenous Picts, Scots and Saxons rebelled against their Romano-Briton overlords, raiding prosperous Roman settlements. Order was restored by the Emperor Theodosius the following year after he based himself and his sea-army in London before subduing the provinces. Roman signal beacons and mounted cavalry units were extended up to the Parisii emporium at York, and Roman fortresses were re-fortified and re-garrisoned.

A generation later Magnus Maximus followed Constantine's example. He declared himself emperor in Britannia, then departed with the finest warriors from Britannia's garrisons to enforce imperium in the east. Theodosius, son of Britannia's saviour general of 368, killed Magnus Maximus and defeated his army. Their loss left Britannia defenceless and prey to civil unrest. In 407 another Constantine, but base-born, usurped the title emperor again and took Britannia's urban garrisons to war across the Channel; he too was crushed. Rival native chieftains warred in an undefended Britannia for supremacy, and Saxon warrior emigrants from the Fresia and Belgica settled in cantons on coasts and waterways to profit from the instability.

Rivalries and unrest in Britannia may have contributed to a decline in agricultural and mineral surpluses, possibly contributing to the weakening hold of the Roman Empire on the continent. In 410 the Roman armies of occupation withdrew from Britannia, leaving only a few ships at southern cantons to guard the coast according to Bede. Romanised Britons were left vulnerable to slaughter and slavery from enemies on all sides, fragmented into rival warring tribes. Client kings and queens sometimes prevailed on Rome to provide military aid, but as exports of surplus production waned so did Roman protection. Meanwhile Dacian-derived Goths from the Baltic and north of Europe and Huns from the east contested Slavo-Dacian and Illyrian Dacian territories, mines and waterways. Loss of secure supplies of British, Slavic and Illyrian salt, salt-foods and iron may have irreparably undermined Rome. The last Roman emperor, Romulus Augustus, was deposed in 476. The eastern Roman emperor ruled from Dacian Constantinople for almost a thousand years, until the Turks captured the Hellespont in 1453.

As emperors lost authority Romano-Dacian sea-lords and sea-armies continued to raid and demand tribute as they had done when they were agents of empire. Dacian sea-armies from York, East Anglia, Freesia and Gallia contested straits, cantons, trade routes and resource rich lands. Dacian sea-lords continued to compact truces with terrorised hinterland chieftains and urban elites for military protection in exchange for coastal protection, commonwealth cantons, stipendiary provisions, tribute and slaving. Meanwhile local kings and prelates far distant from Rome and Constantinople strayed from communion with the Universal Church, resisting the Roman pope and Roman orthodoxy.

Born to a noble Roman family and great-great-grandson of Pope Felix III, Pope Gregory the Great survived occupation and famine in Rome in his youth to rise through the church. When he became pope he sent Augustine, the prior of his own foundation monastery, as his envoy to Frankish and Anglian kings in 595. The Franci tribe had been converted to communion with Rome by Pope Felix III with consecration of the first Merovingian king. Rivalries between Merovingian heirs had since fragmented the Frankish kingdom and church. Pope Gregory understood that Rome needed Frankish military allies to protect it from northern and eastern enemies. He wanted to promote Frankish imperium in Germanic and Gallic realms to secure protection and food for the Roman people and promoting trade and markets. Pope Gregory sent papal agents with Augustine to exhort

Christian communion with Rome among the Merovingian kings and collect past due financial contributions from prelates.

Pope Gregory also sent Augustine to kings in Britain to restore Christian communion with Rome there too. Although likely directed to prosperous East Anglia, Augustine was diverted by the Frankish King Charibert of Neustria to his royal daughter Queen Bertha in Kent. The king's only daughter Bertha had married King Aethelberht of Kent while the youth had lived in Neustria at the Frankish court, possibly fostered by King Cheribert. Charibert had helped his son-in-law seize the Kent throne.

Queen Bertha and King Aethelberht received Augustine in Canterbury, gave him a minster church already established in the city to preach his Romanised Christianity and a port for promoting trade to ensure the clerics' prosperity. The royal couple then wrote to Pope Gregory to secure Christian primacy in Britain for their kingdom. Augustine is commonly given credit for converting Aethelberht to Christianity, but more accurately he secured the king's communion with the Universal Church under papal authority. Bishops and other prelates of the land were less easy to win over.

The ethnonym *Angli*, loosely translated as English, dates from the mission of Augustine and the ethnogenesis of a people in Britain in communion with the Universal Church led by Rome. There was no England nor any English or *Angli* people recorded earlier than the Gregorian Mission.

> *Ad Christum Anglos convertit pietate magistra*
> *Adquirens fidei agmina gente nova –*

> By pious cares he converted the English to Christ,
> Acquiring thereby for the true faith multitudes of a new race.[139]

It was Pope Gregory who named the *Angli* or English as 'a new race', possibly as a barbed jest about a 'far-corner' of Christendom as suggested by his own letters, or as a kinder jest about angelic slave

---

[139] Excerpt of the epitaph on Pope Gregory's as quoted by Rodolfo Lanciani, *Pagan and Christian Rome*, (New York, 1892), p. 232.

boys, as suggested by an anonymous Northumbrian biographer and Bede.

More important, Gregory's designation *Angli* parallels Felix III's naming of the *Franci* as a new race in Gaul a century before. Ethnogenesis of these new races *Franci* and *Angli* promoted imperium of Christian kings consecrated to the service of the Christian God of the Universal Church and his regent on earth, the pope. The ritual of royal consecration common to *Franci* and *Angli* kings binds them to canonical authority and protection of the church.

Kings who resisted papal authority became tyrants and enemies to be excommunicated, reviled and supressed. Seizing power in 1066 after decades of violence against the church and rejection of Roman authority, King Harold was an excommunicate tyrant. The pope looked to Duke William as a consecrated monarch in communion with Rome to avenge the offence against papal authority.

Augustine is often credited with 'introducing' Christianity to England, but that is misguided. Whether or not the Joseph of Arimathea legend has substance, there were likely Christians in Britain even before Saint Peter reached Rome as early Christianity spread along trade routes. The primacy of the Christian church in England was used as a further justification for ending communion with Rome by Elizabeth I in a 1559 letter to Catholic bishops. Christianity remained robust in Britannia even during the Diocletian Persecutions, as evidenced by Saint Helen's instruction of Christianity to her son Constantine. Bishops from Britain attended the Council of Nicaea and later ecumenical councils. Early British bishops continued to convene periodically before the Gregorian Mission. British bishops convened again to negotiate with Augustine when he came into Britain, as recounted by Bede. Augustine's mission was not to bring Christianity, but to promote communion of British Christianity with Rome, enforcing Roman orthodoxy and papal authority so that Rome could share in English church revenues and the pope could influence selection of British kings and prelates.

After Augustine was welcomed into Kent, Pope Gregory wrote to Queen Bertha; he congratulated her on her faith, works and piety, and styled the royal couple of Kent as the first king and queen of the *gens Anglorum* – the 'English people'. In doing this Pope Gregory implied that the Kentish king and queen held imperium of all British

Christians, despite the small geographic scope of Kent in the southeast. Primacy was re-confirmed with the styling of Archbishop Augustine as an apostolic archbishop over all of Britain with an archiepiscopal see at Canterbury. The pope's recognition of Kentish imperium over all British Christians would spur a wider contest as the Dacian realms of Northumbria and Mercia would contest Kentish imperium and seek the pope's assurance of primacy for themselves. Bede wrote his *Historia ecclesiastica gentis Anglorum* to promote the Northumbrian assertion that *Angli* more accurately meant the northern tribes, not the people of Kent or Mercia or Wessex or Essex or East Anglia (all separate kingdoms the time). Bede's fanciful and revisionist history was successfully promoted in Rome to secure an archbishop in metropolitan York.

Saint Augustine became an apostolic bishop to the *gens Anglorum* despite landing and remaining in remote Kent with a Frankish king and queen. Augustine sent further bishops to the king of Essex for a see in London and to the king of Northumbria for a see in York, both Roman freeport trading cantons from ancient times. His envoy to Northumbria accompanied Aethelburga, the royal daughter of Queen Bertha and King Aethelberht, who became queen consort to King Edwin of Northumbria. The ancient Romano-Dacian cantons at York, London and Canterbury were united briefly again in communion with Rome. Metropolitan York was subject to direction from the archbishop of Canterbury, but metropolitan London was reserved to direct papal authority according to a letter of Pope Gregory quoted by Bede.

The 7th century in Britain was marked by wars and unrest as kings and prelates in communion with Rome contested imperium with heretic kings and uncanonical Christian prelates. The wider authority of Rome was also challenged as a new religion rose and spread from Arab lands along north Africa into the Mediterranean. The prophet Mohammed had travelled widely with his merchant maternal uncle, just as Christ was said to have travelled with Joseph of Arimathea. As with Christianity, Islam too spread with sea-armies and merchants as they raided and traded along sea-routes from Jerusalem to Iberia. By the end of the 7th century the Islamic caliphate controlled all the sea-routes from the Levant to Iberia, disrupting British trade to the east and Roman trade through the Mediterranean.

By the 8th century Nordic Dacian tribes of the west had responded to local conflicts and the collapse of long-held mercantile networks and become Viking sea-armies. The 8th century poem *Widsith* recounts the bard's travels among many Dacian tribes from the *Hælsings* – 'strait dwellers' to the *Wicingas* – 'Vikings' – and the *Wicingas cynn* – 'Viking tribesmen.' These are the earliest uses of ethnonyms resembling Viking. Widsith also names South Danes, Geats and Angles – all Dacian diaspora tribes on Baltic, Nordic, British, Irish and Gallic coasts. With settled imperium over hinterlands and cooperating for raiding and trading, these Dacian sea-armies had prospered for centuries, but with hinterlands disputed and war-ravaged by rival kings and trade widely disrupted, these sea-armies turned on each other and on the hinterland tribes destabilised by religious and ethnic wars. Sea-army tribes both allied and competed for treasure, land, provisions and slaves to recover the prosperity they had taken for granted as tribute, stipendiary provisions, and mercantile commerce in better days.

In order to defend against sea-army raids, the diverse tribal kingdoms of 8th century Britain and Gaul began to unify under common military imperium. King Offa of Mercia was the son of Thingfrith, a king of the Anglo-Dacian *Iclingas* who claimed both Christian Anglian and Nordic Dacian descent. As with Iceni, the Iclingas may have been named for Achaeans as an 'outsider tribe' or liminal settlers. Whatever his heritage, King Offa was the first king to hold common imperium of Mercia, Wessex, Essex, Sussex, Kent and East Anglia – the first true king of the realm that became England. Bede styles King Offa a *Bretwalda* – overlord of the Britons – implying royal imperium over the kingdoms of the Romanised south.

Like King Aethelberht, the young Offa had lived at a Frankish royal court during his youth, possibly as foster-son of King Pepin the Short. King Offa also seized power with military support from allies in Gaul, where Pepin the Short had become the first Carolingian king of the Franks in 751. Pepin was succeeded by his son Charlemagne in 768. Charlemagne and Offa corresponded regularly, a correspondence preserved by the cleric Alcuin. The powerful monarchs collaborated on English and Frankish defence against the Vikings and trade with the south and east.

The last region King Offa united with his English realm was *Hastingum* in 771. Symeon of Durham recorded that Offa gained imperium of the *Hastingorum gens* – 'the people of Hastings'. He did not defeat a chieftain or a king. The entry in the annal implies *Hastingum* had remained a Dacian commonwealth republic. *Hastingas* is always separate from Wessex, Kent and Sussex in other English annals too. Very likely the *Lithwicingas*, 'anchorage Vikings' as named by Widsith, had continued to control both the great tidal basin of the Rye Camber and ports in the Baie de Somme opposite, as Roman fleets, the Atrebates client kings, and the Morini fleets of the Veneti city-state had done before them. A stronghold of the *Lithwicingas* at St Valery-sur-Somme would be consistent with the satirical description of the locals as pirates at lines 50-51 in the *Carmen*.

The Queen Cynethryth Silver Penny from the Canterbury mint is in the same style as late Roman silver coins of Helena Augusta, another powerful Anglo-Dacian imperial wife and mother of Christian Emperor Constantine the Great

King Offa married Cynethryth, a celebrated Frankish or Dacian noblewoman, who shared royal imperium and appears on charters from 770. Queen Cynethryth was praised by Alcuin in contemporary correspondence as the literate and numerate administrator of the royal household, and her image appeared on coins of the English realm. She is the only woman represented on early European coins. Her children were offered in marriage to the children of Charlemagne, and her daughter extended English imperium to Northumbria by marrying Aethelred I as his consecrated queen. Queen Cynethryth may have commissioned the songs celebrating her husband passed down through Gallic bards as the legend of King Arthur, a Christian king who brought peace and unity to England with his Gallic queen.

King Offa made many reforms emulating foreign practice, possibly adopting the systems learned at the court of Pepin in his youth or adapted from his wife's kinsmen. He introduced the Burghal Hideage which divided Wessex into hundreds for royal administration, each with a market town and church for civic commerce, tax collection, and manning of militias. Long believed by English historians as a record of King Alfred's Wessex fortifications against the Vikings, 21st century archaeology is raising doubts about any defensive purpose. No 9th century stone fortifications or permanent settlements have been found at the vast majority of the sites. A more rational view is that the Burghal Hideage was a *taxatio* or tribute itinerary for Wessex reeving by King Offa, the first northern Bretwalda to unify Wessex with his realm. Each named place might host a temporary thorn or palisade stockade on a watercourse – *vicus* – for seasonal collection of tribute, provisions and slaves by royal Lithsmen. Anglo-Dacian settlements are omitted, as are prosperous coastal towns most vulnerable to Viking attacks by sea.

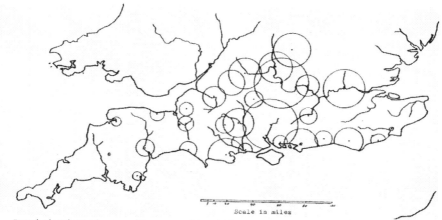

Scale in miles

Burghal Hideage burhs with geographic relative assessments. Note the omission of prosperous Kent, the Rye Camber, Cornwall, Devon, the upper Severn, and lower Thames. Source: Anthony Bradshaw, 1999.

In support of England's communion with the Universal Church, Christian King Offa re-founded the English School for secular clerics and pilgrims in the Holy Apostolic See at Rome and introduced the Peter's Pence tax in England for financial contribution to Rome. Plentiful coins and trade goods once again flowed from Britain to Rome. In return, a grateful pope granted a new Anglian archiepiscopal see at Litchfield in Mercia in 787, displacing the dominance of Canterbury and York, although Litchfield was demoted again in 803 after King Offa's death.

Echoing the pattern of Hellenic and Roman imperium centuries earlier, King Offa imposed a royal monopoly on the salt trade and mines, and minted silver and gold coins of outstanding purity and quality. He presumably sought foreign assayers and moneyers from Rome or his Gallic or Dacian kinsmen for design and manufacture of his coins, as Offa's coinage far surpasses earlier and later coinage of English kings. His silver coinage was standardised to Frankish coinage to promote freer commerce with the Frankish empire.

King Offa may even have negotiated truce with the Islamic Abassid caliphate to secure Mediterranean trade routes. Only three gold coins of King Offa survive, but one is a copy of an Abbasid dinar of 774 and carries Arabic text on one side, *Offa Rex* on the other. The coin may have been standardised to caliphate coinage to promote trade to the Mediterranean. Notably the dinar of 774 does not feature an image, as imagery on coinage would have offended against Islam.

King Offa's coin imitates the Abbasid caliphate dinar of of 774. One side reads 'There is no God but Allah alone' while the other reads Offa Rex.

King Offa made other mercantile truces to promote continental trade. In 785, after time spent at the Abbey of Saint-Denis in Paris for medical treatment, Ealdorman Berhtwald of Sussex ceded a mercantile estate at Rotherfield and the port at Hastingas to the powerful privileged Benedictine clerics. The port is named in the charter as *Portus Hastingas et Peuenisel*. Saint-Denis was the royal foundation abbey of Frankish Merovingian and Carolingian kings and papally privileged as an order of the Holy Apostolic See. Clerics of Saint-Denis had already established ecclesiastical control of many royal estates that had been Roman toll stations and ports, collecting thelony, market tolls and local tribute to share with Frankish kings. Giving the port and canton at the Brede Basin to Saint-Denis promoted trade and prosperity for English overlords while restoring Gallic administration locally to the *gens Hastingorum*. The gift was a sage compromise to promote English-Frankish-Ecclesiastical prosperity, industry and trade. King Offa kept imperium, the *gens Hastingorum* regained semi-autonomous self-rule, and the Benedictine clerics of Saint-Denis received title to salt-pans, iron mines, potteries and port with perpetual revenues of thelony, rents and tolls. King Offa confirmed the Berhtwald charter in 790 with the further gift from two Frankish brothers, probably mercantile clerics of Saint-Denis, of an estate on the Thames at *Lundenuuic* - Londonwick. [140]

Another important English industry may also owe its origins to cooperation between King Offa and Saint-Denis. Charlemagne's father Pepin the Short, who had fostered King Offa and helped him seize power, left a hops garden to the clerics of Saint-Denis in his will. Hops adds flavour to beer, but also stabilises and sterilises beer better than other additives, so that it can be transported and traded further from breweries. Spread by Saint-Denis to its diverse estates, hops began to displace other additives, being preferred by brewers from the 9th century. Most English hops is still grown in Sussex on or near the Rother and Brede Valley estates of Saint-Denis, and oast houses for drying barley still distinguish the East Sussex landscape. Thanks to the two charters from Ealdorman Berhtwald and King Offa, Saint-Denis brought hops to beer brewing in Britain and popularised hops beer by transporting and selling tax-exempt beer in English hinterlands.

Cooperation between the English realm and Charlemagne's empire promoted security from sea-army attacks, prosperity from industrialisation and trade, and unification through Christian secular and monetary reforms. Trade surged as evidenced by widespread coin finds. Popes were grateful for the revenues shared with the church and protection of Christian realms from Viking attack and further Islamic encroachment. Charlemagne was received in Rome as emperor of the west in 800 and consecrated in St Peter's Basilica on Christmas Day to

---

[140] S133 A.D. 790 (Tamworth, Staffs., 12 April). Offa, king of Mercia, to the abbey of Saint-Denis; grant of privileges for land at London and confirmation Rotherfield and Brede Basin, Sussex.

the chanting of the *Laudes Regiae*, as echoed in the *Carmen*.

Peace and prosperity were alike overthrown after both Charlemagne and Offa died and their kingdoms were subsumed in renewed civil strife and tribal rivalries. As described above, a Dacian truce ends with the death of either oath-taker, so the deaths of Charlemagne and Offa opened both kingdoms to renewed Viking attacks until truce could be restored by negotiation with successor kings. In the meanwhile, migrations and opportunist Viking sea-armies put pressure on all coasts. A huge surge in Nordic Dacian immigration to Anglian Britain and coastal Freesia and Gallia in the 9th and 10th centuries coincided with a climatic warming period that simultaneously increased Nordic populations and extended the raiding seasons of spring and fall. Higher crop yields reduced famine and increased infant survivals. A larger population meant wider raiding, trading and migration. Water in the oceans expands as it warms, encroaching on the land, as we observe in our own era of climate change. Lowlying Freesia may have been submerged, displacing a huge Dacian tribe to resettle among kinsmen in Britain. Bede says the Anglians were the only tribe to abandon their continental homeland. Northumbria had long been ruled as an Anglian realm wholly separate from kingdoms of England or the northern Scots. The Northumbrians, East Anglians and Nordic Dacians now confederated to seek more territory for settlement from their neighbours and wider imperium over Britain.

First the Anglo-Dacians settled the isthmus for trade between the Anglian north and Mercia at Repton – 'reeving town' – an ideal place for collecting thelony, seasonal markets, and controlling estuary traffic. Then the Anglo-Dacians claimed iron and salt-rich coasts of Cumbria, East Anglia and northern Mercia. With salt and steel the Anglo-Dacians became a formidable and prosperous army by land and sea. By 871 Anglo-Dacians had defeated King Alfred's older brothers and land army, forcing the young King Alfred to truce. The Anglo-Dacian warriors were paid tribute and withdrew from Wessex, retaining eastern Mercia and making London their political and military capital. In exchange Anglo-Dacians assured security to Wessex from competing sea-army tribes and promoted wider mercantile trade in slaves, wool, agricultural produce and metals from their cantons and commonwealths.

In 876 the Anglo-Dacian sea-army elected a new sea-lord, Guthram, who was not bound by the truce sworn by his predecessor.

Guthram waged war for imperium of all England. Defeated in many battles, King Alfred was forced into hiding. Three years later he rallied a more effective land army to resist the Anglo-Dacians until truce was negotiated. Guthram converted to Christianity and made truce with King Alfred sometime after 878. The terms of the truce modify the ancient Pontic imperium model of truce for protection, tribute and trade by creating the Danelaw as a new Anglo-Danish territorial commonwealth. The first provision of the Alfred-Gurthram truce describes political boundaries, the second sets a high *wergild* or 'man-price' for murder to promote peace, the third requires trial by oaths before a peer tribunal for manslaughter consistent with Dacian peer justice, the fourth requires a witness for trade in slaves, horses or oxen to promote urban markets and curb raiding, and the fifth provides terms for mercantile traffic between the Danelaw and Wessex. The Anglo-Danes retained possession of the iron mines of the Severn, Wash and Weald, and the tin of Cornwall and Devon, depriving Wessex of the ore to make more and better weapons and ships. High taxes imposed on Saxons, west Mercians and other subjugated tribes forced the sale of children as slaves to work Anglo-Dane mines, bloomeries and forges. Slaves made the tools sold back to their farming kindred. King Alfred may have been mostly or even wholly reliant on Anglo-Dane mercenaries for protection, metallurgy and trade. The Anglo-Danes had all the ships, all the mariners, and controlled the estuaries and seas. Nonetheless King Alfred styled himself the first *Anglorum Saxonum rex* - 'king of the Anglo-Saxons'. King Alfred was celebrated for restoring King Offa's unified imperium in England.

The tribal name *Dani* or Danes may have appears to gain usage from this time, assigned as *Franci* and *Angli* as an ethnonym conveying Christian communion with the Roman church. *Dani* or Danish signified a new ethnogenesis. Danish would not be used for the Nordic Dacians of Denmark until the Christian King Sweyn and his son Cnut spread Danish imperium from Eire to St Petersburg.

Guthram died in 889 and the sea-army elected a new sea-lord, Haesten, who was not bound by truce. Haesten must have been a well-regarded Anglo-Danish sea-lord before this time as his sons were godsons of King Alfred and Ealdorman Aethelred of Sussex. Providing sons for fostering as hostages was the traditional way of securing loyalty among coastal elites, so Haesten was almost certainly from Sussex, and perhaps from Hastingas, so protected by Saint-Denis. Haesten had led a series of violent and far-ranging raids into Francia with a young Rollo, who would later become the first duke of Normandy. When relieved of truce by Guthram's death, Sea-lord Haesten mustered a huge sea-army fleet to raid Wessex, a preliminary to renewed truce.

The Anglo-Saxon Chronicle for 893 records Haesten sent a fleet of 250 ships up the *Limne* – 'border river' – from the Rye Camber sea-ford where they destroyed 'a fort within the fen, whereon sat a few churls' while Haesten himself threatened London with 80 ships on the Thames and built a fort at Milton. The annals suggest that King Alfred had not secured the Rye Camber or Thames estuary before this time. Either King Alfred had entrusted defence to Anglo-Danish Lithsmen or he lacked ships and mariners of his own. After King Alfred's land-army sacked Haesten's fortress at Barnfleet in 894, taking much booty and women and children, King Alfred returned Haesten's wife and sons and gave him generous gifts. According to the Anglo-Saxon Chronicle the king treated the brigand sea-lord so liberally because one of Haesten's sons was his godson and the other the godson of Ealdorman Aethelred. It is more likely that the fostering of Haesten's Christian sons promoted the negotiation of truce between king and sea-lord. Restoring the foster sons was a condition of truce along with the generous payment of tribute. Haesten as an Anglo-Danish sea-lord and King Alfred as a client king fits the old Pontic imperium pattern of raiding, settling estuaries and straits to control sea-lanes, and demanding tribute, provisions and trade for truce. Like King Offa before him, King Alfred may have used the Burghal Hideage and the services of Lithsmen to collect royal tribute, thelony and market tolls.

Despite the romantic imaginings of Victorian historians, there is no evidence King Alfred fortified Wessex to any great extent. A more objective reading of Asser's biography of Alfred suggests King Alfred levied forced labour from Wessex for the fortification of Anglo-Danish cantons and emporia at the margins of Wessex. Archaeologists have found no evidence of 9th century fortifications in at boroughs in Wessex. The romantic Victorians who enobled King Alfred with the honorific 'the Great' and attributed a stoic defence of Wessex to him, rather than entertain a more likely collaboration with Anglo-Danish exploitation as a client king.

Having re-established truce in England, Haesten and Rollo began to sack Francia again, adventuring beyond Paris as they looted abbeys and burned towns along rivers. King Charles the Simple was confronted with a massive sea-army leaving a trail of looting, massacre and devastation through a realm he could not secure or defend. He was forced to truce in 911. On the same model that had established the Danelaw and control of sea-lanes in England, King Charles endowed the arrogant and piratical region of Neustria to Rollo as a new semi-autonomous duchy. Under the terms of this truce Rollo became a Christian like Guthram and godson to King Charles. He undertook by oath to defend Gallic coasts and estuaries in exchange for ducal tribute, control of trade, and licence to raid Francia's Gallic neighbours for booty and slaves. As King Alfred claimed to be king of all England, so too King Charles could claim to be king of all Francia, but neither exercised much authority in the Danish commonwealths of Danelaw and Normandy they ceded to Danish sea-lords. Rollo took the name Robert, converted his sea-warriors to Christianity and settled in the land thereafter named Normandy. Ironically, some historians now believe Rollo's sea-army was recruited widely from Anglo-Dacian Northumbria and East Anglia. If so, the Norman Conquest of 1066 was a homecoming of sorts.

The Gallo-Dacian inhabitants of Normandy may have welcomed their new Anglo-Dacian overlords and increased privilege and independence from Francia. Neustrians had cherished the memory of Roman privilege when the region was *Belgium Juliii Caesaris.* They had preserved coastal independence as the fierce *Lithwicingas* until truce with King Offa brought Hastingum under English rule and truce with the heirs of Charlemagne brought coastal Neustria under Frankish rule. The Gallo-Dacian freemen of 9th century Neustria had then demanded a written law on the Roman model protecting liberties and privileges before swearing allegiance to Carolingian kings. Neustrians had also arrogantly required the oaths of their Carolingian kings be sworn in their own Latinate Romana, as well as the Frankish tongue, at the truce-making ceremony.

1745 *Gallia Belgica Rhenus* by Johann Kohler names Neustria and Normandy as *Belgium Julii Caesaris* and shows Romano-Dacian cantons at *Venta* (Norwich), *Villa Faustini* (Bury St Edmunds), *Camulodunum* (Colchester), *Dubris* (Dover) and *Novus Portus* (the Brede Basin).

Duke Rollo's sea-warriors inter-married with the arrogant and mercantile coastal Neustrians, heirs to the arrogant and mercantile *Lithwicingas* and the arrogant and mercantile Romano-Belgae. Normans soon spoke the Latinate Romana of their Neustrian mothers in preference to Nordic and Germanic languages. They embraced the imperial Roman ambitions of Julius Caesar, Caratacus, Carausius, Constantius, Constantine and Charlemagne. They accepted the oral tradition of Neustrian descent from Brutus of Troy as endowing Gallic imperium of southern England and Brittany. Bards spread legends of noble King Arthur who had been raised in Gallia as a Christian king with his Gallic queen before unifying and ruling England as King Offa. Norman sea-lords profiteered from raiding, slaving and trading and soon competed to build massive stone castles and elegant abbeys in emulation of Roman and Frankish imperial grandeur. Norman clerics composed histories in Latin to enhance Norman status in Rome and continental courts.

A shared Hellenic heritage of imperium over Britannia may have made integration of Nordic Dacians, Anglo-Dacians and Neustrians much easier. According to at least two Norman sources, the Dacians believed they had imperium in Britannia before the arrival of the Saxons and the reign of Cerdic, the first Saxon king of Wessex. Richard FitzNagel's *Dialogus de Scaccario*, composed in the 1170s, records that 'the numerous and warlike *gens Dacorum* . . . claimed a right to mastery of England by ancient law' as a justification for demands of Danegeld.

Caesar's *Gallic Wars* with its description of earlier Hellenic imperium was much copied and studied in 10th century Normandy, inspiring Norman dukes to seek conquest not only in Britain, but also in Brittany, Iberia and throughout the Mediterranean as far as Rome and Constantinople. As the 10th century advanced Normans swiftly excelled the Nordic Dacians and Anglo-Dacians in warfare through better military discipline, preparation and technology. The Normans attacked all their Gallic and Britannic neighbours and sent sea-armies to retake Iberia and Mediterranean trade routes from the Saracens. Foreign adventures in distant Constantinople and Sicily gave young Norman warriors wide exposure to different military and naval technologies and tactics. They artfully adapted and improved what they learned. Normans fought on horseback as cavalry, rode saddles with stirrups, invented the couched lance, wrought four types of vicious steel-tipped arrows, adapted crossbows with armour-piercing bolts, and broke down stone walls with mines and siege engines. Norman smiths standardised and mass-produced weaponry and armour. Norman shipwrights standardised ships, rigging and chandlery for coordinated fleet manoeuvres. Norman fleets became expert at materiel and horse transport. By the end of the 10th century the Normans had become a formidable military force with wide imperial aspirations.

Meanwhile a succession of kings had mixed success securing England. King Alfred was succeeded by his son King Edward in 899, son of a Mercian noblewoman. Edward the Elder recaptured the East Midlands and East Anglia from the Anglo-Danes and then consolidated rule over Mercia on his sister's death. It is recorded that Scotland and Northumbria submitted to him as king in 920. He continued use of the title *Anglorum Saxonum rex*.

Edward the Elder's son King Aethelstan ruled from 924 to 939, consolidating royal administration and chancery in England and gaining imperium over Wales. He married one sister to King Charles the Simple, uniting the bloodlines of the two realms as King Offa had once hoped to do, and another sister was married to King Otto I, the Holy Roman Emperor. He imposed Benedictine reforms and copied continental laws to build on Alfred's reforms. The pious Aethelstan never married, left no sons, and was succeeded by his half-brother Edmund.

Edmund the Elder held the throne from 939 to 946, fighting back an invasion by King Olaf III Guthfrithson that initially retook Northumbria and the Midlands. After Olaf's death in 943 King Edmund retook the Midlands and struck a truce with King Olaf of York, who he accepted as godson under truce, leaving York a Danish canton. King Olaf was later ousted from York, but became the Christian King of Dublin. King Edmund also helped restore his nephew, the son of King Charles the Simple, to the Frankish throne.

The Danes that held York and Northumbria became stronger, but held to their truce until the murder of King Edmund in 946. Edmund's brother King Eadred ruled until 955, but the truce had died with Edmund and Danes and Anglo-Dacians grew more aggressive. On Eadred's death the kingdom first went to Edmund's son Eadwig. King Eadwig proved unpopular, and in 957 his younger brother Edgar was declared king north of the Thames by rebels, then succeeded to all of England on Eadwig's death in 959.

What is evident approaching the 11th century is that England remained an easily divided realm with fission lines between Northumbria, Cumbria, Danelaw, East Anglia, London and the south, between coasts and hinterlands, between Anglians, Mercians, Danes and Saxons. England was vulnerable to attacks and uprisings and treachery on all sides. Despite several efforts by English kings to ally with continental kings and the Holy Roman Emperor, the kings of England were incapable of uniting their nobles. Although England was styled as an Anglo-Saxon kingdom from the reign of King Alfred, there was no sense of national cohesion or duty binding the dispersed nobility, urban garrisons and cantonal sea-warriors to the service of any king for long. Such weakness would prove easy to exploit for both Danes and Normans in the 11th century.

APPENDIX II

IMPERIUM IN BRITAIN 966 TO 1066

King Aethelred was born in 966, a younger son of King Edgar the Peaceful by his second wife. By the year of his birth Saxons found themselves surrounded on all sides by Danish cantons and commonwealths in Scotland, York, Dublin, Cumbria, Cornwall, the Severn, and East Anglia. King Edgar may have remained at peace by conceding cantons and commonwealths in truces struck with the fierce Anglo-Danes and Nordic Danes migrating south in increasing numbers.

King Edgar had been a strong king who united York and Northumbria under Anglo-Saxon imperium and forced Roman orthodoxy and Benedictine reforms on reluctant bishops and abbots. When King Edgar died in 975 the succession was contested between his two sons. Elder son Edward was illegitimate, possibly by the Abbess Wulfthryth (a Frisian or Danish name), who Edgar had carried away from Wilton Abbey by force, or possibly by some other Anglo-Danish or Danish noblewoman. Younger Aethelred was the son of a consecrated Christian queen. Aethelred Aethling was given precedence over his elder brother on later charters of King Edgar, evidencing a royal succession preference. Nonetheless, on Edgar's death the Witans chose youthful Edward as king over protests from Aethelred's mother.

Adolescent King Edward died under mysterious circumstances in the company of his step-mother and half-brother at Corfe in 978. His death led to speculation of murder and provoked civil unrest. The youth was venerated almost immediately as a martyred saint, and a cult grew north of the Thames where those Anglo-Danes most loyal to Edward remained aloof and hostile to the martyr's Wessex-bred half-brother.

King Aethelred was consecrated king under his mother's regency, but Edward's death had reawakened Anglian, Mercian and Danish discontent with Wessex imperium over other realms. Anglo-Dacians may have felt cheated of Anglian or Danish imperium with the early death one of their own, King Edward the Martyr.

To heal the breach young King Aethelred was married to Aelfgifu (possibly a royal title rather than a name), the daughter of Earl Thored, the Danish jarl of York. The union may have been intended by the Danes to conceive an Anglo-Danish royal heir. The Anglo-Saxon Chronicle styles Thored with the Danish title *eorl*, uniquely distinguishing the chieftain of cantonal York from English ealdormen elsewhere.

Breach of truce and treachery against Danes are particularly important in King Aethelred's troubled reign. York was a Danish canton under truce with Eorl Thored, a truce probably negotiated with King Edgar and re-confirmed by King Edward. Young King Aethelred married Thored's noble daughter to restore truce on becoming king, but King Aethelred then exiled his father-in-law Thored in 993, inviting Danish retribution. Exeter, which controlled the tin trade from Devon and Cornwall, was also a canton given to the Dane Pallig as ealdorman under truce. Pallig and his Danes joined rebels in 1001, agreed truce in early 1002, and were massacred by order of King Aethelred on St Brice's Day in November 1002. East Anglia and London were given to the Danish sea-lords Thorkell and Hemming under truce a decade later in 1012, then Hemming and other Danes were massacred by order of King Aethelred in a surprise attack in January 1015. King Aethelred's reign shows a recurring pattern of truce, exploitation, breach, truce, exploitation, breach, until the king was finally overthrown by the young Danish Sea-king Cnut who brutally looted and enslaved all of war-weary and leaderless England with a vast sea-army and Anglian allies from the Danelaw. *Angli* used in medieval texts before the Norman Conquest never means Saxon. *Angli* were a conquering tribe. After 1016 Saxons were a subjugated tribe.

Truce having died with King Edgar the Peaceful or King Edward the Martyr, Nordic Danes and their *Angli* allies began to raid again, perhaps to secure truces with factionalised rulers contesting for primacy under a young, weak and unpopular king. The Normans remained allies with the Nordic Danes and *Angli* sea-armies of their kinsmen, continuing alliance by intermarriage, raiding and mercantile interest. Normans harboured and equipped the sea-army fleets, provided weaponry and horses, and hosted continental markets for looted booty and slaves. They provided mustering ports where sea-lords could recruit sea-armies and ships for raiding England, armed them with Norman weaponry and horsed them with Norman-bred war horses.

A mixed Dacian sea-army led by Sea-king Olaf Tryggvason attacked salt-rich Maldon in 991, defeated the local army of defenders, and obtained Danegeld of 10,000 pounds of silver by truce with local chieftains and prelates. A worried Pope John XV then interceded to negotiate truce between Christian rulers of Normandy and England so they might ally in defence against the sea-armies. The pope sent a legate to King Aethelred and Duke Richard the Fearless with a letter requiring in canonical duty as Christian rulers that they compound a truce. A treaty was agreed by king and duke that they would not raid each other or shield each other's enemies.

Olaf and his sea-army were not party to the treaty between king and duke and the sea-armies mustered to raid other localities in 992, 993 and 994. Flanders may have superseded Normandy in providing mustering ports and emporia for booty and slaves from this time. First the sea-armies raided Essex, Kent, Sussex and Hampshire. The attacks divided nobles and prelates who had only loose bonds to a king who could provide no protection. Sea-lords negotiated regional truces with Archbishop Sigeric for Kent, Ealdorman Aethelweard for the south-west, and Ealdorman Aelfric for Hampshire in exchange for huge sums of Danegeld. King Aethelred could not defend his kingdom, unite his nobles, and was ignored as irrelevant in the locally negotiated truces.

In 993 Sea-king Olaf's sea-army targeted Anglian Northumbria, Lindsey and East Anglia, but also threatened the great emporium at London. Hinterland defenders were inept or complicit, possibly compromised by collaborating Danish kinsmen and Anglo-Danish cantons on the coast. Ealdorman Aelfric declined battle, perhaps keeping to his truce, and his son Aelfgar was blinded for his father's offence by a vindictive King Aethelred. Earl Thored was replaced as earl of York by Ealdorman Aelfhelm, half-Danish on his noble mother's side but sworn ealdorman to the English king rather than jarl to a Danish king.

Sea-king Olaf was swiftly gaining imperium over England as each attacked region begged truce. Olaf had lived, fought and traded all through the Irish Sea and the Baltic, from Wendland to Novgorod and Kiev. He had married a Nordic-Dacian princess in Wendland and the powerful widow of an Anglo-Danish ealdorman in Cumbria, a sister of the king of Dublin. The raids may have been opportunistic, but they were more likely tactically motivated to expand Olaf's mercantile trade empire from Cumbria to the Baltic, relying on his royal wives in Cumbria and Wendland for local royal administration. King Cnut would implement the same strategy with his royal wives in Denmark, the Danelaw and southern England.

Olaf agreed truce and mutual security with King Aethelred in 994 in exchange for Danegeld of 16,000 pounds and Anglo-Danish self-rule commonwealths in Cumbria, Devon and East Anglia, each controlling an important strait, salt production, ore mines and trade-route. The treaty replicated the Pontic imperium that the sons of Brutus of Troy had held more than a thousand years earlier. Fitting the pattern established by Guthram and Rollo, the 994 truce required protection of the realm by the sea-army and allowed Olaf's sea-warriors to control Irish Sea, Channel and North Sea trade routes for thelony and tolls, and also permitted raiding neighbouring realms of Wales and Cornwall for slaves.

Olaf had become Christian when he first married a royal wife in Wendland. He reconfirmed his Christianity in the truce with King Aethelred, who accepted him as godson. Olaf spent time at the royal court, presumably learning English methods of secular administration, tax collection, cooperation with the church, and agreeing terms for wider trade. He then left for Nordic Dacia with a cohort of secular clerics in 995. Reaching Nordic Dacia, Olaf declared himself a Christian king. He enforced violent Christian conversion on the non-conformist Christians or pan-theistic tribes of his homeland and tributary realms. He forced his sea-army and a young sea-lord Sweyn Forkbeard to convert to Christianity and be baptised too. Determined non-conformists and pagans were killed or forced to flee newly named Denmark to Eire, Britain, Freesia or the eastern Baltic.

Clerics had begun to protest the sale of English slaves to pagans, so converting to Roman Christianity was good for business. Royal, urban and maritime elites in England and Nordic Dacia cooperated on trade and prospered. Hinterland ealdormen and tribes may have resented King Aethelred's oppressions, taxes, and slaving, but they were powerless to oppose him or his mercenary Anglo-Danish allies.

Richard II, son of Richard the Fearless, succeeded to the duchy of Normandy in 996. The Norman truce died with his father and he eyed England's regained prosperity and trade enviously. A sea-army fleet mustered in Gaul and raided England from the Severn to the Thames from 997 to 999. King Aethelred sent his own Anglo-Danish fleet from Cumbria and Devon against Normandy in 1000, perhaps in retribution or to profit from raiding Mont Saint-Michel.

Meanwhile King Olaf Tryggvason died in 1000 and the Irish Sea and North Sea truces died with him while the Anglo-Danish fleets were away in Normandy. Sweyn Forkbeard had been a sea-lord Olaf's fleet, learning trade routes, raiding and truce. His sister married Ealdorman Pallig of Exeter, giving him intelligence of the English divisions and an advantage in trade with the south. The Nordic sea-army elected Sweyn Forkbeard as both Sea-lord and Christian king of Denmark.

King Aethelred meanwhile raised a land army and raided Cumbria, the Anglo-Danish commonwealth of Olaf's royal widow. He ravaged widely there to slaughter the tribe of his former ally and perhaps to regain some portion of Danegeld paid in 991 and 994. Just as the Roman betrayal of truce with the widow of client King Prasutagus led to the uprising of Boudica and the Iceni commonwealth, King Aethelred's invasion of Cumbria was to raise armies against him with disastrous consequences.

> Now driven in flight from the land
> Is the warrior's bold kinsman.
> Why be so hard, my Lord?
> Evil it is by such a wolf
> Noble prince, to be bitten;
> He will not spare the flock
> If he is driven into the woods.[141]

---

[141] Snorri Sturluson, *Heimskringla*, 'Saga of Harald Fairhair', poem's trans. J. Jesch, *Women in the Viking Age* (Woodbridge, 1991), pp. 163-64.

When the Anglo-Dacian sea-armies returned from Normandy in 1001 they found themselves released from truce with King Aethelred twice over by King Olaf's death and the treachery of the land-army raid on the Cumbrian commonwealth of his queen. The sea-army raided the south, only effectively opposed at Exeter where the Dane Pallig was ealdorman. Ealdorman Pallig then allied with the rebel sea-army against King Aethelred. According to the Anglo-Saxon Chronicle, Pallig combined his forces with the raiding sea-army. They pillaged widely together until truce was negotiated and 24,000 pounds paid in Danegeld in early 1002. The truce restored Ealdorman Pallig's lands and title.

Collecting Danegeld from a war-shocked Wessex and Mercia spurred further unrest among King Aethelred's ealdormen and landowners, again weakening a weak king. Default of geld assessment was punishable by judicial dispossession of land and judicial enslavement and sale of the defaulter, his wife or his children to make good the geld. Slave exports boomed in aas English slaves were sold abroad for gold and silver to raise geld assessments. Ealdormen who failed to raise their burden of geld would lose lands and title. Parents sold children and husbands sold wives, but they hated their king, overlords and reeves for the necessity. Ealdorman Leofsige of East Anglia, who had negotiated the most recent truce with Ealdorman Pallig, killed the king's high reeve for attempting to tax the privileged Anglo-Danish commonwealth and was banished, his lands forfeit to the king. No new ealdorman replaced him, leaving the Anglo-Danes of East Anglia disaffected and without leadership. More and more vacant titles remained unfilled in a divided, impoverished and vulnerable realm encircled by fierce coastal Anglo-Danes and threatening NordicDanes.

Desperate for strong allies, in the spring of 1002 King Aethelred married Emma of Normandy to restore truce with her brother Duke Richard II. Emma was a daughter of Duke Richard the Fearless and Gunnora, a Gallo-Danish noblewoman from a powerful coastal family. Richard II had invaded Brittany and annexed it to Normandy, reuniting two-thirds of the empire of Brutus of Troy. He introduced feudal rule to Normandy. It was Duchess Gunnora, however, who reshaped Normandy as an imperial duchy. She promoted Benedictine reforms of Norman orders, prompted the duke to re-found Fécamp Abbey as the ducal chancery and exchequer with papal privileges of the Holy Apostolic See, founded the episcopal see of Coutances, and made generous endowments to the privileged abbey of Mont Saint-Michel.[142] Gunnora also commissioned the first written history of Normandy from Dudo, a monk of Saint-Quentin, spreading Normandy's fame to Frankish courts and Rome. Gunnora taught daughter Emma how a royal wife promotes royal power through cooperation with prelates, secular clerics, bards, and urban mercantile elites. She schooled her in royal patronage and diplomacy. Gunnora may have lived as late as 1031, guiding her contesting sons Richard and Robert as dukes, advising her daughter Emma as queen consort to successive English then Danish kings of England, and overseeing the education of her royal grandchildren Edward, Alfred and Goda.

Gunnora confirms a charter to Mont Saint-Michel

[142] Ancient Dacian Christian minsters may have required refounding as Benedictine orders to bring them into communion with the reformed Universal Church and to obtain papal privileges reserved for orders founded in the Holy Apostolic See.

The marriage contract for Emma of Normandy and King Aethelred required that Emma be consecrated queen with the Christian rite, that she receive generous dower estates in the privileged royal borough of Winchester, and that her sons by King Aethelred as legitimate issue in Christian marriage should have primacy in inheritance over the six older sons by Aethelred's Danish wife, the daughter of Jarl Thored of York. The family division that had fuelled civil war with King Edgar's second marriage was doomed to repeat with his son's second marriage. Anglo-Danes and settled Danes had looked to the six grandsons of Thored of York to be successors of King Aethelred; they were now threatened with Wessex-Norman imperium from sons of this second marriage.

Learning of their disaffection, a few months after the royal wedding King Aethelred tried to purge southern England of settled Danes by further treachery. With the approval of his southern Witans the king ordered the massacre of all Danes on St Brice's Day, 13 November 1002. Every Danish man, woman and child was to be rounded up and killed. Descriptions of the massacre are horrific, with bound women savaged by dogs, babies heartlessly speared, and churches sheltering terrified Danes torched to the ground. In a charter for a burned church at Oxford, the king coldly justified the genocide as a 'cleansing' and 'most just extermination'.[143] As with any genocide, there would be long memories and retribution.

> Why be so hard, my Lord?
> Evil it is by such a wolf
> Noble prince, to be bitten;
> He will not spare the flock
> If he is driven into the woods

Very few Danes escaped the St Brice's Day massacre, but these few reached Denmark. Among the murdered of Exeter were Ealdorman Pallig and his royal wife, King Sweyn's sister. A vengeful conquest of England began the following year, led by King Sweyn, Sealord Thorkell the Tall, and joined by thousands of Anglo-Danish and Nordic Danish kinsmen of those slain.

---

[143] S909, *The Cartulary of the Monastery of St Frideswide at Oxford.*

The next few years were quite horrible in England, at least in the south. In 1003 King Sweyn sacked Exeter, avenging his sister and Ealdorman Pallig, possibly aided by the queen's Norman reeve, who was appointed on Pallig's death. Then prosperous Wilton and Salisbury fell. In 1004 Sweyn's armies raided East Anglia, leaderless since the banishment of Ealdorman Leofsige. A great famine in 1005 provided a brief respite as the Danes returned home, but famine can cause as much civil strife as war. In 1006 Ealdorman Wulfgeat, who Aethelred 'had loved almost more than anyone' was dispossessed of his lands and banished as a rebel, perhaps in default of tribute to the king. Ealdorman Aelfhelm of Northumbria was lured south to a royal council then murdered and his two sons blinded. Having betrayed and banished his Anglo-Dacian protectors, having taxed his own people into penury and slavery, having dispossessed his most capable ealdormen, the kingdom that remained to King Aethelred was weak and leaderless, ripe for conquest.

In the late summer of 1006 King Sweyn returned with another sea-army and raided inland to the very centre of England and looted every shire in Wessex. Saxon attempts to repulse the raiders always failed. The sea-army settled on the Isle of Wight and raided from this base wherever they wished. A great council was convened which determined that the king should petition for truce. In 1007 Danegeld of 30,000 was paid to the sea-army, and Eadric Streona – 'Eadric the Acquisitor' – was rewarded for viciously collecting the geld with the office of ealdorman of Mercia, vacant since 985.

In 1008 a further great council convened which agreed to try new tactics. The council banned the export of English slaves abroad and commissioned a royal fleet of ships for defence of the realm under the king's direct authority. The first royal navy would rise to take the place of truce with Anglo-Danish sea-lords. Both reformist policies threatened Anglo-Danish mercantile and maritime elites. Slaves sold at cantonal markets for export were a great source of profits to raiding sea-armies, mariners and slave traders. Anglo-Danish defenders of the coasts held valuable royal privileges for tax collection, sea-borne trade, self-rule and hinterland slaving that could be lost to a royal fleet.

According to the Anglo-Saxon Chronicle, Wulfnoth Cyld rebelled in 1009, a year after the great council. *Cyld* is interpolated in Version F of the Anglo-Saxon Chronicle as meaning 'nobleman', but it may more specifically denote an Anglo-Dacian sea-lord. *Scyldings* were the descendants of legendary Nordic Dacian royalty. Wulfnoth was probably mixed Saxon and Anglo-Dacian heritage as he is also recorded as the son of the Saxon Ealdorman Aethelmaer of Wessex, who held primacy among ministers on royal charters from the mid-990s to 1006, and in one source is a nephew of Ealdorman Eadric Streona of Mercia, who assumed primacy from 1006. Both ealdormen would submit to King Sweyn in 1013. Wulfnoth Cyld's estuarine manor in Sussex, his command of a fleet of ships as sea-lord, and his successful raids on the south coast all agree with noble Anglo-Danish heritage and youthful fostering by an Anglo-Danish sea-lord.

Wulfnoth's son Godwin would also become a sea-lord and earl after King Cnut's conquest of England. Wulfnoth's grandson Harold, who bore a royal Danish name, would become earl of East Anglia, then earl of Wessex, then *subregulus*, and then king of England. Wulfnoth and Godwin are names that do not follow the pattern of Saxon royal names, but they are common Frisian names attested in 10th century East Anglia. Like his king, Ealdorman Aethelmaer may have taken a noble Anglo-Danish wife to promote Wessex trade and placate the Anglo-Danish sea-armies settled on his coasts.

Wulfnoth's rebellion against King Aethelred was triggered by Beorhtric, brother of Eadric Streona. Beorhtric set himself up as sea-lord of the new royal fleet and then accused Wulfnoth of an unspecified offence. According to the Anglo-Saxon Chronicle, Wulfnoth recruited 20 ships of rebels and violently raided the southern coast of England and 'wrought every kind of harm'. The king sent Beorhtric and 80 ships chasing after Wulfnoth, but the inexperienced commander and crews foundered the royal fleet during a storm. Wulfnoth burned their ships with flaming arrows, a classic Frisian sea-army attack. Beorhtric and the crews were left dead or drowning on the next tide. The remainder of the royal fleet returned to London.

> Evil it is by such a wolf
> Noble prince, to be bitten;
> He will not spare the flock
> If he is driven into the woods.

Godwin would have been a youth about the same age as King Sweyn's second son Cnut when Wulfnoth Cyld rebelled and led his sea-army and fleet of ships into exile. Wulfnoth would have prudently taken young Godwin with him or sent him ahead with the rebel families rather than leave the boy to be judicially enslaved, murdered or blinded as other sons of offending nobles had been. Victorians who suggested Godwin was a loyal Saxon who stayed in England to resist the Danes were indulging unreasonable romantic fantasy.[144]

Nordic oral tradition suggests Wulfnoth's wife was a Danish noblewoman descended from King Gorm the Old, which renders Wulfnoth's rebellion even more reasonable. If true then Godwin was at least half-Dane and possibly descended from both Saxon and Danish royal houses. Godwin's youthful preferment as sea-lord and earl by King Cnut, his rising quickly from earl to *subregulus* when King Cnut was abroad, Tostig Godwinson's royal marriage to Judith of Flanders, and Harold Godwinson's ambition for the crown of England are all better explained with dual English and Danish royal heritage.

Wulfnoth and his 20 ships almost certainly fled to exile in Flanders. Coastal Flanders offered mustering free ports for sea-army fleets and Bruges had become the favourite emporium for sea-army raiders and slavers after Normandy closed its ports and markets under truce. Bruges was the logical place to sell Wulfnoth's looted booty and English slaves and resettle a seafaring family in sanctuary one tide's sail from England. If she survived the St Brice's Day massacre and lived to 1009, then Wulfnoth's wife may have fled to Denmark or Flanders earlier and prepared for the family's resettlement in exile. Danish royal connections and a settled family presence in Flanders would explain the family's influence with Count Baldwin IV and Godwin's lifelong alliance with Count Baldwin V. Raids against England from Flanders with mercenary sea-armies became a Wulfnoth family tradition for four generations, common to Wulfnoth Cyld, Wulfnoth's son Godwin, four

---

[144] Edward Bulwer Lytton's popular novel *Harold, The Last of the Saxon Kings* (London, 1848) cast Godwin and Harold as loyal Saxon Englishmen. The novel established a romantic public mindset in which Godwin and his sons were patriotic Saxon defenders of England rather than Anglo-Danish allies of the invading Danes and traitorous rebels against English kings.

of his earl grandsons (Sweyn, Harold, Tostig and Gyrth), and even his great-grandsons, the twin sons of King Harold.

Wulfnoth and Godwin with their 20 ships and accomplished sea-warriors would be welcomed in any mustering sea-army fleet. They brought sure knowledge of the coasts and could disclose the defences and value of prosperous hinterland targets. By Nordic custom freemen mariners of any origin could join a sea-army at any general fleet muster. Oaths of loyalty were demanded, but these only bound the skippers and mariners until geld and booty were distributed at the end of the campaign.

In spring 1009 another huge sea-army fleet was mustering along the Flanders coast, preparing to cross the strait to attack England. In command were Thorkell the Tall and his brother Hemming. Thorkell was a famed Jomsviking sea-lord with wide experience of war, said to be foster-father and military mentor to King Sweyn's second son Cnut. A connection as foster-sons may explain the lifelong devotion of Cnut and Godwin to each other.

The *Knytlinga Saga* says Wulfnoth gave young Godwin as a foster-son to Thorkell's son Ulf. It was customary to give a son to be fostered as hostage when forming an alliance. Fostering by Ulf would explain Godwin's early command of fleets, his preferment as a sea-lord until 1021 by King Cnut, command of fleets and sea-armies in two Nordic and Baltic campaigns, his early preferment as earl, promotion to *subregulus* after Thorkell, and Godwin's ready skill attracting Danish mercenary fleets to join his raids on England as an exile and rebel in 1051 and 1052. Ulf would marry Cnut's royal sister Estrith, giving Godwin another connection to the Danish royal court.

Thorkell and Hemming's fleets sailed in the late spring and summer of 1009 and relentlessly raided throughout England. Nothing the English could do kept the raiders from looting and slaving. A massive 84,000 pounds in Danegeld was collected and paid in 1012. Under the terms of the Pontic truce Thorkell and Hemming agreed to serve King Aethelred and defend England from other Vikings once the geld was paid and the fleet dismissed in exchange for self-rule commonwealths in East Anglia and London and control of Nordic trade-routes. Thorkell and Hemming remained in England with 45 ships and perhaps 5,000 men. The truce also required payment of the first stipendiary *Heregeld* – 'army tax' – to the Anglo-Danish sea-army.

Thorkell's truce may have brought Godwin safely back to England as a youthful sea-lord in the mercenary fleet and restored royal favour and protection. Multi-lingual and nobly-born Godwin may even have negotiated the truce with King Aethelred or Ealdorman Eadric Streona for Thorkell and Hemming. The *Vita Aedwardi* describes Godwin as *profundus eloquio* – 'profound in eloquence'; this is echoed in the description of youthful Godwin as 'a well-spoken fellow' when he meets Ulf in *Knytlinga Saga*.

The settlement of Nordic defenders in England did not stop aggression by King Sweyn or heal the divisions among English nobility. Collection of the Danegeld and Heregeld caused greater famine, poverty and resentment as more landholders were dispossessed of lands and more defaulters and family members were sold into slavery to meet assessments. It was around this time that Wulfstan, archbishop of York and bishop in plurality of the sees of London and Worcester, began protesting the massive slave trade. William of Malmesbury recounted of Bristol at the time:

> You could see and sigh over rows of wretches bound together with ropes, young people of both sexes whose beautiful appearance and youthful innocence might move barbarians to pity, daily exposed to prostitution, daily offered for sale.[145]

King Sweyn invaded again in early 1013 and raided widely from Sandwich to Northumbria. The Anglian nobles of the north and people of the Danelaw submitted to King Sweyn's imperium. Royal son Cnut was married to the daughter of the murdered Ealdorman Aelfhelm of Northumbria to seal the Danelaw alliance and provide continuity of royal administration in the Danelaw. The Danes also took many hostages to secure Anglian and Anglo-Danish oaths.

Crossing the border from Danelaw into King Aethelred's Wessex realm, King Sweyn's army raided more widely and more cruelly. Oxford and Winchester submitted to him and gave hostages, possibly preferring Danish imperium as ancient Dacian trading settlements. Only urban London resisted the Danish army, defended by stout walls

---

[145] *Vita Wulfstani*, as translated by M. Swanton, *Three Lives of the Last Englishmen* (London, 1984), p. 126.

and an urban garrison of Danes under command of Thorkell the Tall. King Aethelred sheltered in London under Thorkell's protection. King Sweyn then turned from London to Bath, and received the surrender of Ealdorman Aethelmaer, grandfather of Godwin, and all the western thegns, and they too gave oaths and hostages. Ealdorman Eadric Streona of Mercia followed their example and submitted too. Seeing all of England had fallen, London's citizenry convened and agreed to seek truce with King Sweyn, offering geld and hostages.

Queen Emma and the royal children Edward, Alfred and Goda were sent from London to sanctuary in Normandy. King Aethelred remained with Thorkell and the mercenary fleet in the Thames for a time, but the king soon joined his queen in Normandy. The royal family took sanctuary at Fécamp Abbey, refounded by Emma's parents Richard the Fearless and Gunnora as a papally privileged Benedictine order. Literate and numerate secular monks of Fécamp had become expert administrators of Normandy's ducal chancery and exchequer.[146] Then as today it was record-keeping and communication networks which enabled efficient government, industry and trade.

Fécamp Abbey monks provided both education and protection for the royal children. Fécamp clerics also introduced the children to the court offices and entertainments of Duke Richard II and dower Duchess Gunnora. Eldest son Edward would never be comfortable living anywhere but a palace adjacent to an abbey, and would rebuild Westminster Abbey and a new palace for himself on the model of the Benedictine foundation and ducal palace at Fécamp.

In February 1014 King Sweyn died, ending the truce sworn by English elites. The sea-army in England elected youthful second son Cnut as their sea-king. By Nordic custom younger son Cnut could be elected sea-king by the sea-army, leading raids abroad, while his elder brother Harald succeeded to King Sweyn's terrestrial kingdom by consent of the terrestrial jarls.

---

[146] The name Fécamp may derive from *fisc-campus*. One meaning of *fiscus* is imperial exchequer. Fécamp was a Roman imperial treasury. It was not uncommon for Frankish royal residences to take over Roman imperial palaces, as at Cologne and Paris.

Instead of confirming Sea-king Cnut as successor to King Sweyn in England, the English Witans sent to Aethelred, offering to restore him as king if he would rule better.[147] Perhaps they hoped he had learned Norman royal administration while in exile. Adolescent Edward Aethling was sent to negotiate with the Witans, a display of royal favour for the presumptive heir and an insult to Aethelred's half-Danish older sons. One condition of Aethelred's return was the outlawing of all Danish kings, which the Witans conceded, outlawing Sea-king Cnut. King Aethelred then returned and led a land-army against Sea-king Cnut's forces in Lindsey. The Danes returned to their ships, but before leaving England the outlawed Cnut sailed to Sandwich and set ashore all the hostages yielded to King Sweyn by English nobles. He cut off their hands, ears and noses as punishment for their kinsmen's treachery.

> Evil it is by such a wolf
> Noble prince, to be bitten;
> He will not spare the flock
> If he is driven into the woods.

Young Godwin likely remained with Thorkell and the mercenary fleet, perhaps promoting alliance with the Anglo-Danish sons of King Aethelred against the youthful Edward Aethling. Godwin is mentioned in the 1014 will of Aethelstan, then the eldest surviving grandson of Jarl Thored of York. The will recommends restoration of an estate at *Cumtune* – 'combe manor' – to *Godwine Wulfnoðes suna* – Godwin Wulfnothsson. Other lands are restored to Ealdorman Aethelmaer, Godwin's rebel grandfather. A prized sword of King Offa was left to brother Edmund Ironside, perhaps suggesting Aethelstan's succession preference. Step-mother, half-brothers and half-sister in Normandy were omitted entirely. *Cumtune* was an estate near *Aetheledene*,

---

[147] The Witenagemot was a great council of high ecclesiastic and secular English rulers; members were Witans. A great council might convene to enact laws or to select a new king. Abbot Aelfric of Eynsham wrote in the 10th century: 'No man can make himself king, but the people has the choice to choose as king whom they please; but after he is consecrated as king, he then has dominion over the people, and they cannot shake his yoke off their necks.'

Aethelstan's seat on the navigable Cuckmere estuary near Exceat.

Once restored to the throne, with Sea-king Cnut outlawed from England, King Aethelred raised Heregeld of 30,000 pounds to reward the loyal mercenaries of Thorkell and Hemming, whose fleet and sea-army remained defending London, East Anglia and the Thames. The geld distribution may have ended the truce between king and Thorkell as being the end of the campaign contracted between them.

Cumtune, Exceat and Aetheldene have not survived to modern times, abandoned as the Cuckmere estuary closed to navigation.

King Aethelred then turned on his Danish mercenaries once again, perhaps to retake the generous geld collected and paid in 1012 and 1014. He ordered the surprise slaughter of all the Danes in East Anglia and London in January 1015. Hemming was murdered in East Anglia. Thorkell with sons Ulf and Eilaf sailed from London to Denmark and reconciled with Sea-king Cnut. King Aethelred's treachery broke any truce with Thorkell, leaving him free to attack the land he had before defended.

> Evil it is by such a wolf
> Noble prince, to be bitten;
> He will not spare the flock
> If he is driven into the woods.

Cnut's reconciliation with his foster-father Thorkell and foster-brothers Ulf and Eilaf gave him powerful allies with intimate knowledge of England's vulnerable ports, emporia, coasts and defences. Thorkell's fame as a sea-lord would attract an even wider fleet and sea-army from the Baltic, Ireland and Orkneys to join the conquest led by Sea-king Cnut. The treacherous slaughter of Danes and Anglo-Danes in East Anglia and London had once again stirred a Nordic Dacian lust for vengeance.

Divisions among the scanty nobility remaining in England would worsen too. At a great council at Oxford later in 1014, Ealdormen Siferth and Morcar from Northumbria and the Danelaw were murdered so the king could seize their lands for sale to others. The Anglo-Danish ealdormen, sons of the Dane Arngrim, might be suspected of continuing some alliance with the Danes. The north was less war-ravaged, so had remained more productive and prosperous than the south. War-hardened Edmund Ironside, the eldest surviving half-Dane son of Aethelred, now openly rebelled against his father at this injustice. He rescued Siferth's widow from his father's imprisonment, married her for royal continuity of administration in the north, and they jointly led an opposition regime attracting supporters away from the southern king.

Sea-king Cnut returned with a fleet of 160 ships in the summer of 1015 and ruthlessly subdued an exhausted and impoverished south. By this time Godwin may have become a sea-lord in Cnut's raiding fleet in his own right. A runestone in Uppsala, Sweden, long a favoured sea-army muster port, confirms Godwin held a military command: *Bjor Arnsteinsson fandt sin død i Godines hær dengang da Knut drog til England* – 'Bjor Ansteinsson found his death in Godwin's raiding-army when Cnut sailed to England'.

Ealdorman Eadric Streona of Mercia switched sides again and allied with Sea-king Cnut, bringing 40 ships from the king's fleet. The combined sea-armies moved north and raided Eadric Streona's own Mercia and Warwickshire. Exacerbating the vulnerability of the realm, a huge flood coincided with the autumn high tides at harvest time and caused massive loss of lives, crops and cattle, threatening famine. In the late autumn Edmund Ironside gathered an army north and south, and sent for his father to jointly lead it, but the discouraged king soon returned to London rather than confront Sea-king Cnut and the rebel

Eadric Streona. Edmund Ironside then rode north and took to raiding his own lands for his own profit, following Eadric's example. Cnut continued raiding all the way to Northumbria, where he killed the ealdorman appointed to replace the sons of the Dane Arngrim and put the sea-lord Eric, son of Danish Jarl Hakon, in his place. By Easter 1016 Cnut had control of all England, and he returned to besiege London, where Edmund Ironside had taken refuge with the king.

King Aethelred died on St George's Day, 23rd April 1016. The Witans of England unanimously elected Cnut as king, repudiating the sons of Aethelred. Only London, long a cantonal commonwealth, resisted King Cnut, choosing Edmund Ironside for London's king. The two kings clashed repeatedly, alternately raiding and warring throughout England, until they met at the Battle of Assendun in September 1016. King Edmund was injured and his army was defeated; he surrendered on terms and lived only until November. His infant sons by Siferth's widow, more than half-Danish by blood, were sent abroad into exile. There were few noble English survivors among a nobility depleted by decades of wars, rivalries and civil disputes. The Anglo-Saxon Chronicle records 'all the nobility of England was destroyed' in the many battles. The surviving Witans and aldermen of London unanimously confirmed King Cnut, who was consecrated king of all England in London on Christmas Day 1016. As a measure of the eradication of Saxon nobility, there appears to have been no further resistance to King Cnut's rule, which started and remained peaceful and prosperous.

Cnut the Great was the second son of King Sweyn and his second wife Świętosława, a Polish princess, daughter of King Mieszko I of Poland and Dobrawa of Bohemia, and sister of King Boleslaw I of Poland. She was queen first to King Eric the Victorious of Sweden, who had defeated King Sweyn to briefly rule Denmark and invade Germany. After Eric's death she married King Sweyn, providing continuity of royal administration in Nordic realms and trade connections through her Slavo-Dacian kinsmen in the east. Cnut's Slavo-Dacian heritage and his mother's knowledge of eastern realms may have contributed to King Cnut's later determination to dominate all sea-borne trade from the Irish Sea to St Petersburg.

Almost the first act of King Cnut was to confirm by charter the privileges of St Paul's church in London to display his Christian piety and willingness to cooperate with secular clerics for English royal administration and wider European mercantile prosperity. King Cnut made London his military, economic and political capital. St Pauls could provide the literate and numerate secular clerics essential to royal administration of markets and shipping. The multi-cultural, talented, mercantile burgesses of London could quickly re-establish trade with the continent and Nordic markets.

Following the example of his royal father and mother, King Cnut swiftly negotiated to marry Queen Emma, the widow of King Aethelred, reinforcing his royal legitimacy as successor and providing continuity of royal administration in England. Their marriage contract, like Emma's first, stipulated that Emma would be consecrated Cnut's queen with the Christian rite, she would retain her royal estates in Winchester and the south, and King Cnut's sons by her as legitimate issue of a Christian marriage would have primacy for succession over the son Cnut had fathered with his Mercian first wife. Queen Emma would bear a son Harthacnut, future king of England and Denmark, and a daughter Gunhilda, pledged in infancy for marriage to the son of the Holy Roman Emperor to secure trade routes to the Mediterranean. Emma's three older children would remain in exile at Fécamp.

Another demand at the time of Emma's marriage may have been endowment of *Rameslege* – 'Rome's lowey' – to Fécamp Abbey in fulfilment of a promise by King Aethelred.[148] The two Brede Basin manors of *Bretda* and *Hastingas*, and their vast estuarine port, had been dispossessed for treason of Wessex Ealdorman Aethelmaer. The name Rameslege may derive from centuries of 'Roman law' and Romana language in the basin, long a Gallic possession of Saint-Denis Abbey of Paris. The name *Rameslege* parallels *Danelege* for the autonomous Danelaw, implying an autonomous commonwealth.[149]

---

[148] A lowey was an extrajudicial estate granted freedom from royal demesne by charter. The toponym may also have been used for designating cantons ceded as Anglo-Dacian settlements.

[149] The four Anglo-Saxon charters were copied in an 11th century portfolio preserved in Paris. While some Victorians dismissed these as forgeries, more recent analysis suggests they were accurate copies of original early charters. Early Saint-Denis churches at Rotherhithe and London confirm long-term possession.

The last of Anglo-Saxon charter for Saint-Denis evidences a jealous preservation of freedom from royal and manorial taxes in the ecclesiastical commonwealth. The reeve who had dared collect taxes on the estate was forced by King Edgar to carry the charter restoring the abbey's immunities to Paris and lay it on the altar of the three martyrs, Dionysus, Elutherius and Rusticus.

The 1017 charter of King Cnut thus restored Gallic possession and liberties to the manors and port that had dominated Anglo-Gallic trade for centuries, but secured its rich forests, potteries, iron mines and salt-works for the clerics and sea-armies of Queen Emma's native Normandy in preference to Paris. The charter grants *terram que Rammesleah dicitur cum portu suo omnibusque rebus ad se perinentibus* – 'the land which is called Rome's Lowey with its port and all affairs of business that pertain to it'. The similarity of the wording used by King Aethelred in the 1005 charter for Eynsham Abbey suggests that Fécamp Abbey had either received a charter from King Aethelred which is now lost, or King Cnut employed royal chaplains familiar with the forms of King Aethelred.

Queen Emma may have promoted the royal chaplain Aelfwine, a former secular monk of Fécamp Abbey who had accompanied Queen Emma to England and managed her royal affairs. Aelfwine likely negotiated for Queen Emma's marriage and related endowments as her secular cleric and chaplain; he is named in one charter as her *praepositus* or administrator of royal estates. He became principal chaplain to King Cnut and later bishop of Winchester. It would be customary to negotiate privileges for his order in recognition of his services to the royal couple.

Sea-lord Godwin made himself useful to King Cnut after the Danish conquest by violently serving wherever violence was wanted, usually in command of sea-armies or Lithsmen for the king. Bilingual Godwin may have led collection the king's Lithsmen with Ealdorman Eadric for collection of the huge geld assessed on the conquered English after 1016, which far exceeded any earlier Danegeld or Heregeld. The single attribution of Godwin as a nephew of Eadric Streona may stem from this association. It may have some literal basis if the youthful Godwin became foster-son to Ealdormen Eadric as hostage during the Aethelred-Thorkell truce, a post which would give him first-hand expertise of English collection of stipendiary provisions and Heregeld during the truce interval, and collection of Danegeld in

2014, before the pay off to Thorkell's fleet. Such a connection better explains Ealdorman Eadric's defection with 40 ships to join Sea-King Cnut. Godwin's ambition to succeed Eadric as king's reeve may also better explain King Cnut's decision to kill Eadric in 1017, when Godwin was mature enough and experienced enough from the 1016 Danegeld collection to have earned the promotion. Young Godwin signed his first royal charter as *Godwine dux* in 1018, indicating military command and early royal favour. There is no record of a terrestrial estate at this early date, but *dux* could designate command of the London urban garrison or royal Lithsmen, consistent with Norse tradition of using *dux* for war-lords or sea-lords without any manorial seat.

Judicial dispossession and judicial slavery for geld arrears on the methods perfected by Eadric Streona would allow Godwin as high reeve to quickly amass wealth, land and influence in a similar manner. Buying judicially forfeit land for the price of geld assessments was a perk of office for the king's reeve, and would explain Godwin's rapid rise from landless exile as a boy to the wealthiest nobleman in King Cnut's realm. Eadric the Acquisitive, as he is styled in Hemming's cartulary, was also a high reeve before gaining an earldom, and famed for appropriating church land and treasuries for himself, as Godwin would also do wherever he could get away with it.

King Cnut based his royal fleet of 40 ships and Lithsmen in London, once again a Danish financial, military and administrative capital. King Cnut employed a proven model for military cooperation, occupation, taxation, peacekeeping, and exploitation. Terrestrial rule and tax collection were organised through the Huscarls, a fraternal order of elite warriors modelled on the Jomsviking Brotherhood (*thinglith* in Old Norse). The Jomsvikings had been established by Thorkell the Tall a generation earlier for control of tribute and trade on the south shore of the eastern Baltic above the Polish and Slavo-Dacian fluvial trade routes. The site of Jomsborg or Vineta (a cognate of the Romano-Dacian *Venta* as at *Venta Belgarum* and *Venta Icanorum*) is disputed, but may be Wolin Island in Poland or Tollense Island (literally 'toll-river island') in Germany. Archaeologists have found the remains of thousands violently killed in the Tollense Valley around 1250BC, nearly the same time as sea-army attacks on Troy and Egypt.

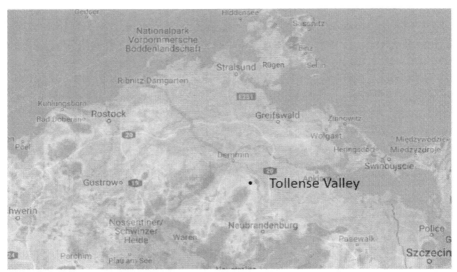

Jomsburg may have been on a hill above the Tollense Valley overlooking a confluence of rivers and islands controlling the southern Baltic sea routes to the east and south, a perfect stronghold for coordinating piracy or demanding thelony on authorised trade.

The Huscarls replaced the few inferior Mercian and Saxon nobles as survived the wars of 1016 as royal guardians, tribute collectors, and military elite. Members could be manorial lords and household retainers, sea-warriors, or warriors of urban garrisons. Competition for the limited election to the brotherhood was fierce. All Huscarls were sworn loyal to King Cnut and fraternally loyal to brother Huscarls. To qualify for the elite brotherhood, prospective Huscarls had to be experienced veterans, extremely wealthy, and possess body ornaments and weapons richly decorated with gold and silver. All inferior warriors were relegated to the service of earls with the new rank thegn, or urban magistrates as garrison guards. London's goldsmiths and silversmiths were kept hugely busy in 1016 and 1017 as the first recruits sought ornamented weapons to qualify for the order.

Some have suggested that the Huscarls had two divisions, Danish and English, based on Godwin's command of *Angli* troops on a Baltic campaign, but the English unit was almost certainly limited to Anglo-Danish sea-warriors and the London Lithsmen. Some Saxon and Mercian landholders and collaborators will have survived and peacefully cooperated with the Danish regime of military occupation, but subjugated Saxon nobles, in particular, were unlikely to be elected by the conquering Danes into the elite military brotherhood of the Huscarls, or retain sufficient unappropriated wealth to qualify for the rank. After the Danish conquest Saxons would be despised by the victors as inept, weak, unreliable and undisciplined military prospects. Queen Emma was unlikely to promote Saxon interests once she married King Cnut, preferring many Normans and encouraging Frankish and Norman emigration instead.

The Huscarls had their own legal code, meaning one law for the commoners of the realm and another law for the Huscarl military elite. A Huscarl tribunal for settling disputes among members could only convene in London after a call for assembly among Huscarls. 21st century achaeologists believe the forum or hall where the Huscarls convened was located near the site of the present Guildhall, in a corner just outside the old city walls, where aldermen of London still convene. Discipline among Huscarls was maintained by promoting or relegating Huscarls up or down the table of the great hall according to their communal merit or offences. Violence against a fellow Huscarl was a crime, a stricture intended to prevent inter-regional raiding and squabbles among the military elites. If a Huscarl stood accused of a crime he could demand trial by oath of witnesses before other Huscarls, even for an offence against the king. King Cnut willingly submitted himself to the justice of the Huscarl tribunal when he killed a fellow Huscarl in anger.

Whatever his ethnic heritage may have been, young Godwin was raised as a proficient sea-lord like his father Wulfnoth Cyld. He probably travelled, raided and traded widely with the raiding fleets of King Sweyn, Sea-Lord Thorkell, Ulf and Cnut after his father's exile, as a mercenary in England with Thorkell, and in command of a raiding-army as sea-lord to King Cnut. Godwin undoubtedly self-identified as Danish or Anglo-Danish. Godwin spoke Danish, was early favoured by King Cnut with military command, became earl of Wessex and Kent from 1021, married Thorkell the Tall's powerful daughter Gytha, and gave all his children noble Danish names.[150] After Cnut was consecrated as king of England, King Cnut's first earls were foster-father Sea-lord Thorkell, foster-brothers Sea-lords Ulf and Eilaf, Sea-lord Hakon, and Sea-lord Godwin Wulfnothsson. Eadric Streona was briefly allowed to retain Mercia as earl, but was soon killed as an

---

[150] Eadgytha Godwinsdottir was renamed Edith only when she married King Edward in 1045.

untrustworthy traitor.[151]

In 1021, on the death of his brother King Harald, King Cnut succeeded to the kingdoms of Norway and Denmark, uniting the three crown kingdoms after defeating a few rebellions with Godwin's aid as sea-lord. As ruler of three kingdoms, and a wider mercantile empire from Eire to the eastern Baltic, and his mother's Polish realm, a new chapter opened in more efficient, harmonised and deliberate royal and mercantile administration. Common control of all trade routes provided a long interval of security from pirates and raiders, promoted industrial-scale exploitation of agriculture, fisheries and mines, and fostered wider mercantile prosperity. King Cnut's first aim after securing the Baltic, again with Godwin's aid as sea-lord, was to travel to Rome through the Slavo-Dacian realms of his mother's kinsmen to negotiate fluvial and Mediterranean trade routes with the pope and Holy Roman Emperor. The Saracens then held the Mediterranean, so the Baltic and fluvial Germanic and Slavo-Dacian trade routes were a lifeline for Roman trade with Western Europe. Wool, salt-fish, salt-meat, grain, furs and slaves were major export commodities from Cnut's realms to the east, while gold, silver, wine, oil, fruits, spices and dyes flowed back to the prosperous west.

Godwin was promoted to earl of all Wessex and Kent in 1021, taking control of the prosperous earldom King Cnut had initially reserved to himself in 1017. Being earl entitled Godwin to one-third of all judicial levies as agent of the king's justice in addition to other thelony, tribute and trade privileges. By 1023 Earl Godwin held primacy among secular witnesses to royal charters, a primacy he retained until his death. He was left in charge of England as *subregulus* when King Cnut was abroad, supplanting Earl Thorkell.

At King Cnut's instigation Godwin married Gytha, daughter of Thorkell the Tall and sister to Earls Ulf and Eilaf. Earl Ulf married Cnut's sister Estrith. Thorkell had become the earl of prosperous East Anglia in 1017, *subregulus* for King Cnut until a 1021 breach, and later

---

[151] Romantic Victorians suggested Godwin was favoured by King Cnut for his loyalty to King Aethelred or Edmund Ironside, but this is very unlikely given Wulfnoth Cyld's exile and Godwin's early command of sea-armies for Cnut.

jarl of all Denmark. Ulf was foster-father to King Cnut and Queen Emma's royal son Harthacnut, although Cnut would later order Ulf killed for revolt in Denmark in 1026.

The Godwin family settled at the historic Wessex emporium of Winchester. Godwin and his Danish wife and kinsmen may have regarded the Saxons of the region as a subjugated tribe, a convenient chattel pool for slave exports, and soft targets for judicial fines and dispossessions of land.[152] The family amassed wealth very quickly.

Godwin and Gytha had eleven children together. All but the youngest son Wulfnoth were raised as enterprising sea-lords. The elder five sons also became earls under King Edward. Unusually for such a large family, no sons entered the church. Godwin only appears as a church benefactor once, apparently leaving management of clerical affairs and promotion of spiritual interests to his wife and daughters. It was Godwin and Gytha's daughters who were educated to be pious Christians, speak several languages fluently, and be literate in Latin. The eldest daughter, Eadgytha Godwinsdottir, was educated at Wilton Abbey, the abbey of King Edgar's abducted Abbess Wulfthryth. She would become Queen Edith, assuming a Saxon name as the wife of Edward the Confessor in 1045.

Godwin's wife Gytha Thorkellsdottir oversaw her husband's household and wider landed estates, his bondsmen's family welfare, church patronage, and the family fortunes and reputation. Her

---

[152] William of Malmesbury identifies Godwin's 'first wife' as a 'sister of Cnut' who sold Saxon slaves to her homeland, preferring young girls. As others confuse son and foster-son, he confuses sister and foster-sister. Gytha was Godwin's only wife and foster-sister to Cnut, not sister, but otherwise the account makes sense for a sea-lord's daughter and then wife. Danish wives had responsibility for marketing what their sea-lord or noble husbands seized, including slaves, and for distribution of shares or proceeds to the families of their hustband's men. Certainly slavery boomed under Danish rule, and Saxons, as the largest subjugated tribe, were the main source of slave supply. Girls were preferred for export to support prostitution, agriculture and weaving. Slaves were taken both in raids by shipmen and in lieu of geld by reeves. As late as 1086, when Domesday Book was compiled, about 20 per cent of the English population were still slaves.

responsibilities included marketing tribute, trade goods, booty and slaves in domestic and foreign markets, providing payment for service and making gifts on Godwin's behalf for the welfare his men and their families, endowing the church for the benefit of the family's souls, and providing an enduring legacy through commissioning songs and sagas. Gytha would have been well-positioned to guide her husband's ambitions with her father Thorkell jarl in Denmark, her brother Ulf as royal consort to King Cnut's sister Estrith, and brother Earl Eilaf ruling Glouscestershire on the Irish Sea. Both Winchester and Bristol became great mercantile and slaving ports, booming while Godwin was earl. According to the *Vita Eadwardi*, Gytha's household was multi-lingual, with mercantile agents from Dublin and Flanders teaching her children fluency in coastal languages additional to their parents' Danish and English, while clerics schooled them in Latin, mathematics and other subjects.

Earl Godwin supplemented his wealth by raiding the church where it was vulnerable, dispossessing bishops and abbots of prosperous lands, as well as looting church treasuries. Sources are anecdotal about his abuses, but form a cohesive pattern of targeting sites where thelony and tolls could be extorted from the control of trade. Earl Godwin took the port manor of Berkeley in Gloucestershire from a convent of nuns who were either killed or sold into slavery, so that his wife Gytha refused to eat produce from the estate. He acquired the port of Bosham by seizing the port, settling armed retainers there, and daring the archbishop of Canterbury to complain to King Cnut. Godwin gained the port of Plumstead by fraud and the port at Folkestone by bribing the archbishop. He likewise seized the port at Steyning by occupation on Bishop Aelfwine's death in 1047, and violently occupied the great Sussex port at Rameslege, taking control from Fécamp Abbey, after his rebellion in 1052. The Canterbury monk Eadmer described Godwin as 'a bitter enemy of the church of Canterbury', with the worst atrocities against 42 English pre-conquest religious foundations occurring during the reign of the weak King Edward when Earl Godwin was at his most powerful.

Raiding and dispossession of church lands was common throughout Danish-occupied England, but particularly in the south where Godwin and his sons ruled.[153] Churches and abbeys were custodians of Anglo-Saxon gold and silver before the Norman nobility built stone castles. Pre-conquest nobles and kings were expected to continuously move about collecting tribute or warring, so they appointed secular clerics of Benedictine orders or founded their own abbeys to manage their estates and secure their treasuries. Literate and numerate secular clerics would collect local land tributes, market levies and taxes and keep local records. These Anglo-Saxon clerical orders were soft targets for conquering Danes. Excommunication was the punishment for raiding the church, but damnation may not have been much of a threat to forcibly converted or near-pagan Danes.

King Cnut seems to have ignored violence against the church during his early reign, before unification of England with the kingdoms

---

[153] The curious text of King Cnut's 1018 writ confirming liberties of Christ Church Canterbury (S985) indicates that the possessions and liberties of the Church of England were then widely eroded:

And I inform you that the archbishop spoke to me about the freedom of Christ Church, that it now has less [possessions] than it once had. Then I gave him permission to draw up a new charter of freedom in my name. Then he told me that he had charters of freedom enough, if only they availed anything. Then I myself took the charters of freedom and laid them on Christ's own altar, in the witness of the archbishop and of Earl Thorkell and of many good men who were with me — with the same provisions as King Aethelberht and all my predecessors [had] freed it: that no-one, be he ecclesiastic or be he lay, shall ever be so presumptuous as to diminish any of the things that stand in the charter of freedom. And if any one do this, may his life here be shortened and may his dwelling be in the abyss of Hell, unless before his end he make amends for it more severely according to the archbishop's instruction.

The 1018 writ references the first written law of Kent, the Dooms of Aethelberht, enacted in the year 600. The first provision of that law is protection of the property of the church, bishops and clerics, with restitution and compensation as the penalty for infringement. Godwin may have taken Cnut's writ either literally or in jest as permitting him to seize and enjoy church property at peril of his soul, with the the option to later repent and make good his thefts. The writ was witnessed by Emma and Thorkell, but not Godwin.

of Sweden and Denmark gave him a vast mercantile empire to exploit on common standards and practices. After his trip to Rome in 1021 King Cnut harmonised church and state administration. It is likely that Queen Emma guided King Cnut toward better relations with the church as Duchess Gunnora had guided Duke Richard the Fearless. Queen Emma's own chaplain Aelfwine, originally a secular cleric of Fécamp Abbey and manager of the queen's estates, became King Cnut's royal chaplain before becoming bishop of Winchester.

Emma and Cnut endow a gold cross to Old Minster, Winchester. Queen Emma is given the title Alfgyfu, a title similar to King Aethelred's Danish first wife.

A second charter for Fécamp Abbey, attributed between 1028 and 1035, suggests possession of the northern manor *Bretda* in Rameslege had become contested so that Fécamp's Abbot John de Ravenna was forced to sue for royal protection.[154] Earl Godwin may have seized the port manor with its profitable port, potteries, saltworks and iron mines with the same irreverence he had displayed towards other church possessions. King Cnut clarified in the second charter that the extent of *Rammesleah* included *unam terram que Bretda vocatur alia vero que Rammesleah dicitur cum portu suo omnibusque rebus ad se pertinentibus* – 'that manor which is called *Bretda*, which is otherwise properly called *Rammesleah*, with its port and all affairs of business appertaining to it.' Rather than witness the charter with *ego Godwinus dux*, as usual for him, Godwin was forced to subscribe that 'the gift was by his most willing consent' after the attestations of the king and queen. This suggests Abbot John of Fécamp Abbey had prevailed over Godwin temporarily, but made an enemy who would seize all of Rameslege in 1052.

Under this second charter Fécamp Abbey also shared in *duas partes telonei in portu qui dicitur Wincenesel*[155] – 'two-thirds of the thelony in the port which is called *Wincenesel*. *Telonium* for toll house and thelony for tolls come from the Greek, τελώνιον, and was the oldest sea-army tax collected in coin. The king retained the other third share for protection of the port. The Brede Basin was used for receiving and taxing large continental shipments of wine and oil for centuries. A coastal cell at the sea-ford also controlled access to the tidal Rother and Tillingham rivers, so the thelony on traffic using the anchorage at the sea-ford would provide very great revenues. *Wincenesel* - 'wine channel cell' - may have been the anchorage the Saxons named *Pefenesea* – 'nearly the ness anchorage'. Elaborate tracery stones found off

---

[154] John de Ravenna had been prior of Fécamp from its refounding, when his uncle William of Volpiano became its first Benedictine abbot. He succeeded as abbot from 1028. Restoring order to the abbey's English affairs may have been an early priority when he succeeded as abbot as the loss of Rameslege revenues would lead to disaffection among the monks of the abbey after 1052.

[155] *Wincenesel* is the earliest cognate for Winchelsea in an English record. The Danes might prefer it to Saxon or Frankish names. It appears Flemish or Frisian in origin, but also could be *Venta*-river-cell, echoing the Jomsviking Tollense / *Vineta*.

Winchelsea Beach near the turn of the last century at a particularly low tide after a storm may be all that now remains of this cell. Spectroscopic testing of the stone may confirm Caen quarry origin.

King Aethelred and King Cnut's dispossession of Rameslege from Godwin, the heir of Aethelmaer, in favour of Fécamp Abbey may have contributed to Earl Godwin's enduring enmity against Normans. If he was indeed the son of Wulfnoth Cyld and grandson of Ealdorman Aethelmaer he would doubly resent the finest heavy cargo port in Sussex and its oak, pottery, salt and iron going to Norman clerics. The prosperous Norman and Anglo-Gallic clerics, craftsmen, merchants and settlers in the Brede Basin were perhaps the only people living in Earl Godwin's vast earldom that he could not tax, raid, loot or enslave – at least while they enjoyed a Danish king's protection.

Meanwhile Aethlings Edward and Alfred grew to manhood in exile at Fécamp Abbey and the ducal court. The aethlings were half-Norman by their mother Emma and thoroughly Norman in language, education, occupation and outlook as young men reaching maturity. Young Edward regarded both Edmund Ironside and King Cnut as illegitimate tyrants, relying on descent from King Aethelred for his better claim to the crown. Edward witnessed charters in Normandy during this period as *Edguardus Rex,* and granted charters for lands in England to Norman and Frankish religious orders as if he were himself the rightful king of England.

Usurped first by his half-brother and then by his step-father in 1016, Edward observed more family strife in Normandy when Duke Richard II died in 1026. Richard III succeeded his father as duke, but younger brother Robert rebelled against him. Richard III died quite suddenly, leading to wide speculation that Robert had killed him. The duchy of Normandy was roiled by factional violence and instability. Robert was excommunicated by the pope for arresting his uncle the archbishop of Rouen, who may have denied him consecration, and for raiding the treasury at Fécamp Abbey to fund his army in the civil war.

After defeat of his rivals, Duke Robert committed himself to mending ties to the church. He restored his archbishop uncle to his see at Rouen, restored looted treasure to Fécamp Abbey, and displayed his contrition to the pope with very generous gifts to the church and Rome. He was given papal reinstatement to communion with the church, consecration as duke, and a new sobriquet, Robert the

Magnificent. The duke also helped his young cousins Edward and Alfred attempt an assault on England in 1032, but the adventure was abandoned after a storm dispersed the Norman fleet.

Duke Robert set out on a pilgrimage to Rome and Jerusalem in 1034, leaving his only son William, a child by his handfast wife Herleva, as his designated heir. Duke Robert arranged for William to have the protection of the French king and four guardians during his minority, and for Herleva to marry Herluin de Conteville should he fail to return. William was just eight or nine when his father died on the return journey from Jerusalem in 1035. It took many years for the young duke to secure his duchy, with his noble kinsmen in Ponthieu foremost among those seeking his early death.[156] The duke learned military and diplomatic skills alike in gaining and holding his duchy.

England had been prosperous and secure during King Cnut's reign, at least for Anglo-Danes and Danes, but brother soon contested against brother when he died in 1035. Raised mostly in Denmark by Ulf and Thorkell, Harthacnut was clearly Cnut's favoured heir, but King Cnut's death had dissolved the binding oaths in both Nordic and British realms. Sweden fell to King Magnus, splitting the realm unified with Denmark since King Sweyn Forkbeard's defeat of Eric the Victorious. Harthacnut appointed his older half-brother Harold Harefoot as regent in the north of England and his mother Queen Emma as regent in the south while he went to secure the crown of Denmark and contest the crown of Sweden. Appointing separate regents for the Anglian Danelaw and Saxon south suggests the political divisions between Anglians and Saxons remained entrenched even after 20 years of Anglo-Danish unified rule. The two powerful wives of King Cnut had remained as competing royal agents in each domain. As soon as Harthacnut was abroad the elder son Harold Harefoot sought the English crown for himself.

Queen Emma may have invited her older sons Edward and Alfred to return to England in 1036 to counter Harold Harefoot's ambition to rule in the Saxon south of England, ceding the Anglian

---

[156] Enguerrand I and Hugh II, counts of Ponthieu and kinsmen of Guy d'Amiens, were particularly troublesome, repeatedly conspiring to kill the young Duke William.

north to her rival. Edward returned to Normandy after a skirmish at Southampton, but Alfred and his retinue were intercepted by Earl Godwin, treacherously betrayed after pretended friendship, and then turned over to Harold Harefoot. Ninety-nine men out of every hundred were killed, and the handful of survivors were sold as slaves in Dublin. Alfred Aethling died a horrific death after being blinded and mutilated. Perhaps alienated from Emma and Harthacnut by his role in Alfred's murder, Earl Godwin supported Harold Harefoot as king in 1037.

Queen Emma fled Winchester to sanctuary in Bruges where she sought support in retaking England from her surviving sons. Edward refused, remaining in Normandy. King Harthacnut sailed with ten ships to join Emma in Flanders where he mustered a much greater fleet for attack. Harold Harefoot died in 1040 before the Danish fleet sailed, leaving King Harthacnut uncontested king of both Denmark and England.

Before leaving Denmark in 1040, at the urging of his Danish nobles, King Harthacnut agreed a treaty with King Magnus of Norway that whichever of the two survived the other should reunite the Nordic kingdoms. That treaty would be the basis for Norwegian claims to the crowns of both Denmark and England after Harthacnut died in 1042.

King Harthacnut was angered by Earl Godwin's betrayal and involvement in his half-brother's death and so put Godwin on trial for murder before the Huscarls. Godwin swore an oath that he had only acted on orders from King Harold Harefoot which was attested by witnesses. Godwin also bought forgiveness with the gift of a highly decorated ship, fully manned with eighty magnificently armed warriors with gold and silver ornaments and weapons. Some think this gift confirms Godwin's command of the Huscarls, the military elite owing military service to the king and collecting royal taxes, or the London Lithsmen, the royal naval fleet instrumental in coastal defence and controlling foreign trade. The real purpose may have been to seal a compact between the young king and his most powerful earl as the gift of a ship implies a reciprocal grant of martial authority.

The gift of a ship in Nordic sagas always implies a mutuality of military service and obligation. With this gift of a ship and sea-warriors Godwin reminded Harthacnut that he retained many more ships with many more sea-warriors as earl and sea-lord. If denied land and protection of the law by the king then Godwin could cause great harm as an outlaw.

Perhaps in response to the implied threat of his most powerful earl, or perhaps at his urging to loot the kingdom, King Harthacnut raised the number of Lithsmen ships in royal service from sixteen, the number under King Cnut, to seventy-two. He also demanded 21,000 pounds to pay off his useless mercenary raiding-army from Flanders and Denmark. When the burgesses of Worcester rebelled against enormous and unanticipated taxes and killed two of the king's Huscarls, the king ordered the town sacked and burned. The destruction of Worcester can be viewed as a reminder to the hinterland burgesses and peasants that a Dacian truce demanded tribute in exchange for protection and mercantile privileges. Godwin loyally led the army that fulfilled the command, but he allowed the townspeople to flee well in advance with their goods, and he thus avoided any violent confrontation.

King Harthacnut invited his remaining half-brother Edward to return to England from exile in 1041, possibly at Queen Emma's urging or on the advice of Bishop Aelfwine of Winchester. The bishop had been a monk of Fécamp and royal chaplain to Queen Emma and King Cnut. King Harthacnut might have promised the strong King Magnus of Norway the succession of Denmark by treaty, but the English Witans and Queen Emma might prefer his weak Anglo-Norman half-brother succeed to the crown of England, at least in the Saxon south. According to the *Encomium Emmae* Edward was invited to 'share the kingdom' with Harthacnut and the Anglo-Saxon Chronicle Version C says he was 'sworn in as king'. It may be that the Saxon south and Anglian north were still being ruled as separate realms. Harthacnut may have intended to rule the Danelaw with Denmark, allowing his Norman mother and Edward to rule in the south. It was such a brief time before Harthacnut died that it is impossible to know for certain what was intended.

King Harthacnut died while 'standing at his drink' at the wedding feast of Tovi the Proud and the daughter of Osgod Clapa, an East Anglian staller, in June 1042.[157] King Magnus duly became king of

---

[157] Tovi the Proud refounded the Abbey of the Holy Cross and St Lawrence at Waltham, rebuilding the church around a large stone

both Sweden and Denmark and pressed his claim to the crown of England also.

Clever and resilient Queen Emma still had one son left and a great deal of influence among Saxons, Anglo-Danes and the many Anglo-Normans she had settled throughout England's lands and church during four decades' patronage as England's queen and queen-mother. Norman-raised Edward was put forward as the rightful heir and last male of the Saxon royal line of Cerdic of Wessex.[158] It may have been to Edward's advantage that he was some part Dacian nobility too by his grandfather Richard's descent from Rollo and his grandmother Gunnora's powerful Gallo-Dacian heritage. The Normans and Anglo-Danes had long inter-married and collaborated in raiding and trading. King Edward therefore represented a unity of bloodlines: Saxon, Dacian and Norman.

Lacking any warriors, land or treasure of his own, a weak Edward was forced to negotiate with England's Witans to secure a kingdom whose nobles might justly regard the middle-aged, childless, Norman-bred prince as impoverished, useless in battle, and foreign in culture. Church prelates among the Witans would favour Edward for his royal hereditary claim, Emma's generous patronage, and Edward's proven generosity to the church. Queen Emma had settled many Normans in England on lands as well as in influential posts in the church, so there would be many Anglo-Norman Witans to support a Norman-bred prince in 1042. King Edward would also secure an important alliance with kinsman Duke William of Normandy and brother-in-law the Count Eustace of Boulogne, married to Goda, for defence against Nordic raids should King Magnus press his claim. Saxon Witans, such as there were, would have preferred a weak King Edward to the strong

---

cross he found following a dream in 1030. Tovi built a church to house the cross and bestowed his own sword as protection. Waltham also oversaw an important ford on the River Lea for taxing road trade and river traffic. The church was favoured by Earl Harold Godwinson from 1044, and may have housed the treasury of Earl Harold, and later King Harold, as evidenced by his founding a school there for the training of secular clerics.

[158] The survival of Edward the Exile, an illegitimate son of Edmund Ironside, was then unknown in England.

King Magnus, fearing higher tribute, yet more slaves and greater Heregeld would be demanded by a remote Nordic king, a concern reinforced by Harthacnut's recent massive Danegeld and Heregeld demands. The Anglo-Danes and Danes ruling England from 1016 and providing the elite Huscarls would naturally prefer to retain the generous Heregeld collected by self-exempt Huscarls to enrich themselves and their retainers and garrisons, rather than pay more abroad to King Magnus and lose status to his Nordic warriors. Whatever the rationale, the Witenagemot consented and King Edward was consecrated king in 1043.

King Edward reconciled with Earl Godwin, the most powerful earl in England, despite Godwin's role in the betrayal and murder of Edward's brother Alfred. Earl Godwin gave King Edward another, larger and more fabulously worked gilded ship, this time manned with 120 warriors equipped with gold and silver weapons. The gift would remind the powerless king that Godwin remained his most powerful earl and sea-lord with command of hundreds of ships and thousands of manorial retainers and sea-warriors.

There was a high price for Godwin's military and political support. In 1043 Godwin's eldest son Sweyn was given a vast earldom once held by his uncle Eilaf, embracing Gloucestershire, Herefordshire, Oxfordshire, Berkshire and Somerset. Godwin's nephew Beorn Estrithson, brother of the Danish king, was given a massive earldom in the Midlands and command of the London Lithsmen. Godwin's second son Harold became earl of prosperous and mercantile East Anglia in 1044, former earldom of his grandfather Thorkell the Tall. Weak King Edward was surrounded by powerful Anglo-Dacian earls, military elites and prelates, leaving him little scope for independent action.

King Edward's early reign shows he tried to secure some measure of royal independence. He made some appointments of Normans and Franks to lands and ecclesiastical offices that fell vacant, and he reorganised the exchequer and chancery on Frankish royal principles. One of his earliest acts was to take the royal treasury Queen Emma withheld from him in Winchester.

Earl Godwin promoted and aided this attack on the powerful dower queen. The treasure may have given King Edward some wealth to hire his own retainers and to rule and reform England, but dispossession of Queen Emma's prosperous dower estates also created a vacancy well suited to a new queen. Aged over 40 and childless, King Edward married Godwin's eldest daughter Eadgytha in 1045, making her Queen Edith by consecration.[159] Queen Edith succeeded to Queen Emma's prosperous estates in Winchester.

No doubt Earl Godwin and Queen Edith hoped that the kingdom won fighting alongside young Sea-king Cnut and Thorkell the Tall might pass to Godwin's heirs through Edith's sons. King Edward had no children by any woman in Normandy to his middle-age and he had no children in England with his queen.

It is unclear whether King Edward moved the royal treasury from Winchester after securing it from his mother, but he may have moved it to cells of Gallic clerical orders he preferred. Saint-Denis, Frankish and Norman clerics were recruited as royal chaplains. King Edward may have distrusted less well educated, less literate and less commercially sophisticated English or Danish prelates and chaplains. He might expect them to obey Earl Godwin and other lords rather than their king. Advised by the royal physician Baldwin, a monk of Saint-Denis, King Edward re-founded Westminster Abbey as his own royal foundation, with a school, a treasury and a palace for himself as he had known for nearly three decades at Fécamp. Thorney Island had been a Romano-Dacian fortress and the site of the first royal foundation abbey of the East Saxons.[160] King Edward now made Westminster his seat of royal administration and a Gallic sanctuary in a land otherwise ruled by Danes.

---

[159] Unfamiliar foreign names often changed with consecration, so that Queen Emma was styled Aelfgyva in English annals and Gytha Godwinsdottir became Queen Edith.

[160] Thorn or Thorney is a toponymic name for Dacian island fortresses because the arced walls were traditionally fortified with high thorn hedges. Early papal envoys and missionaries often settled royal minsters at the same sites to provide sanctuary to merchants and mariners to promote wider foreign trade.

Further strain arose between the king and his in-laws in 1048 after Earl Sweyn Godwinson abducted the Abbess of Leominster. It is possible Sweyn intended to dispossess her of the abbey treasury and her vast estate strategically located on the Welsh border. Leominster offered a secure fluvial island base where several rivers joined together, flowing to the upper Severn. It was ideal for a fortress for raiding into Wales and the border country for slaves to export from the market at Bristol or put to labour in Sweyn's new earldoms of Herefordshire and Gloucestershire. Earl Sweyn may even have been emulating King Edgar, who had abducted the Abbess Wulfthryth from Wilton Abbey. Instead of being pleased with the young earl's enterprise, King Edward returned the abbess to her abbey and exiled Sweyn from England for his violence against the church.

> Evil it is by such a wolf
> Noble prince, to be bitten;
> He will not spare the flock
> If he is driven into the woods.

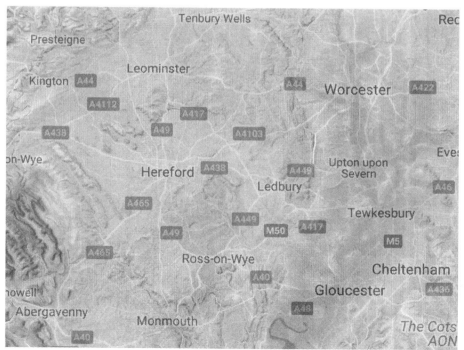

Leominster was on a hill overlooking a confluence of rivers above the tidal Severn. Herefordshire and Gloucestershire had a disproportionate number of slaves in Domesday Book, perhaps related to the convenience of neighbouring Wales for raiding.

The outlaw Sweyn had no trouble recruiting allies. By the autumn of 1048 sea-armies from Flanders and Ireland were attacking England's coasts for the first time since 1016. Church estates, ports and urban emporia were targeted for looting and slaving, putting pressure on prelates, merchants and king, just as Pontic imperium raiding sea-armies had practiced for thousands of years. King Edward mustered a royal fleet at Sandwich in 1049 to counter the attacks and contain Baldwin V, the lifelong ally of Godwin, who was raiding the empire on the continent with his own sea-army in parallel. Earl Godwin brought the most ships by far to the royal muster.

Sweyn Godwinson boldly sailed with a mercenary fleet to Bosham and came among the royal muster at Sandwich overland to seek reinstatement from King Edward. He must have come at Earl Godwin's urging, and certainly under Earl Godwin's protection for an overland passage defying exile. Earls Harold and Beorn were reluctant to give back lands of Sweyn's earldom that had been allocated between them. King Edward again exiled Sweyn, ordering him from England within three days. Ships were despatched with Earls Godwin, Harold and Beorn in command to ensure Sweyn and his ships left England. Tostig Godwinson accompanied or followed them in command of another ship. Once the ships were away from Sandwich they reunited with Sweyn, which must have been pre-arranged in secret. Earl Beorn was prevailed upon by the outlaw Sweyn to intercede with the king for Sweyn's reinstatement. Instead of returning to Sandwich, however, Sweyn lured his cousin Beorn to his ships at Bosham, murdered him, and fled again to Flanders after a stop at Exeter.

The London Lithsmen lost their Sea-lord with Sweyn's murder, frustrating the king's naval mission against both the Vikings encouraged by Sweyn and Godwin's ally Count Baldwin V. Humiliated, with no one to lead the Lithsmen, the king became even more vulnerable to violence from raiding sea-armies. The Witans declared Sweyn an outlaw and the Huscarls declared him a *nithing*, but that did not stop sea-army attacks on rich English targets. Earl Godwin has been deemed aloof from these events by modern historians, but such irrational romanticism is nonsense. England's most powerful earl and sea-lord was in his prime. He had more ships and sea-warriors than any other earl. The fierce warrior who had helped found the Huscarls and the London Lithsmen in 1017 could not abdicate responsibility for Sweyn's crimes, his insolence in demanding reinstatement, the murder of Earl Beorn, or renewed and unopposed sea-army attacks on English targets.

> Evil it is by such a wolf
> Noble prince, to be bitten;
> He will not spare the flock
> If he is driven into the woods.

The costly raids continued from both Ireland and Flanders with disastrous losses to England's targeted churches and trade. Archbishop Ealdred of York finally interceded on Sweyn's behalf and urged a trial before the Huscarls as Sweyn's right. King Edward may have preferred the Witans to a Huscarl tribunal as he himself, neither warrior nor Danish, was unlikely to have been elected to the Huscarls. The Witans decided in 1050 to reinstate Sweyn to his earldom and reduce the royal fleet of Lithsmen from 14 ships to just 5, and those 5 were to be paid off after just one more year. With Earl Sweyn reinstated the sea-army raids ended just as suddenly as they had begun, and the murder of Earl Beorn remained unavenged.

The reduction and dismissal of the royal fleet of Lithsmen after intensification of sea-army raids on both coasts makes no sense at all, unless the Witans understood very well that Sweyn and Godwin were together coordinating the attacks on England. Father and son had used the ancient Pontic imperium protection racket to hold a weak king and defenceless hinterland to ransom for Sweyn's truce and reinstatement, as Ealdorman Pallig had done decades before. The raids accordingly stopped when Earl Sweyn regained his earldom under truce. Sea-lord Tostig likely succeeded to Earl Beorn's command of Lithsmen, many now becoming the *butsecarlas* – ship-warriors – of Earl Godwin. From this time the Godwin family exercised unopposed military mastery by land and sea.

King Edward repealed the hated Heregeld tax entirely in January 1051, perhaps as revenge for his humiliation by the Huscarls and disbanding of the Lithsmen, both of whom were sworn loyal only to the king. The elite Anglo-Dacian Huscarls had for more than 50 years received the generous Heregeld stipendiary tribute for defence of England. Huscarls were exempt this tax on their own lands, so repeal deprived them of tributary revenues while benefitting landowners and burgesses who were not members of the elite military order. Saxons, Mercians and Normans would have likely been excluded from election by Anglo-Danish Huscarls, so the repeal of the hated Heregeld may have fuelled ethnic divisions and resentments. Earl Godwin and his sons might have particularly resented the loss of generous revenues.

In the spring Tostig Godwinson married Judith of Flanders, sister of Count Baldwin V. The match may have been arranged without King Edward's assent, a customary requirement for a minister's first marriage, especially a union with such diplomatic importance.[161] King Edward had backed the emperor against Baldwin V the year before, so was unlikely to have approved the match. Tostig had no terrestrial earldom, but if he commanded the Lithsmen or his father's mercantile fleet and *butsecarlas* then he held status, power and wealth as a sea-lord that would justify the royal connection. Tostig may even have been fostered by Count Baldwin V in Flanders. A Flanders charter of this time has Tostig witness as *Tostig dux*.[162]

Tostig's landholdings in Domesday Book are concentrated in coastal Cumbria, once the commonwealth of Olaf Trygvasson, and in Northumbria, on the coast controlling the estuary below York. They evidence possible control of Irish Sea and North Sea trade routes. It was alleged that Godwin 'by fraud and injustice' alienated the estate at Plumstead on the tidal Thames from St Augustine's Canterbury for Tostig. Plumstead with its vast tidal sand flats offered an excellent naval anchorage dominating the tidal Thames approach to London, controlling also access to the River Lea and the Medway, ideal for assessing thelony on trade to the continent.

---

[161] All liegemen were required to seek their lord or king's assent to a first marriage. Tostig's marriage to the sister of the powerful and rebellious count of Flanders would have been particularly offensive to King Edward after Baldwin V's promotion of sea-army attacks and raids on England and the Holy Roman Empire the year before.

[162] The Anglo-Saxon Chronicle at 1049 in Version E has Tostig in command of a king's ship at Sandwich. The *Vita Aedwardi* styles Tostig as *dux* at his marriage to Judith, despite his not receiving an earldom until 1055. In Nordic culture *dux* might be a military title for a sea-lord even without a landed estate. *Dux* as sea-lord is consistent with Godwin *dux* witnessing early charters of King Cnut before he held a terrestrial earldom.

Plumstead is east of London on the tidal Thames estuary. Plumstead would be an ideal tidal anchorage for mercantile fleets trading along the coast and abroad, controlling access to the Medway, Thames and Lea rivers.

Tensions rose over the summer as King Edward appointed Robert of Jumièges the first Norman archbishop of Canterbury in preference to one of Godwin's kinsmen. Robert had been royal chaplain and was an able secular administrator who could promote Roman orthodoxy and continental reforms within the English Church. After returning from Rome with his pall Archbishop Robert refused to ordain Spearhafoc, an East Anglian ally or kinsman of Earl Harold, as bishop of London. Instead the archbishop's protégé William, a Norman priest who had replaced him as royal chaplain, was ordained to the privileged see of London. Relations between King Edward and his in-laws were at a new low as the church, long a soft target, hardened against the influence of Godwin.

In the autumn King Edward had a visit from Count Eustace II of Boulogne, husband of his sister Goda. Eustace and his retainers attempted to commandeer the rich homes of burgesses in Dover while awaiting their ships to sail home. The Dover burgesses resisted, leading to deaths on both sides. Count Eustace took his remaining men and a biased account of the combat to his brother-in-law King Edward and demanded redress. The King ordered Earl Godwin to punish the burgesses as earl of Kent by wasting Dover. Godwin refused and instead raised an army to threaten King Edward as the dispute intensified. King Edward in turn summoned northern Earls

Edwin and Morcar to his aid. After a standoff in the west at Beverstone, near Godwin's western naval stronghold at Berkeley, the two sides agreed to a Huscarl tribunal in London three weeks later. Godwin was denied land passage so returned by ship from Berkeley, while his land army melted away leaderless on the long march east back to London. Godwin would not forget their desertion a year later.

Godwin had demanded trial before the Huscarls, as was his right even in a dispute with the king under the laws of Cnut. King Edward put the matter instead before the Witans, again, where church prelates, non-Danes, and urban aldermen would have more influence than within the Huscarls. At the end of September Godwin and his sons Sweyn and Harold were stripped of their titles and earldoms by the Witans in council. Godwin, Sweyn and Gyrth fled to Bruges. Harold and Leofwine fled to Ireland. Queen Edith was stripped of her wealth, royal possessions and estates and sent to a convent. Spearhafoc had until now stubbornly refused to cede London's episcopal see to bishop William. Around the same time as Harold and Godwin were sailing into exile, Spearhafoc looted 'many bags of gold' from the London diocesan treasury before disappearing, probably in one of the rebel ships.

> Evil it is by such a wolf
> Noble prince, to be bitten;
> He will not spare the flock
> If he is driven into the woods.

According to the different versions of the Anglo-Saxon Chronicle, the outlaw Godwin raided either *Thorney* or *Pefenesea* before fleeing to Bruges with a ship loaded with treasure and sons Sweyn, Tostig and Gyrth. Thorney may have been Westminster, where Edward had built his palace and royal treasury, although Thorney is a name common to fortifications at many Romano-Dacian ports.[163] *Pefenesea* in Sussex also may have held a royal treasury secured by the Fécamp Abbey cell at *Wincenesel*. Whichever site was raided, the recruitment of mercenaries in Flanders for further raiding in England was likely funded with the treasure of both church and king. A weak

---

[163] Dacian temporary fortifications had deep moats topped with dense thorn bushes and high palisaded walls.

king was rendered even more vulnerable and in need of allies.

Duke William soon paid a visit to his cousin King Edward and great-aunt Queen Emma, bringing many men from Normandy with him. The duke had been a youth of fifteen or sixteen in 1041 when Edward had left for England. Now in his prime and mid-twenties, the duke may have been invited by King Edward to help secure the kingdom against attacks by Godwin and his sons and to help fill manorial vacancies in earldoms and military leadership forfeited by the outlaws. The Gallic recruits soon started building castles on the Norman model and commanding kings' ships.

The *Carmen* suggests Duke William was named as heir by King Edward and accepted as heir by the Witans in 1051. Many Normans and Franks had been settled by Queen Emma since 1002, and more had been settled by King Edward during his eight years as king, so Norman and Frankish nobles and prelates would have been a sizeable cohort among the Witans in 1051. The Normans were the traditional allies of the Anglo-Danes of Northumbria and East Anglia, with many inter-marriages among coastal families. Aelfgar of Mercia was given Harold's earldom in East Anglia, perhaps as the price of his acquiescence to the king's appointment of a Norman heir. Whatever Saxon freemen had survived as landowners since the Danish conquest would have wanted to preserve the repeal of the Heregeld tax and curb slave exports to the east.[164] Duke William was a kinsman of King Edward and Queen Emma and a proven warrior and capable ruler. As a young King of England he could bring Frankish allies to England's defence to deter both the Godwin family outlaws and Nordic kings.

Perhaps to secure truce and forestall Baldwin V from aiding further attacks on England, Duke William stopped in Bruges on the way back to Normandy to treat with Count Baldwin V. He contracted marriage to Mathilda, Count Baldwin's only daughter, which indicates his successful negotiation of truce. As designated heir of King Edward, returning in triumph with the consent of the Witans, William was a much better ally for Count Baldwin than the treasonous exiles he

---

[164] Slavery had been banned in Frankish lands since King Dagobert and Saxon clerics had long sought to stop the sale of English slaves abroad.

sheltered. His grandsons would be kings of England.

Duke William's favourable reception in both England and Flanders must have enraged Godwin and his sons. They mustered mercenary sea-army fleets and determined to foment a rebellion against King Edward. First Godwin raided *Pefenesea* again in the spring of 1052 and sought support among his own Hastingas ship-warriors and manorial bondsmen. He returned to Flanders with a promise of welcome and support in southern England.

Godwin recruited a larger mercenary sea-army with the proceeds of a second raid on *Pefenesea*, and returned later in the summer to raid the prosperous Isle of Wight and Portland. Harold Godwinson meanwhile recruited a mercenary sea-army from Dublin and raided in Wales, Cornwall and Devon. The outlaws then combined fleets, raided the Isle of Wight again, and then proceeded to *Pefenesea* once more and, according to the Anglo-Saxon Chronicle Version E, 'got out all the ships that had put in there' to supplement their joint fleet.[165]

King Edward soon raised an English fleet and dispatched Norman loyalists as commanders to intercept Godwin and his sons, but these ships failed to confront the rebels. Perhaps the Anglo-Danish crewmen on the hastily mustered ships resented repeal of the Heregeld tax or disbanding of the London Lithsmen. They may have remained loyal to their former sea-lord, Tostig Godwinson. The Anglo-Saxon Chronicle implies they were inattentive to their duty and frustrated the mission of their unfamiliar Norman commanders.

Land forces were no easier to raise or to command. The Norman and Frankish lords King Edward had settled on the forfeited lands of Godwin, Sweyn and Harold had no time to learn the English tongue, nor gained respect from the thegns, garrisons, bondsmen and fyrd they would command to defend the Norman-bred king. Huscarls, thegns, bondsmen and urban garrisons preferred as Anglo-Danes for

---

[165] The context of all occurences of *Pefensea* cognates in the Anglo-Saxon Chronicle is as a fleet mustering place and sheltered anchorage. Modern Pevensey is not said to have a port in the 12th century navigation guide *De Viis Maris* and there is no archaeological evidence for either port or significant pre-13th century settlement at Pevensey, founded by charter in 1207.

generations would resent the imposition of Gallic overlords as their new masters.

The much-feared Godwin and his popular son Harold[166] landed in the south and urged open rebellion against the king and violence against all Normans and Franks in England. According to the Anglo-Saxon Chronicle the *butsecarlas* – ship-warriors – of *Hastingas* joined bondsmen of Kent, Sussex and Surrey in supporting the outlaws, an act of sedition encouraging other military elites and bondsmen to open rebellion. This time Godwin took hostages of every recruit into his ships to ensure the land army would march on London. No one in the south would have forgotten the outlaw Cnut's harsh treatment of hostages in 1014 at Sandwich; none could take the implied threat lightly. Godwin's enlarged rebel fleet sailed up the Thames. The garrison of London let Godwin's fleet pass the causeway or bridge.[167] Godwin's fleet blockaded King Edward on the Thames while the rebel army besieged the king overland.

King Edward was surrounded by Godwin's hostile fleet and army. His northern earls and thegns were sympathetic to Godwin and reluctant to wage a civil war that would see only English warriors killed. Civil war would leave England vulnerable to King Harald Hardrada of Norway, who still pressed his claim to England's crown. King Edward's Norman and Frankish nobles were useless to him, already murdered by rebels or fleeing abroad.

William of Normandy was unable to aid King Edward as he

---

[166] Orderic Vitalis wrote of Harold that he 'was very tall and handsome, remarkable for his physical strength, his courage and eloquence, his ready jests and acts of valour. But what were these gifts to him without honour, which is the root of all good?'

[167] Archaeologists have found no evidence of an 11th century bridge spanning the Thames at London, leading some to conclude *pons* meant a tidal causeway, perhaps with tidal canals, flash-locks, and bridges for ship passage at northern and southern ends of the barrier. The London Lithsmen may have controlled access upriver and downriver for thelony at the barrier. London boatmen would later purchase control of all Thames navigation and revenues from the king after Magna Carta.

might have intended the year before. William's command of the duchy of Normandy had been undermined by papal excommunication following marriage to Mathilda of Flanders in defiance of a papal interdict. The pope had not forgiven Baldwin V's attacks on the Holy Roman Emperor, and perhaps feared an alliance of the young duke with Flanders. The excommunication had provoked renewed civil unrest and violence in Normandy.

Bishop Stigand, a venal Anglo-Dane holding the episcopal sees of Winchester and Elmham in plurality, negotiated King Edward's capitulation as a partisan of the Anglo-Danes. The Witans reinstated Godwin and his sons and daughter to their titles and property, except Sweyn who remained outlawed.[168] In exchange, according to William of Jumièges, Duke William of Normandy was confirmed heir and successor to King Edward by Godwin and Harold as a condition of reappointment. Outlaws in 1051, it makes sense that they alone were required to confirm the Witans' assent given in their absence. Godwin gave his youngest son Wulfnoth and Sweyn's son Hakon as hostages to Duke William to warrant his future good conduct. Sweyn himself had gone on pilgrimage to the Holy Land and died during his travels.

Stigand siezed the see of Canterbury as his own reward for negotiating the settlement between king and rebels, usurping Archbishop Robert of Jumièges who had fled abroad. Anglo-Norman and Anglo-Frankish courtiers, noblemen and settlers were violently purged everywhere as outlaws, except a few retainers allowed to remain in the royal court of King Edward and the sanctuary of the church. Lands and possessions were seized and redistributed by Godwin and Harold, who either kept these for their own profit or rewarded retainers and rebels with them. Earl Godwin finally seized prosperous Rameslege and its great port from Fécamp Abbey knowing weak King Edward was powerless to interfere.

Stigand was excommunicated by five popes for his refusal to relinquish the see of Canterbury, or even the see of Winchester. He did release Elmham, but settled the see on his own brother as its new bishop. Stigand also refused to concede his canonical duty to the pope

---

[168] Already outlawed twice before, when refused reinstatement Sweyn travelled to Jerusalem and died on the journey.

or pay Rome its traditional share of English Church revenues. The gold and silver that once flowed from England to Fécamp and Rome was diverted instead to personally enrich Godwin, Harold, Stigand and their partisans.

The Heregeld tax was reinstated, rewarding the Anglo-Dacian elite Huscarls who had refused service to the king or allied with the rebels. A confederation of Channel ports was organised about this time as a defensive union of ship-warriors with each port under obligation to supply the king ships and crews for royal service on demand and coastal defence at all times in exchange for generous stipends, liberties and immunities.[169] Earl Godwin became the first Constable of Dover Castle under these arrangements, which permanently replaced the king's standing fleet of Lithsmen, disbanded the year before.

The Normans, Franks and Roman Church never forgave the rebels or the violent seizure of Norman, Frankish and church lands by Godwin, Stigand and their partisans. All stayed their hands while King Edward yet lived. Perhaps they trusted William of Normandy might put things right as the royal heir.

Earl Godwin was gripped by a violent seizure while dining with King Edward at Winchester at Easter in 1053 and died a few days later. Several contemporary accounts report Godwin choked on a piece of bread handed to him by the king after protesting his innocence of Alfred Aethling's murder, suggesting either poison or God's judgement on his crime. Whether or not he was the agent of Godwin's death, King Edward may have felt satisfaction at seeing the man who had betrayed his brother to a hideous death, repeatedly raided and robbed royal and church treasuries, rebelled against him twice, deprived him of any military command, and wreaked great violence on Normans, Franks and clerics succumb at his table and die a lingering death.

---

[169] This early confederation became the model for the Confederation of the Cinque Ports under later Norman kings. The Hellocis –'strati places' – at line 504 may refer to the warriors of the coastal commonwealths.

Earl Harold Godwinson succeeded to his father's titles, lands and wealth. His influence grew as King Edward weakened. Earl Harold openly ruled England as *subregulus* or regent from 1053, an office only exercised in the past during a king's absence abroad. King Edward retired into the church, devoting himself to the construction of the Chapel of St Peter at Westminster and rebuilding the privileged royal abbey at Bury St Edmunds with his friend and physician Abbot Baldwin on the model of Frankish continental abbeys.

Harold's remaining brothers now received earldoms of their own. Tostig Godwinson was made earl of Northumbria. Gyrth Godwinson was made earl of East Anglia, Cambridgeshire and Oxfordshire. Leofwine Godwinson became earl of Kent, Essex, Middlesex, Hertford and Surrey. The four sons of Godwin together held more than two-thirds of England's lands and tribute. Exempt from Heregeld themselves as Huscarls, the burden of taxation will have concentrated further on those who held less land and influence.

John de Ravenna, abbot of Fécamp Abbey, came to England in 1054 to seek restoration of the abbey's possessions at Rameslege and Steyning. The abbey was suffering financially from the loss of such great revenues. King Edward approved the abbot's suit, but Earl Harold refused to return the abbey's manors and ports. In compensation King Edward gave Abbot John a further written promise under seal of a minster church at Eastbourne and nearby land and meadow, as well as land at *Caestra* – now Pevensey Castle – with its salt-pans and twelve dwellings.[170]

Earl Harold began to run the affairs of the kingdom for his own profit. He endowed Waltham Abbey, probably as his own chancery and exchequer, and founded a school to train secular clerics for his own service as administrators. The stronghold and church at Waltham

---

[170] The very poverty of *Caestra*, corresponding by proximity to Eastborne to Pevensey Castle, indicates the site is unlikely to be the *Pefenesea* raided and looted three times by Godwin. Surrounded by shallow tidal saltmarsh at the western extent of the Pevensey Levels, with little fresh water or pasture, and no timber even today, the site would have been useless for anything except fishing and modest saltworks in the 11th century. There is no mention of a valuable church, market or port in the 1054 writ.

had been re-founded by Earl Tovi the Proud after Thorkell the Tall returned to Denmark, and had passed to Earl Harold in 1045 as a favoured Anglo-Danish order. Earl Harold probably continued to use Waltham Abbey for his personal treasury after ceding East Anglia to his brother Earl Gyrth in 1053. He would not keep his fortune in Winchester or London, having seen Winchester looted by his father in 1044 and London looted by Spearhafoc in 1051.

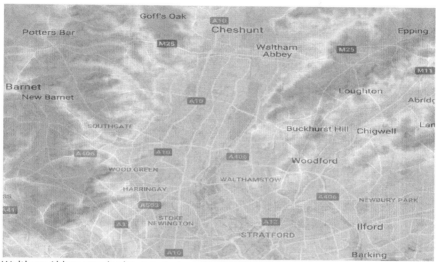

Waltham Abbey stands above a strategic ford at the top of the Lea estuary leading to the tidal Thames. The abbey collected thelony on trade from East Anglia to Mercia and from water traffic coming up the river from the Thames, a pound first canalised by the Romans.

Stripped of his Norman noblemen, possibly denied tribute by his earls and Huscarls, and impotent with no military force personally loyal to him, King Edward all but retired from public life. He devoted himself to religious works. The Thorney Island site of Westminster Abbey had been granted to papal envoys in 604 for the first royal foundation abbey near London, and had been a Romano-Dacian trading settlement long before. From this sanctuary King Edward corresponded with popes, emperors, and prelates, expressing a personal piety while living a quasi-monastic life. King Edward also gave generously to the abbey at Bury St Edmunds, now under Abbot Baldwin, the Saint-Denis monk who had been his royal physician and guided him on refounding Westminster Abbey. Childless and in failing health, King Edward left the running of the realm to the young and ambitious Earl Harold, perhaps comforted by the knowledge of his Norman kinsman Duke William's succession.

Earl Harold began travelling to the continent, and may have gone as far as Rome. He began to collect relics to endow holy protection to Waltham Abbey. He stopped with Count Baldwin V of Flanders, brother-in-law to Tostig Godwinson and father-in-law to Duke William of Normandy in 1056. The witness list of a Flanders charter from September shows that Earl Harold also met then with Count Eustace of Boulogne, Count Guy of Ponthieu, and even Bishop Guy d'Amiens, composer of the *Carmen*.

The prospect of William of Normandy as heir to the crown threatened civil war in England as the duke might still be opposed by Godwin's powerful and wealthy sons. In addition, King Harald Hardrada of Norway, son of King Magnus, still threatened invasion from the north. Archbishop Ealdred, Earl Tostig and his wife Judith of Flanders all travelled to Rome in 1056, perhaps to seek papal advice. Tostig and Judith were well received by the pope, who sat Tostig by his side in council. Perhaps to avert the calamity of civil war or foreign invasion, Archbishop Ealdred was told on this trip of the survival of Edward the Exile in Hungary, son of Edmund Ironside and grandson of Thored of York. Likely hoping another weak figurehead king nominally descended from the line of Wessex and nominally connected to the Anglians of York and Northumbria might succeed the aged King Edward, the archbishop convinced Edward the Exile and his family to immigrate to England in 1057.

King Cnut had sent Edmund's two young sons to Norway intending permanent exile. The jarl of Norway entrusted Edward to his daughter, who raised the boy secretly in Kiev where she was queen of the Russo-Dacians. As a man Edward became a retainer of his royal foster-brother, following him from Kiev to the Hungarian court when his royal foster-brother married the Slavo-Dacian princess of Hungary. Edward spoke no English and was fully Slavo-Dacian in language, education, character and habits. Archbishop Ealdred had perhaps thought a blended Saxon and Slavo-Dacian heritage might prove acceptable to Witans in England, hoping to prevent civil war in England or invasion and conquest from Nordic realms or Normandy.

Edward the Confessor, Edward the Exile and his infant son Edgar were the last three heirs of Cerdic of Wessex, founder of the Wessex royal dynasty. The mature Edward the Exile and infant Edgar might continue the long bloodline of Saxon royalty, but they commanded no men, brought no useful allies, possessed no land or personal fortune, commanded no ships, and they only spoke foreign languages. They were not welcomed in England. Edward the Exile died suspiciously two days after arriving, and King Edward showed no regard for his widow or the infant Edgar and his sisters, Margaret and Cristina. King Edward may have regarded the boy as tainted by illegitimacy and a living reminder that half-brother Edmund Ironside was the first usurper to deny him the English crown in 1016. Despite the title aethling in Victorian and modern histories, Edgar was not styled aethling by King Edward or the Witans of 11th century England. Edgar does not appear on any charters, indicating King Edward refused the boy royal recognition or protection.

Attempts to improve relations between the English Church and Rome were otherwise irregular and unsuccessful. Stigand travelled to Rome in 1058 to get his pall as archbishop, but he received it from anti-pope Benedict X who was soon deposed.[171] Stigand was soon excommunicated again when pope replaced anti-pope. Earl Harold meanwhile continued to dispossess and raid the church opportunistically. In 1060 Harold raided and looted the diocesan treasury of Wells after Bishop Dudoc died, and dispossessed the diocese of its prosperous lands before Bishop Giso could be appointed.

England had security with Earl Harold as *subregulus*, but peace does not train men for war. Anglo-Danes who had won conquest of England as a vast sea-army had become soft manorial hinterland chieftains in the next generation. Perhaps to train his men for war, in 1062 and 1063 Earl Harold led raids into Wales. Like the Vikings and the ancient Dacian raiders, he and his men moved unpredictably around from place to place, rather than risking a pitched battle, as mobile sea-armies had always preferred. Gerald of Wales wrote of Earl Harold's violent campaign of surprise night attacks that they 'left not one that pisseth against a wall', killing all Welsh men, boys and male infants wherever they were found, 'they destroyed [the Welsh] almost to a man'. Only young women and girls were taken captive for slaves. The raiding ended when King Gruffydd was betrayed by his own men,

---

[171] After deposing and exommunicating Pope Benedict X in 1058, Pope Nicholas II held a synod that rescinded the right of Romans to vote for future popes in 1059, limiting votes to the college of Cardinals.

and his severed head was sent to Earl Harold in token of Welsh submission.

Earl Harold's only other military adventure was as companion to Duke William of Normandy. According to the *Carmen* and other Norman sources, the ailing King Edward reconfirmed Duke William of Normandy as his heir about 1064. A record from Colchester says the king sent a two-handled sword and other tokens of succession to Duke William by the envoy Hubert de Rie, loyal protector and dapifer to the Norman duke since childhood. Hubert de Rie was old enough to have been familiar to King Edward from his long residence in Normandy, despite years of separation.

In 1064 King Edward also sent Earl Harold to Normandy. The *Carmen* suggests at lines 295-96 that Harold accompanied the Norman dapifer's return. Some suggest Harold hoped to negotiate release of his youngest brother Wulfnoth and nephew Hakon, fostered at the Norman court since 1052 and now nearing manhood. Whatever the motivation, the *Carmen* and other accounts say Earl Harold became a vassal of Duke William, swore loyalty to the duke as the future king of England, and betrothed or married a Norman noblewoman whom he later spurned and dishonoured. A marriage was often contracted as a longer-term basis for cooperation and alliance when hostages were released as freemen.

In 1065 Harold started building a hunting lodge at Portsoken, at a strategically crucial narrowing of the tidal reach of the Severn. The Anglo-Saxon Chronicle says the Portsoken stronghold was to be a hunting lodge for the king, but it is doubtful the failing health of King Edward left him much strength for hunting. If hunting was to be done from Portsoken, it would more likely be Welsh slaves for sale in Bristol across the Severn. Harold had made a good profit on slaves taken in his earlier Welsh raids and might want to secure a more permanent supply.

Brother warred with brother again as King Edward weakened. Tostig Godwinson, Earl of Northumbria, was a kinsman of Count Baldwin V and Duke William by marriage, and these connections may have incurred ambitious Earl Harold's distrust and resentment. A Nordic saga has Tostig as the older son who was fostered and favoured by King Edward as a royal heir. Tostig and Judith's embassy to Rome and reception by the pope indicated favour and status denied to Earl

Harold. Both sea-Lord and earl, Tostig might side with Duke William in hopes of greater lands and prosperity as a kinsman of the duke, perhaps supplanting Earl Harold as *subregulus* in England.

The northern thegns revolted against Earl Tostig in 1065 for doing in the north what Godwin and his sons had always done in the south. According to the Anglo-Saxon Chronicle Tostig taxed the northern thegns heavily and was violent against churches. The Anglian regions had before been treated respectfully as allies and kinsmen of the Danes from 1016. Northumbrians in general, and Anglo-Danish thegns and prelates in particular, were not accustomed to harsh treatment by overlords as subjugated Saxons and Mercians endured in the south. Northern churches and abbeys had not been dispossessed and looted as the southern churches and orders had been.

Earl Harold, acting as *subregulus* for the king, sided with the rebel thegns, stripped Tostig of his earldom, and outlawed him, denying him a trial before the Huscarls. Tostig fled to Bruges and urged revenge against Earl Harold to his kinsmen by marriage, Count Baldwin V and Duke William. Released from any oath by denial of the Huscarl tribunal, he mustered a mercenary fleet from Flanders and the Orkneys.

> Evil it is by such a wolf
> Noble prince, to be bitten;
> He will not spare the flock
> If he is driven into the woods.

King Edward took ill over Christmas and died in the first days of 1066. He was buried near the altar he had erected in the Chapel of St Peter he had constructed at Westminster, the church of the abbey privileged by the pope in 1061 as an order within the Holy Apostolic See. It was as close as Edward would ever get to Rome. The chapel constructed in Frankish grandeur had been consecrated just a week earlier.

Earl Harold asserted the king's deathbed assent to his own succession and next day declared himself the king of England. According to Elizabethan antiquarian William Camden, the Witans were convened to confirm Harold's accession as king after the fact, in contravention of English tradition of election and affirmation. Camden says that Harold had no claim to nobility on his father's side, whose ethnicity was unknown, and only a claim to noble blood by his Danish mother. The Witans submitted, however, hoping King Harold's Danish influence and proven abilities as a leader would preserve them from Nordic and Norman conquerors.[172] Indeed, King Harold would be regarded as 'the last Danish king of England' until Nathan Bailey's *An Universal Etymological English Dictionary and Interpreter of Hard Words*, under the entry for Battle Abbey in 30 editions from 1721 to 1802. Later Victorians transformed Harold into a Saxon hero to please Germanic royalty ruling England.

Pope Alexander II promptly excommunicated King Harold, denying him the service of the church and secular clerics in canonical duty. As the English Church had been estranged from Roman communion since 1052 this may not have had any importance in England. The excommunication signalled to the rival royal claimants in Norway and Normandy, however, that the pope would welcome a war to depose a tyrant and restore the English Church to communion with Rome.[173] King Harold may have tried to heal the rift with Rome by making some restitution to the church in 1066, but his hasty generosity was not enough to make the pope overlook decades of violence against clerics, dispossessions and looting.

Duke William determined to conquer England. Lanfranc, as abbot of Bec, had won favour with the duke by securing reinstatement to communion with Rome after the duke's own excommunication for marrying Mathilda of Flanders. The duke had promoted Lanfranc to abbot of Saint-Etienne at Caen, a privileged foundation abbey generously endowed to the Holy Apostolic See in settlement of the dispute. In 1066 Lanfranc interceded with Pope Alexander II to aid the duke again. The pope had been a student of the illustrious Lanfranc and was well-disposed to his suit. The pope declared Duke William the rightful heir of King Edward and sent a papal banner, ring

---

[172] *Britannia*, The Normans, §5.

[173] Holy war could be very profitable, making it easy to recruit mercenaries. Pope Urban II (pope 1088 – 99) would decree soon after the Norman Conquest that it was not culpable homicide to take up arms against the excommunicate and not theft to take property from heretics to redistribute it to Christians. The decree was a papal pardon for the violence of the Norman Conquest.

of St Peter, and holy relics to carry into battle. The pope also provided an open letter to the clergy of England instructing them in canonical duty to recognise William as king, entitling him to the rite of consecration as monarch and the services of secular clerics.

William immediately began recruiting seasoned warriors and commanders from Normandy and its Frankish and Mediterranean allies. Mediterranean fleets brought horse transports, weapons, sea-warriors, archers and crossbowmen from Norman possessions in Calabria, Apulia and Sicily. Norman forges, smiths and armorers mass-produced armour, helmets, swords, spears, lances, maces, steel tipped arrows, and many, many iron bolts for crossbows. The crossbow had never yet been fired in England, but its power to wreak havoc on massed infantry was well-proven in Norman campaigns in the Mediterranean. In parallel Norman shipwrights built a fleet of ships to carry men, horses and arms to England, financed by assessments on the manorial nobles of Normandy. The manorial nobles assembled their warriors, drilled them in attack and defence, and equipped them with horses and weaponry. Every warrior was promised great riches in land and booty to follow the conquest.

The duchy of Normandy had been won by a great sea-army of widely-recruited Normans in 911. The pope had recently been restored to supremacy in the Roman church and to the Holy Apostolic See in Rome by sea-faring Normans in the Mediterranean. Apulia, Calabria and Sicily in 1058 had been retaken from the Saracens by sea-faring Normans under a pope's banner. So too might the kingdom of England be profitably conquered and ruled by sea-faring Normans, and brought back into communion with the Roman church.

Skilled and seasoned commanders trained eager manorial recruits in battlefield and fleet manoeuvres. The Mediterranean Normans had proven they could defeat Germanic and Nordic infantry by annihilating Swabian-German mercenaries allied to the Lombards in Apulia in 1053 to the last man. They had practiced and proven how alternating artillery and cavalry charges could weaken massed ranks lacking archers or the mobility of horsemen. That victory won Roger de Hauteville the hereditary fief of Apulia from a grateful pope, with the promise he could be king of Calabria and Sicily, founding another Norman kingdom with further conquest. Normans would have schooled themselves in cavalry and infantry tactics from these earlier campaigns when making plans and strategy against the defenders of England in 1066. They might even have believed from their prior conquests that they were divinely favoured by God and instruments of His will in defeating excommunicants and heretics as agents of the pope.

In the spring of 1066 the outlawed sea-lord Tostig Godwinson raided the Isle of Wight and the south coast of England with a mercenary fleet, suborning ship-warriors to join him as his father Godwin had done in 1052. Tostig's command of the ship-warriors in 1066 is further confirmation that he had been their sea-lord before he became an earl in the north. He took the combined fleet north to raid unwary Norfolk and Lincolnshire. Defeated by the northern thegns, then deserted by most of the ships and ship-warriors, Tostig spent the summer in the court of King Malcolm of Scotland treating with King Harald Hardrada of Norway, who still pressed his own claim to the English crown.

Tostig may have suggested to King Harald that he could unite the Danelaw with the Nordic realms, leaving the south for Tostig to rule either as king or as *subregulus*, the title his father and brother had held. Alternatively, Tostig may have conveyed an offer of alliance from Count Baldwin V and Duke William, offering on their behalf Nordic imperium over the Danelaw in exchange for support reunifying the south with Gallic realms. The *Carmen*'s regret at Tostig's death at line 136 suggests he was valued as an ally.

King Harold of England assembled a fleet and land-army and kept them on the south coast to defend against further attacks. When provisions were exhausted at the end of the summer, the men were permitted to return home. According to the Anglo-Saxon Chronicle many ships of the sea-army were wrecked by a sudden storm in the Channel before reaching London. If the best of Harold's warriors and commanders went by ship, as seems likely with the Huscarls based in London, the loss of his fleet may have been a more tragic weakening of the realm than the land-army losses at Stamford Bridge a few weeks later. The long-deployed Anglo-Dacian land-armies left to make their own way north may well have savaged the Saxon and Mercian hinterlands on the way. They returned north unrewarded for their service by King Harold, a breach of Dacian military tradition. Some of the wasting later blamed on the Normans was probably done by the bands of the disaffected and hungry land-army, who returned home to the north under arms but without pay.

On the other side of the Channel the Normans were preparing their fleet. Fécamp Abbey founded, armed and manned a warship for the invasion fleet with twenty warrior monks under the command of Remigius, a noble-born monk of the abbey. The fleet sailed from sheltered Dives where it had mustered to coastal Fécamp on one tide. Before the fleet left Fécamp Duke William promised *per unum cultellum* – 'swearing on a knife' – to restore the Fécamp Abbey possessions in England appropriated by Godwin, the manors of Steyning in 1047 and Rameslege in 1052, as well as the lands near Eastbourne promised 'under seal' in 1054. It is likely a skilled Fécamp navigator accompanied and directed the invasion fleet heading for England's coast.

King Harald Hardrada was an accomplished warrior of wide military experience. In his youth Harald Hardrada led the Varangian Guard for Constantinople during the campaign to retake Sicily from Saracens in 1038, allied with three-hundred mounted Normans led by the elder de Hauteville brothers. It is possible in 1066 that the Normans and King Harald had struck a further military alliance through Tostig or the de Hautevilles. Danelaw would go to the Nordic king, reuniting the three Nordic kingdoms. Southern England would reunite with Brittany and Normandy, restoring the three kingdoms ruled by Brutus of Troy to common rule under King William.

Harald Hardrada's fleet and sea-army arrived in Northumbria in August 1066. The Norsemen and Tostig began raiding together. They defeated the northern earls at Fulford on 20th September and then pressed the region to bring rich tribute to them. They met defeat themselves when King Harold and his forces attacked their camp unawares at Stamford Bridge on 25th September. King Harold's surprise night attack, a technique perfected in the Welsh campaigns, preceded a prolonged battle throughout the day. King Harold of England won with both his brother Tostig and King Harald Hardrada killed in the battle, but the losses were great on both sides. Evidencing Anglo-Dacian sympathy for the Nordic invaders, King Harold allowed the son of Harald Hardrada to return to his ships with the surviving Nordic warriors.

King Harold then seized all the tribute collected from the surrounding region as booty for the Nordic raiding army and carried it south.[174] Rather than returning the vast treasure to local nobles and townsmen from whom it had been collected, or even distributing the treasure among those fighting with him as allies and auxiliaries, King Harold kept the treasure. William of Malmesbury suggests King Harold's earls, thegns, garrisons and bondsmen dispersed to their homes greatly dissatisfied with this excessive greed. King Harold had violated the most basic Dacian maxims: all military service must be compensated and booty should be shared out equitably. King Harold's lack of generosity at Stamford Bridge may have discouraged these warriors and many others from promptly joining for the next battle against the Normans at Hastingas.

According to the *Carmen* King Harold was met on the march from Stamford Bridge 'laden with rich spoils' and told of the Norman invasion. Having rushed north, King Harold now rushed south. On his way south King Harold raised an army of those who would join him to meet the Norman threat. There were doubtless many earls, thegns, urban garrisons, bondsmen and fyrd in the English army, but according to William of Malmesbury the core of the Harold's forces were paid Danish mercenaries - *stipendiarios et mercennarios milites*. This could mean the Anglo-Danish garrisons of urban settlements and the Anglo-Danish Huscarls and ship-warriors relied on for raiding, slaving and trading when not at war. Version E of the Anglo-Saxon Chronicle styles Harold's army at Hastings as *here*, a word used otherwise only for mercenary sea-armies raiding England and Godwin's sea-army of mercenaries from Flanders in 1052.

If visual proof is needed that King Harold self-identified as more Dacian than Saxon it is found in his battle standard. The so-called 'red dragon' of the Bayeux Tapestry by King Harold as he fell to the Norman onslaught was not a dragon at all. *Draco* means battle standard, and Harold's was a red-dyed wolf-skin, exactly like the wolf-skin standard of the Illyrian Dacian army defeated by Trajan in the 2nd century and exactly like the red wolfskin standards of medieval Dacian Romania in the east and of medieval Nordic kings from Halfdan the

---

[174] William of Malmesbury's criticism of King Harold echoes the charge against Carausius in 296: that he allowed pirates to loot Gaul and then captured their ships fully laden to keep the spoils himself.

Black in the west. Wherever the Dacians had settled along the sea lanes and rivers of Europe, the diaspora used a red-dyed wolfskin as the unifying totem and as a battle standard.

Dacian standard from Trajan's Column and Harold's standard from Bayeux Tapestry

Patriotic, protestant, and imperialist Victorians cast King Harold as a Saxon because they preferred identifying with Protestant Germans, as did the monarch. Their error has persisted long enough. The south of England was defeated from the north in 1016 with Saxons leaders slain and their sons enslaved; those who survived were subjugated, impoverished and enslaved over the five decades that followed. King Harold identified with the Danes, not the Saxons.

If the Saxons of 11th century Wessex and Mercia marched to battle at all they were ill-armed, ill-trained and reluctant. Those Saxons that survived to collaborate with their Anglian and Danish masters would be unlikely to receive military commands. As Huscarls were an elected body and exempt the Heregeld tax, those not favoured by the Danish elite would have borne heavy taxes, could afford fewer and poorer weapons. Contemporaneous accounts of Harold's army mention only *Angli* and *Daci*, Anglians and Dacians, never Saxons.

We can guess at other social and economic divisions. Thanks to Domesday Book we know that Godwin's sons controlled more than two-thirds of England's manorial lands and the church held most of the rest. There was not much land of value remaining for a subjugated Saxon or Mercian population to own. As the Huscarls exempted themselves from the taxes they collected, the minority of non-Huscarl landholders of whatever ethnicity would be forced to meet all the geld and Heregeld demands of their overlords by 1066. It seems reasonable to suggest this vast economic inequality and injustice may have weakened social cohesion. We resent vastly wealthy elites who pay no taxes in our own times, but we do not force the sale of wives or children into slavery for geld. At the time of the Domesday survey in 1086, which only covered the south of England, about 20 per cent of the population were slaves. The proportion in 1066 must have been higher, and many more slaves would have been exported abroad.

Intensive slavery had reduced the manpower to defend the kingdom as slaves were not armed or trained for war as freemen might be, nor did slaves have a duty to defend the land as freemen did. One of King William's first acts was to set forth the conditions for freeing English slaves. He then banned the sale of English slaves abroad. Slavery was entirely outlawed within a generation and had disappeared almost entirely within a century. In 1066, however, the painful legacy of Anglo-Danish slaving of subjugated Saxons and Mercians would have weighed heavily on the kingdom, and particularly on the south where the Normans chose to land, fortify and fight.

King Harold and his land army of Anglians and Dacians stopped in London after their march south. His mother Gytha and brother Earl Gyrth urged him to remain. Gyrth offered to lead the English army so that Harold would not break his vassalage oath to Duke William. King Harold angrily rejected the offer. He set out for Sussex in haste with such land-army as had assembled already. The *Carmen* and other sources suggest King Harold intended another ambush, sending a fleet of coastal vessels to blockade the Norman camp while he rushed southward with the land-army. As in Wales and Stamford Bridge, Harold hoped to surprise an unwary camp and defeat an unprepared enemy with a night attack. Discovered and taunted into rash action, King Harold led his army forth to seize high ground and fight an unfamiliar pitched battle prematurely.

Despite their superior numbers and bravery, the massed ranks of the English were defeated. King Harold lost his life and his kingdom. The Danes and Anglians lost imperium over Saxon England. Duke William became King William, first by acclamation of his troops on the battlefield, next by claiming divine succession by conquest at the graveside of defeated King Harold, and finally by ritual of royal consecration at Westminster Abbey with the election and approval of England's Witans and aldermen. England at last became a united realm under a Norman king.

APPENDIX III

THE NEW GEOGRAPHY OF THE NORMAN CONQUEST

'History is not intelligible without geography,' wrote H.B. George.[175] Geography misleads historians, however, when they use contemporary maps to explain medieval and ancient history. We know that there has been significant geomorphic change, especially in coastal areas of Britain subject to land-raising earthquakes, fluctuation of sea levels with cycles of global warming and cooling, violent seasonal and storm surge flooding, siltation and coastal erosion. Contemporary historians have largely ignored the geographic changes over the centuries, consistently using contemporary maps to describe ancient events. When Elizabethans and Victorians mapped the Norman Conquest they used the maps and place names familiar to them without considering that landscape, seascape and human settlements had all been altered. Modern historians credulously followed them. If contemporary geography was misguided then it is likely the history we have received from contemporary historians was flawed too.

British coasts 1000 years ago were more porous and open to the sea, and 2000 years ago Britannia referred to an archipelago of islands from Freesia to Eire, and tidal estuaries deeply cut across England east and west, dividing north from south. When the ancient Hellenes, forefathers to the Romans and Nordic Dacians, explored the coasts of the *Cassiterides* at the dawn of the Iron Age, they described an archipelago of large islands.

---

[175] *The Relations of Geography and History* (Oxford, 1901).

It is important to understand that the ancient British coast was exposed to all the violence of nature. There were no sea defences. Tides, then as now, averaged about 7 metres in variation along the Sussex coast, but seasonal high tides in spring and autumn were, then as now, much higher. The narrower Dover Strait, later widened and deepened by a series of large medieval earthquakes, made tidal surges inland much more frequent and violent. Turbulence in the strait from tidal surge and storms was more likely to sink ships. Fierce tidal bores would have scoured and widened estuaries near the straits. Tsunamis from earthquakes and huge violent storm surges caused occasional massive inland flooding.

The landmass of Britain was lower too, perhaps by 2 to 4 metres. Earthquakes, shingle shift, sedimentation and siltation over successive centuries have forced the landmass of Britain steadily upwards. The medieval warming period – like today's global warming – caused sea levels to rise for a few centuries as icecaps melted and warmer sea water expanded its physical mass, raising water levels by as much as 6 metres. Ridges and hills subject to erosion were higher and steeper; valleys and marshes subject to siltation were lower and deeper. Using topographical maps, we can still see the extent of former tidal seascape on the Sussex coast floodplains.

This topographic map of East Sussex shows modern elevations. Landmass was 4 to 8 metres lower in 1066, so much of the low-lying landscape was then navigable seascape.

Perhaps there is a very simple reason why a century of archaeology at Battle, Hastings and Pevensey has yielded no evidence of the Normans of 1066: the places may be wholly irrelevant to the Norman Conquest. Archaeologists have been digging in the wrong places guided by inaccurate interpretations of historical records using contemporary maps and place names. The geographic clues in the *Carmen* and other original sources, combined with scientific advances in archaeology, geology and coastal geomorphology might better locate the events of 1066.

The Sussex coastal region changed a great deal between the 11ᵗʰ century and the Elizabethan era, when the first comprehensive English histories were compiled. Earthquakes, siltation, and coastal shingle shift all re-shaped the landscape and seascape boundaries. Earthquakes forced the coastal plains higher while deepening and widening the Channel to reduce tidal surge. Storm surge wiped out the settlements at Old Hastings and Old Winchelsea in the 12ᵗʰ century, forcing their 13ᵗʰ century relocation to the modern settlements. Siltation closed the port at *Peuenesel* and all the Rye Camber and Pevensey Levels, leaving just narrow, winding channels to the sea. Fishing and trading settlements relocated with the coastline, but often the burgesses kept old place names associated with historic privileges. Early antiquarians like William Camden, who published *Britannia* in 1585 as the first geographic survey of Britain, little appreciated the scale of coastal change and resettlement between the 11ᵗʰ and 16ᵗʰ centuries, although Camden often notes oral traditions of landscape change.

Geological core samples and topographic maps now evidence the coastline of England a thousand years ago. Highlands, especially the sandstone ridges of Sussex, were higher. Lowlands, marshes and fens were lower and subject to deep seasonal flooding and tidal inundation. The Rye Camber extended inland so far that Tenterden, now 22 miles from the sea, was a tidal settlement accessible by estuarine navigation. The Rye Camber itself was much more extensive, with the main rivers – Rother, Tillingham, Brede and Pannel – flowing east to west, debouching into a wide basin with a complex of navigable creeks. Much of the south of England that is now densely settled was then uninhabitable wetlands. The now pastoral landscape of the Brede Valley and Tillingham Valley was then saltmarsh, tidal estuary or seascape.

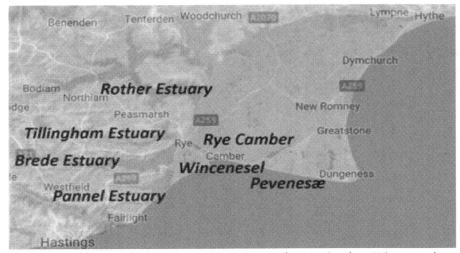

Rother, Tillingham, Brede and Pannel estuaries in the Rye Camber, Wincenesel as a toll island (drowned in the 13th century) and Pevenesæ as an anchorage.

Historians unfamiliar with the sea have often failed to grasp the narrative of maritime coastal navigation in medieval sources. All navigation in the 11th century was tide-to-tide, advancing with a flowing or ebbing tide and anchoring during slack water, adverse tides, and adverse winds. This is consistent with navigation described in the *Carmen*. Safe anchorages in the seascape had names familiar to all mariners for coastal navigation. Ships always tried to cross the Channel or North Sea on a single tide to reach a familiar safe anchorage. An anchorage was not a port, although modern historians too often use the term port to describe them. Wissant in coastal Gaul, for example, was a wonderful, sheltered, sandy tidal anchorage but never had a port. Mariners would come out of an anchorage or port on an ebb tide, anchor during the slack tide on a coastal anchorage, then progress toward their next anchorage on the following ebb or flow tide, whichever suited their destination. Then, as now, experienced sailors took wind, coastal geography and tides into account in every carefully planned voyage. Spring and autumn were favoured for markets and raiding alike because the seasonal high tides made cross-sea voyages in heavily-laden ships much safer and more certain on a single tide.

Derivation of coastal place names may also require reconsideration to recognise the commonality of Dacian maritime navigation and trade dialects in coastal settlements from the Black Sea, up the Danube through Nordic regions, throughout the Britannic isles to Iberia, and back to the Mediterranean. Victorian toponymists categorised all British place names parochially as either Celtic or Germanic, unless there was an obvious Roman association. They ignored Gallic and Dacian dialects, even though the 11th century Danes – *Daci* – progressively conquered and ruled Romania and Poland, the Baltic, Nordic realms, various North Sea and Irish Sea straits, coastal Freesia and Gaul, and ultimately England. Dacians particularly sought to settle and hold strategic straits, saltworks and metallurgy regions. These show a significant commonality of Esc-, Ex- and Isca- place names and Thorn or Venta place names.

With imperium in England contested in the 10th century and two military conquests of England in the 11th century, a great confusion of names was inevitable as Danes, Saxons, Frisians, Normans, Franks and Latinate clerics all used different names for the same places. Adding to the confusion, there were no consistent spelling conventions and some languages had no written form. Translation to the written forms in histories and charters, often penned by foreign clerics, might be inexact or careless.

Victorians preferred to assume indigenous and parochial name origins, and too often imagined personal name associations, whether a personal name was attested or not. Domesday Book, a treasure trove of 1086 data on names, landholdings and land uses, has led many English historians and toponymists to only look at land as a measure of the 11th century realm, ignoring maritime imperium, trade, fishing and seafaring as sources of English employment, wealth and power – and maritime naming conventions.

Controlling a strait was the best way to control and tax water-borne traffic and suppress piracy. *Hels* was strait in Old Norse as *hellas* was in Greek. The *Hælsings* tribe in Widsith were probably the Dacians of Helsinki or the Danish Hellespont, but the straits most contested for tribute, salt, metals and slaves were the Irish Sea, North Sea, Celtic Sea and Channel strait. The opportunistic and enterprising Dacian diaspora tribes collaborated, inter-married, raided and traded among their cantons on all coasts. They terrorised interior tribes and elites to gain resources, tribute, market privileges and security of tenure without ever fully integrating.

Given the wide diaspora of seafaring Dacians, the modern association of Vikings with Nordic tribes may be too narrow an ethnic and nationalist conceit. The *Lithwicingas* – 'estuary Vikings' –controlled trade between Britain and Gaul from port settlements on both sides from a very early date, successors to King Commius and Emperor Carausius. *Lith* or *lið* meant limb but also 'arm of the sea' or a tidal estuary. The Lithsmen of London were likewise ship-warriors established by King Cnut for control of the tidal Thames. *Here* too had no geographic import; it meant 'sea-army' whether the ship-warriors were based in Britain or abroad.

The toponymic origins of ex-, isca-, -ic, -ich, -vic, -wick and -wich names in Britain have long been disputed, but ancient Greek may provide better inspiration than Celtic, Germanic or Roman names. These places are almost always on or near ancient watercourses or anchorages controlling Hellenic-era trade in the British mineral wealth of salt, tin and iron. These settlements would attract ancient Dacian sea-armies, merchants and cantonal settlers. Incorporating εϰ – 'outsider or outflow' – into place names may have advertised Dacian cantons to hinterland merchants and sea-farers and advertised Dacian commonwealth rule or Romano-Dacian mercantile law. In this context it may be significant that King Offa granted *Lundenuuic* – Londonwick - to Saint-Denis in 790 for a Gallic trading canton at London as well as confirming the earlier grant of Rotherfield priory and *portus Hastingas et Peuenisel.*

There are other intriguing Greek toponymic parallels. Λιμάνι (limani) means harbour or strand in Greek, and there are Limne rivers at the main estuaries of the English coast in Devon, East Anglia and Sussex. Κανάλι (kanali) may be the Greek basis for the English Channel and other watercourses with canal or channel names. *Nas* or *ness* is a headland from Iceland to the Holy Land. *Os* meaning mouth or port is likely the source of the names for the rivers Ouse in Yorkshire, East Anglia and Sussex. A better approach to toponymy on the coasts of Britain would more widely consider the nautical or mercantile function of a place or region during the Bronze Age and Iron Age in seeking to derive names, and comparing Hellenic and Dacian naming in other coastal and riparian regions of Europe.

Analysis of the name Winchelsea provides a good example. The received Victorian etymology is that Winchelsea should be derived indigenously as a diminutive of a personal name *Wine*, though the suggested name is wholly unattested for Sussex. Old English *-ea* meant flowing water, so 'little Winece's river'. A more rational, objective and functional approach would take the 11th century charter name *Wincenesel* and look across to Flanders where the channel to Bruges is still called *Wijnkanal* – 'wine canal' – and dates to the same era of trade cooperation between Godwin in Sussex and Count Baldwin in Flanders. *Wincenesel* makes better sense as 'wine channel cell' – the toll station for the wine canal where thelony was collected – often a barrel of wine from the front and back of every ship. This derivation is supported by the second charter of King Cnut to Fécamp Abbey's Abbot John endowing the abbey with two-thirds of the thelony collected at *Wincenesel*.[176] We know Old Winchelsea was an island or spur of sloping shingle at the mouth of the Rye Camber. We know Winchelsea was a wine port from Roman times. Ships crossing to or from the continent would anchor on the sloping shingle at *Wincenesel* during slack tide and pay tolls for the anchorage before onward navigation inland through the sea-ford in the shingle or along the coast tide-by-tide.

The early Frankish name *Peuenisel* could similarly mean 'almost the ness cell' or the more obvious 'peninsula'. A tidal island or shingle spit is consistent with consistent usage of *Pefenesea* in the Anglo-Saxon Chronicle as a place for securing, mustering or raiding ships, perhaps the same place as the *Pevenesæ* in the Bayeux Tapestry where the Norman fleet moored after crossing the Channel. 'Almost the ness anchorage' makes more sense of the name than any modern associations with Pevensey.

Complicating the task of separately identifying places in the landscape and seascape, ancient ports often took the same name as their fortress or emporium, even if they were quite distant, on the example of Rome and Paris. The port of Rome at Ostia is 30 miles from Rome, but was the first colony established as a mercantile republic with Roman citizenship in common with urban Roman citizens. The Port de Paris at Saint-Denis is 6 miles distant by land from the emporium on the Ile de la Cité, and more than twelve miles by river, but both held common Paris citizenship. The *Carmen* uses the

---

[176] S982 Grant of King Cnut to Abbot John of Fécamp Abbey: *concedo duas partes telonei in portu qui dicitur Wincenesel* – 'I concede two parts of the customs tolls in the port which is called *Wincenesel*'.

port naming convention in identifying St Valery-sur-Somme as the port of Vimeu, a fortified town 9 miles inland from the Baie de Somme. Ancient *Hastinge portus* might be similarly distant from ancient *Hastingacaestre*, wherever that was, but holding common citizenship. The 12th century *De Viis Maris* says bluntly that *Hastinges* town and castle had no port as the port was 7 miles distant at *Winchelse*.

The name Hastings may even derive from *ostia* (mouth) or *aesca* (estuary). The great Roman port at Ostia was being developed at the same time the ports in Roman Britannia were improved and secured by imperial planners. The road from from Rome to Ostia is the Via Hostiensis. *Hostiensis* might easily be corrupted to *Hastingas*.

Improving our grasp of the geography, navigation and names of 1066 necessarily changes our understanding of events. The Norman ships sailing in September 1066 were very heavily laden with men, weapons, horses and supplies. They knew where they were going and had planned the navigation diligently. The Norman fleet set out from Dives-sur-Mer in Normandy two days before the full moon of 6th September 1066, near the peak of autumn high tides. The highest tide occurs two days after the full moon. They navigated along the coast to Fécamp Abbey with a flooding tide, hoping to cross from there. Like Julius Caesar more than a thousand years earlier, they hoped to take advantage of the seasonal high tides to accomplish their cross-Channel passage on a single tide.[177] Had they crossed on the next flood, they might expect the peak lunar tide would carry their heavy vessels securely into port.

The Normans' plan was frustrated by adverse winds and surging seas. The fleet took shelter at St Valery-sur-Somme, a large estuarine bay a single tide's sailing from Fécamp opposite the Sussex coast. They impatiently waited there fifteen days for a favourable turn in the weather. The *Carmen* describes Duke William's prayers for a south wind and dismay at the north wind and unrelenting rain.

---

[177] An advantage of raiding in September might be the assurance of plentiful tribute and booty. Mid-October was the traditional time for reeves and portreeves to remit tribute and tolls to the king. Gold, silver and agricultural surplus would be ready for delivery.

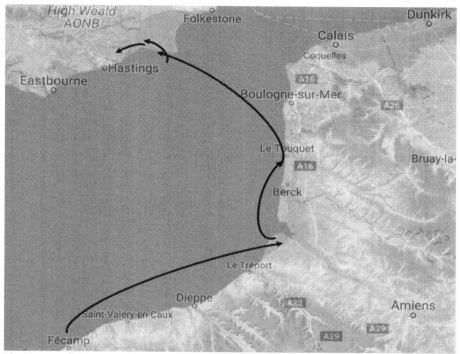

The Norman fleet cross-Channel navigation to *Hastinge portus* was in tidal stages:
(1) September 5th the fleet left Dives for Fécamp, the day before the full moon, hoping to cross on September's highest tide variation, but adverse winds and surging seas forced them to seek shelter in St Valery-sur-Somme.
(2) On September 26th the ships came out of the estuarine port at St Valery on an afternoon ebb tide and formed an orderly fleet along the coast off-shore at slack tide.
(3) With the next flooding tide and south wind the fleet crossed at night by lantern light to *Pevenesæ* where they moored off-shore in a 'sea-harbour' formation while lagging ships caught up with the fleet. The ships struck their heavy sails.
(4) With daylight and the next flooding tide they raised light sails, weighed the sea-harbour anchor, and passed the sea-ford in the coastal shingle into the Rye Camber.
(5) With the flooding tide they navigated the channel between Rye and Winchelsea into the shallow, calm loch of the Brede Basin three hours from the sea. They garrisoned the signal beacon fortress at *Peneuessel* (Udimore). They then poled their ships across the loch to *Hastinge portus*, beaching their heavily laden ships on the level, sandy strand at high tide in the shelter of Iham and Icklesham. They could then safely empty the vessels of men, horses and material securely as the tide receded. They rebuilt the signal beacon fortress at Iham (Winchelsea) and erected a palisaded camp near Icklesham.

The weather cleared, unusually warm weather followed, and the fleet left port again on the afternoon of 27th September, with a steady south wind. The fleet formed up on the coast at slack tide, awaiting the next flood tide for crossing. The fleet crossed the Channel in procession on a single tide, using the south wind to trim their sails for the Sussex coast. Flood tide and ebb tide each last for six hours off Dover, but critically the turn of flow comes two hours after the turn of elevation, allowing trailing vessels to catch up to the moored fleet.

The *Carmen* is testimony to both preparation and patience. The anchored Norman ships form an orderly fleet on leaving St Valery while they await the next flooding tide at line 103. They use a 'sea-harbour' formation when moored off the English coast at line 116. Both would require rehearsal of fleet manoeuvres to perfect for a diverse fleet of hundreds of warships, horse carriers and supply vessels. For the 'sea-harbour' larger ships had to form an arc by chaining themselves stern-to-stern, while the smaller vessels sheltered in the calmer, defended centre. As the *Carmen* tells us, the Norman fleet had the benefit of Norman sea-armies from the Mediterranean campaigns. The 'sea-harbour' was a standard Norman defensive formation for mooring in enemy waters there.

The fleet could safely muster in the shelter of the shingle spit at the sea-ford while the crews rested and the ebb tide ran against them. The *Carmen* adds the details the heavy sails were taken down. Light sails – *carbasa* – are raised for onward navigation with daylight and a flowing tide.

Bayeux Tapestry Scene 38: *Willelm dux in magno navigio mare transivit et venit ad Pevenesæ* – 'Duke William in a great ship crossed the sea and came to *Pevenesæ*.' The ships are clearly not landed indicating *Pevenesæ* is in the seascape.

Pevenesæ is named as the anchorage where the Norman fleet mustered in the Bayeux Tapestry. In the scene the masts are raised, the sails are still billowing and the ships are still making progress. The implication therefore is that *Pevenesæ* was not a landing or port ending the journey but a well-known anchorage along the way. *Paene* in Latin and *peue* in Old French both mean almost. *Ness* means a headland. *Ae* in Old English and *sea* in Old French mean flowing waters. *Peue-nes-ae* therefore means 'almost the ness waters' or 'almost the ness anchorage'. It is notable that every usage of *Pefenesea* in the Anglo-Saxon Chronicle likewise refers to the mustering of a fleet of ships, the sheltering of ships, or the raiding and seizure of ships, confirming a well-known anchorage in the coastal seascape rather than terrain on the land. Anglo-Saxons commonly substituted f for v rendering Latin names and words, so *Pevenesæ* and *Pefenesea* are likely Frankish and Anglo-Saxon names for the same place, now possibly Lydd – a corruption of Lith – above Dungeness.

Pevenesæ certainly does not mean modern Pevensey, which did not exist in 1066 as a named settlement, unless it is *Caestre* in King Edward's 1054 grant to Fécamp Abbey. The ruined 3rd century fortress built by Roman rebels under the Gallo-Dacian rebel Carausius, now Pevensey Castle, offered no fresh water springs, no forage for horses, no firewood for forges or kitchens, and was strategically useless, even vulnerable. There is no archaeological evidence of an ancient port. The island on which the castle sits was surrounded on all but one side by sea and salt marsh in 1066 and accessed by only one causeway to a barren cape toward Winchester. King Edward's 1054 writ describes *Caestre* as having a few cottagers and salt-pans – no port, no town and no church. The 12th century navigation guide *De Viis Maris* similarly mentions *Penenesse* - 'fort-on-the-headland' - only as a landmark, not as a town, port or anchorage even a century later. The modern town was founded on nearby shingle in 1207 by royal charter after the ancient settlement of *Peuenesel*, somewhere further eastwards, closed to the sea.

Wherever *Pevenesæ* was in the seascape on 28th September 1066, the Normans raised anchors at sunrise and set light sails, as detailed in the *Carmen*. The next flood tide carried the Norman fleet into 'a calm basin' – *sinu placido* at line 128 – three hours' navigation from the sea after sunrise. These details are consistent with navigating the Rye Camber channel to the prosperous Brede Basin, then known as Rameslege to the Danes and *Hastingas* to the Gauls, a region held by

Saint-Denis from King Offa to King Aethelred, and then held by Fécamp Abbey from King Cnut's charter of 1017 until Godwin's dispossession in 1052. The same basin may have been a Gallo-Roman port commonwealth going back to the Morini – 'sea people' – before Julius Caesar. A rising tide would sweep the fleet up the estuary and ensure an increasing depth of water beneath the heavily-laden ships to forestall grounding. The hundreds of ships were safely beached on the sandy bosom of the basin, a haven with no rocks to threaten the hulls as the heavy ships settled on a receding tide. Men, horses and materiel could be safely unloaded onto a firm strand. The spars, masts, rigging and sails could all be re-used within a palisaded camp, while the stripped-down ships could be employed for estuarine raiding locally, powered by oarsmen or punted. Boats were preferred for raiding as they could bring away far more supplies, slaves and booty.

The account of the navigation in the *Carmen* has echoes of Julius Caesar's *Commentaries on the Gallic Wars*. Caesar similarly sailed for Britannia at night, anchored off-shore in the fourth hour, waited until his fleet had mustered by the ninth hour, then used favourable wind and flooding tide to advance eight miles deep into a harbour bounded by steep cliffs lined with defenders near enough to throw darts to the strand. Caesar's fleet likewise landed on an 'open and level shore' - *aperto ac plano littore*. The similarity of these accounts, and the alignment of all geographic features with the Brede Basin, may indicate Julius Caesar and Duke William both sailed to the same sheltered, cliff-lined basin.[178]

The Bayeux Tapestry provides visual confirmation of an estuarine port landing in 1066. It shows the Norman ships poled to the gently graded strand, sails taken in, the masts lowered, and the beached ships lined neatly along the strand above high water with their oar ports opened. This last detail is significant, telling viewers that the

---

[178] Victorians suggested Deal or Sandwich for Caesar's landings, but these bear no geographic resemblance to details in his description. The Brede Basin is a perfect match, with steep cliffs either side of an eight mile loch and level strand for the battle. The ruin of Caesar's ships may be accounted for by a tidal bore surging up the narrow valley, a phenomenon common in estuaries near a strait and most severe at full moons, as in 55 BC, or with storm surge, as in 54 BC.

boats are where they will be poled or rowed rather than sailed. Horses are shown being led from the ships onto the strand without ramps by men who are wearing knee-length breeches. There are no anchors.

Bayeux Tapestry Scene 39: The ships are punted ashore, sails stowed, rigging taken in, the masts lowered, and oarports opened.

This scene's imagery contrasts vividly with the scene of Harold's 1064 landing at coastal Ponthieu earlier in the tapestry. There the ships are under sail, steersmen guide them to the coast, massive anchors hold the ships, and the men wade ashore with their breeches tucked high into their waistbands. These clues in the tapestry signal to the knowledgeable mariners of the medieval era that Harold landed on an exposed coast whereas the Norman fleet of 1066 landed in a sheltered estuary.

Other traceable features are offered in the *Carmen*. The calm basin where the Norman fleet landed held ruined fortlets – *diruta castella*. The diminutive plural *castella* would be the right word for alien cells of Fécamp Abbey or subsidiary fortlets of a regional fortification like *Hastingacaestre*, but the same term was also used for Norman signal beacons. William of Poitiers and Orderic Vitalis called the first *castellum* taken and garrisoned *Peneuessellum* - 'fort in the wash'. The 'fort in the wash' is more likely to be at Udimore, a strategic signal base where a port beacon could be seen from anchorages at Wissant, Boulogne and Le Touquet. The narrow Udimore ridge was then a natural fortress, a steep peninsula surrounded at high tide by the sea, except to the west. Udimore is more than 30 metres higher than Iham on the point of the

Hastingas cape, which is 30 metres higher than Lydd, an approximation for Wincenesel. Aligning the three beacons would provide sure navigation from the continent.

Bayeux Tapestry Scene 6: The ships sail to port, oarports closed, are secured by heavy anchors and chains, and the men go ashore with their tunics gathered high.

As with Pevensey, there is little evidence for any port, fortifications or settlement at modern Hastings before the Norman Conquest, except a Roman pharos on the heights at Ore. The 12th century navigation guide *De Viis Maris* is quite clear that the post-conquest settlement *Hastinges* in the late 12th century had a castle and town but it had no port; the port of *Hastinges* was seven miles distant at *Winchelse*.[179] The oldest traceable settlement near modern Hastings was a Fécamp Abbey cell and hospital in Priory Valley.[180] This land was not even considered part of Hastingas until much later. The 12th century *Taxatio* of Pope Nicholas II lists the Priory Valley church as within the parish of Brede, not Hastings.

---

[179] *Deinde est Hastinges villa et castellum, sed non est ibi portus, que distat a Winchelse vii milaria* – 'Next is Hastings town and fort but there is no port there; it is seven miles distant at *Winchelse*.'

[180] The Priory Valley church is listed as being in the parish of Brede in the 12th century *Taxatio* of Pope Nicholas II, suggesting that the western side of the Hastings ridge was not within Hastings parish.

Victorians anachronistically derived the regional name Hastingas from the 9th century Sea-lord Haestens, but that name and *Hastingacaestre* are attested much earlier. The place name more logically derives, like Estonia, from *Aestienses* – 'place of tidal shores' – topographically describing the vast sandy basin for mariners. The coastal tribe *Aestiens* – 'tidal shore people' – was mentioned by Tacitus as occupying Freesia before resettlement to the Baltic, Britannia and Armorica. He describes the Aestiens as capable warriors and skilled sailors. The early 5th century *Notitia Dignitatum* names the leader at *Anderidos* – 'great ford' in Old English – as *Praepositus numeri Abulcorum* – 'governor of many Belgae', suggesting Frisian or Belgic auxiliaries of the Aestiens resettled at Hastingas. Alternatively, the name may come from *Hostiensis*, derived from Ostia, like the Via Hostiensis leading from Rome to the port at Ostia.

The *Notitia Dignitatum* lists command of *Litus Saxonicum* – 'the Saxon shore' – to *Dux Belgicae Secundus* and the fleet at *Anderidos* to a maritime command in Paris. The *Comes Britannicarum* – 'count of the Britannia archipelago' – commanded a mobile field army of cavalry and infantry units for support of the frontier armies wherever needed, like the confederation of Emperor Carausius. Victorians parochially assumed that the count was located somewhere in England, but it is more likely the base of his command was Arx Britannica in Freesia. From there his sea-army could support the frontier commands across the Brtiannic Sea or anywhere needed along the Rhine.

In the *Carmen* the land where the Normans landed had been stripped of its terrified tenants - *colonis*. Colonists would be right term for settlers in a Romano-Dacian commonwealth canton, auxiliaries at a Romano-Dacian imperial settlement, or ecclesiastical tenants on Fécamp Abbey lands. Ecclesiastical tenants held land by covenant, not birth-right. These clues together indicate the Norman landing was in the estuarine Brede Basin. Not only would the vast sandy basin be an ideal safe harbour for the Norman fleet, Norman navigators would have been familiar with navigation to *Hastinge portus* above the sea-ford and coastal anchorage at *Wencenesel*, both owned by Fécamp Abbey. They knew the valley offered fresh water springs, forage, firewood and fish to sustain them until King Harold came to battle. Familiar terrain, hundreds of horses and massive quantities of ship-borne weapons gave the Normans a decided advantage.

Praetorium van Agrippa at Brittenburg by Engelbertus Matthias Engelberts, 1797 – 1799, as preserved in the Netherlands Rijksmuseum. The image portrays the Roman imperial fortress and treasury at the enisled *Arx Britannica* in Freesia, with Dacian wolf-head ships for sea transport, and slaves pulling fish traps ashore in the foreground. The subsidiary forts of the Saxon Shore in Britannia and Gallia served as local treasuries for collection and forwarding of tribute and salt-food provisions to Arx Britannica at the mouth of the Rhine. From there provisions were transhipped to the Roman armies and auxiliaries defending the empire along the northern riparian borders.

Insiginia of the Count of the Saxon Shore from the Bodlian Library, Oxford, manuscript of the *Notitia Dignitatum*. The forts are suggestive of imperial storehouses or treasuries rather than military fortifications. Romano-Dacians may have built these coastal fortlets in the late Roman Empire at the direction of Constantine the Great to collect and secure provisions from the tributary agrarian tribes and coastal fisheries.

The 12th century Icelandic bard Snorri Sturluson in the *Saga of Harald Hardrada* adds further confirmation. He names *Helsingia-port* for the battle place. In the oral tradition the battle was near to the port camp of Duke William. *Helsingia* must be a region on a *hels* or strait consistent with the Brede Basin at the sea-ford of the Rye Camber.

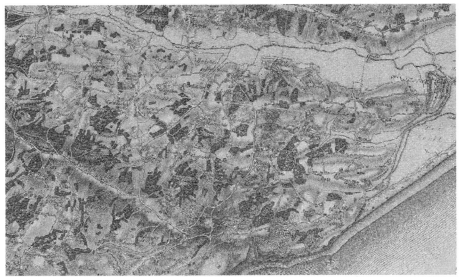

Ordnance Survey 1st Series map of the Brede Basin (1869) still shows a sandy loch or lough.

The Brede Basin finally makes sense of the name Orderic Vitalis uses six times in his *Historia*. The Old English name Senlac quite simply means 'sandy loch'. A loch or lough is a narrow, long estuarine pound cut off from the sea at low tide, both today and in the 11th century. Although modern Britons think of lochs as Scottish, the word was in common use by Anglo-Saxon and Irish navigators when England's coastline had many more sheltered inland estuaries. Lochs were valued as fish traps, so that fish came in with the flooding tide and could be caught with nets as the tide receded from a calm, shallow pound. The Battle Abbey Chronicle lists a landholding on the Udimore ridge in the same basin as the manor *Santlache* just a few decades later.

Lac in Old English always implies flowing water, appropriate to the tidal reach of an estuarine river. There is no sandy stream or any other running water on Battle Hill, making a nonsense of the name's use in any context there. The low ridge near Battle Abbey commonly called Senlac ridge was only recently given the name to promote Victorian and modern tourism.

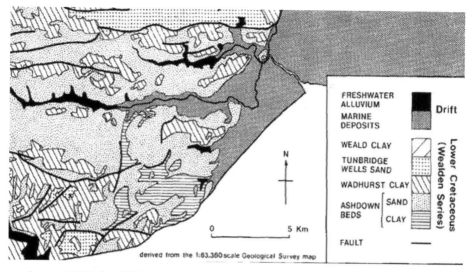

Source: M. Waller, P.J. Burrin and A. Marlow, Flandrian Sedimentation and Palaeo-environments in Pett Level, the Brede and Lower Rother Valleys and Walland Marsh (1998).

Geological surveys confirm a sandy loch in the Brede Basin exactly as the historical sources suggest. Core samples reveal that a thousand years ago the Brede Basin was covered in deep marine sands and subject to tidal inundations. The 100 salt-pans of *Rameslie* recorded in Domesday Book similarly confirm an extensive tidal basin in 1085.

The identification of the offshore mooring and inland port are supported by a more ancient name used in the 8th, 9th and 10th centuries: *Portus Hastingas et Peuenisel.* That name was used in four Anglo-Saxon charters for the Brede Basin when it was the possession of Saint-Denis Abbey in Paris from 785 to at least 960. Centuries of possession by the papally privileged monks of Saint-Denis who spoke the coastal *Romana* and controlled Gallic trade under Roman law probably gave rise to the Saxon and Danish name Rameslege – 'Rome's lowey'. The 790 charter is particularly telling, as it confirms the gift *de receptaculo suo Ridrefelda quod est in pago qui vocatur Successa super fluvium Saforda et de portu super mare Hasting as et Peuenisel* – the gift 'of his [Duke Berhtwald's] storehouse at Rotherfield which is in the country called Sussex above the river Sea-ford [the Rye Camber] and of the port [singular] above the sea *Hastingas et Peuenisel.*[181]

[181] S133 A.D. 790 (Tamworth, Staffs., 12 April). Offa, king of

Sometime in the late 10th century, perhaps 978, the port and manors were dispossessed from Saint-Denis and passed to the family of Ealdorman Aethelmaer of Wessex, grandfather to Earl Godwin and great-grandfather to King Harold. Anglo-Danes had settled the coasts as mercenaries since King Alfred, and may have inter-married with the Saxon elites to promote hinterland trade. Rameslege was next recorded in the foundation charter for Eynsham Abbey in 1005 as the possession of Godwin's kinswoman Wulfwyn, who left it as legacy to the Ensham order, founded with Aethelmaer's son as abbot.

Topographic projection of *Portus Hastingas et Peuenisel* with *Peuenesæ* being the mooring on approach to the estuarine port

The ancient name of *Portus Hastingas et Peuenisel* may have regained Gallic currency in the mid-11th century as Saint-Denis sought King Edward's compensation for estates seized during the reign of his father. A portfolio of Anglo-Saxon charters for Saint-Denis estates at Rotherfield, *portus Hastingas et Peuenisel* and *Londonwick* was copied at this time and is still partially preserved in Paris. Baldwin of Saint-Denis, physician to King Edward, may have commissioned the portfolio for his suit to King Edward. In 1058 Saint-Denis gained a generous estate at Taynton, Oxfordshire (then navigable from the

---

Mercia, to the abbey of Saint-Denis; grant of privileges for land at London and confirmation Rotherfield and Brede Basin, Sussex.

Thames), and Baldwin himself was given a port priory on the Severn at Deerhurst, Gloucestershire, which later also passed to the abbey. Baldwin was then promoted abbot at Bury St Edmunds, a royally privileged order refounded by King Cnut with massive lands around the Romano-Dacian emporium *Villa Faustini*. The pattern of Saint-Denis possessions at former Romano-Dacian trading cantons on the Severn, Thames and Wash suggests Parisian clerics had long memories of prosperous trade networks. No doubt their Anglo-Danish rivals resented King Edward's favours to the Gauls.

The industrialisation and fortification of the Brede Basin would have been a major investment for both Saint-Denis and Fécamp Abbey. Each side of the Brede Basin port would have been overseen by a fortified monastic cell on higher ground for collection of tolls and taxes, maintenance of signal beacons, and protection of settlers in case of attack. As can be seen at Dover today, early coastal churches were often built next to Romano-Dacian beacon towers (*pharos*) as coastal monks were also watchmen and responsible for maintaining beacons and port security as part of their duties.

The landing on the south side of the great port was known to both Saxons and Normans as *Hastinge portus* – the port of Hastings. The broad sandy estuary was the favoured place for landing heavy cargo ships bearing wine and oil from the continent, and taking salt, iron, timber and wool back. The harbour was sheltered by the heights of Iham hill to the east and the Icklesham ridge to the south. In the *Carmen* the Norman *castra marina* – 'seaside camp' – is on the shore at *Hastinge portus* which the 12th century *De Viis Maris* later identifies as *Winchelse*. King William takes King Harold's body back to the camp for burial on the heights of the cliff and remains five days at the camp after the battle.

William of Poitiers and Orderic Vitalis both say the Normans landed first at *Penevesellum*[182] - 'fort in the wash' or 'fort in the basin' –

---

182 11th century Norman sources use *Peneuesel, Peneuessellum* or *Pebessellum* for the Norman landing place. 12th century Battle Abbey clerks changed the name to *Peuenesel*. The Bayeux Tapestry tituli reads *ad Pevenesæ*, but visually references an anchorage in the seascape rather than a fortress in the landscape.

an apt name for Udimore. The narrow peninsula of the Udimore ridge provided a natural stronghold, excellent topography for bloomeries, salt-pans, and iron-smelters, and a chokepoint across the Romano-Dacian causeway for taxing trade between Hastingaport and hinterland Kent and Wessex.

Roman pharos and restored Romano-British church at Dover Castle

Udimore was also a magnificent place for a signal beacon that could signal to other beacons neighbouring the Brede Basin and across to Battle, Cap Gris Nez and to St Valery-sur-Somme. The strategic significance of Udimore as a beacon base explains why the wily old soldier William Poitiers ascribes such importance to seizing and garrisoning this place first on landing in England, such that he says the name *Penevesellum* should be celebrated by Normans.

Wherever *Peneuessel* was, the name was not celebrated long. Count d'Eu made Court Lodge at Udimore his eponymous moated stronghold while he built Hastings Castle on the far side of the ridge. By the time Domesday Book was compiled in 1086 the manor had taken his name as *Dodimere* - 'd'Eu-by-the-sea'. Court Lodge at Udimore was large enough to host the king and all the court, and convenient to the port hostels, kitchens, baths and entertainments of Hastingaport opposite. The port and its markets would make providing food and drink for hundreds attending an extended royal court much easier. Court Lodge is consistent with the royal residence of King William described by William of Poitiers as the mustering place before the Norman fleet is paid off and returns to Normandy for the Easter celebrations at Fécamp in 1067. The manor is recorded as the place of courts for William Rufus and later Norman kings. The Court Rolls record support of a royal chaplain, a sign of secular administration and royal residence.

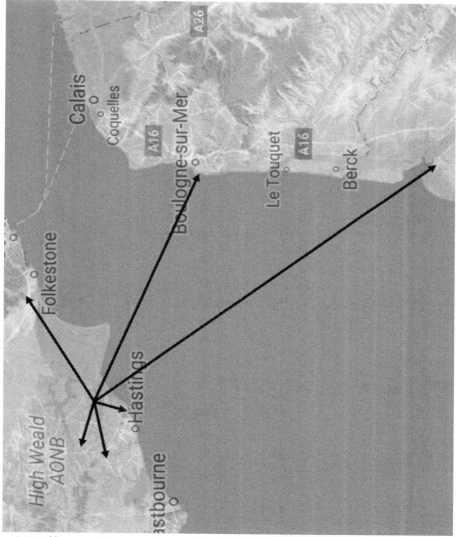

A signal beacon at *Penevessel* near either Court Lodge or the Fécamp Abbey church at Udimore would offer communication and navigation guidance to ships crossing from the anchorage at Wissant, Boulogne or Le Touquet, as well as communicating to neighbouring coastal beacons at Folkestone, Romney, Ore and Battle for coordinated coastal defence.

It is more difficult to locate the historic *Pevenesel*, assuming it is quite a different location to the *Peneuessellum* of William of Poitiers. The profound changes in the region from war, earthquakes, siltation and shingle shift leave this more of a mystery. The earliest mention of *Pevenesel* is in the four Anglo-Saxon charters for Saint-Denis of Paris, which describe the port holding in Sussex as above the sea-ford at *Portus Hastingas et Pevenisel*. Hastingas must be the cape of Hastingas, extending from the great ridge to Winchelsea along the Icklesham Ridge below the Brede Basin. That manor was given to Fécamp Abbey in 1017 and again in 1066 as Rameslege. By implication Pevenisel should be the manor of *Bretda* or the Udimore ridge, but it seems only part of this was included in Rameslege.

Pevenisel might have been at Boreham Street above the port channel between Wartling and Hooe. The location suits exploitation of the clay, iron and forests of the region by Romans, Anglo-Saxons and Normans. The entry for *Pevenesel* in Domesday Book includes *gablo* – urban tribute, *telonei* – customs tolls, and *portorium* – bridge or ford levies, and modest pasturage. There are no salt-pans, indicating a fluvial rather than estuarine settlement. The population increased from 24 burgesses in the time of King Edward to 60 burgesses in 1086, indicating substantial Norman settlement. Intensive exploitation of iron in local foundries and smithies would explain the rapid siltation of the port, requiring resettlement of the borough by 1207.[183] The charter for the modern town of Pevensey describes the place of the modern town as on the shingle between Langeney (Eastbourne) and 'our port of *Pevenesel*'. Wartling held a royal manor with a chaplain, indicating a royal residence and treasury on the site, consistent with a nearby port.

The names *Penevessel* and *Pevenesel* became inextricably confused in the 12th century when the monks of Battle began to promote their order with a history tying the abbey to the Norman victory, claiming *Pevenesel* for the landing-place and the altar of the abbey church for Harold's death. A settlement at Boreham Street makes sense for this fabrication as it would have been in the circular soke of Battle Abbey.

---

[183] Gallic cargo vessels crossed the Channel with sand ballast, and dumped it on reaching a port. This combined with ash and debris from saltpans, founderies and forges rapidly clogged Norman ports.

The fishermen of *Hastingaport* likewise moved to the valley below Hastings Castle as the Brede Basin silted up and shingle shift on the coast closed access to the sea from the Brede river. Winchelsea was also attacked by the French several times, with massacres of civilians encouraging migration.

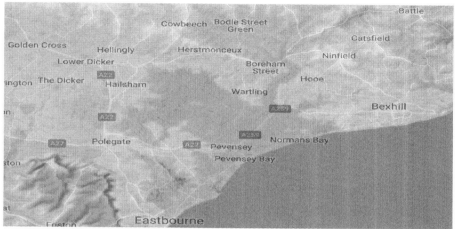

Portus Pevenesel before the 1207 charter for relocation may have have been the settlement Pevensel, probably at Boreham Street. Hooe had 34 salt-pans in Domeday Book while nearby *Pevensel* had none, indicating a fluvial settlement. Wartling was used as place of signing in a forged charter, which suggests some royal residence near the port.

By the time antiquarians began compiling histories of the Norman Conquest in Elizabethan times the Rameslege settlements had been long forgotten. William Camden in 1585 mentioned that the old town of Hastings had been 'swallowed up by the sea'. He sensibly expressed scepticism modern Hastings ever had a port, noting fishermen of the day had to winch their boats from the hard, making it unsuitable for cargo vessels.

Archaeology in the Brede Basin may yet find the Romano-Dacian and Norman port and fortifications. Dacian fortresses had distinctive arced walls topped with impenetrable thorn brush. Islands or settlements with Thorn in their English names may therefore merit particular investigation, especially near salt or iron works. Guestling Thorn could be ancient *Anderidos* or *Hastingacaestre*.

The Normans entrenched Udimore with a deep moat that can still be seen today. There have only been preliminary investigations of the port opposite, but archaeologists found wide Roman roads had been raised on stone foundations and metalled with iron slag. The roads extended from the Udimore ridge across a causeway through the Brede Basin and up over the Icklesham ridge to the Pannel river seaward. A spur of the ridge road forms a further causeway east to Wickham and Iham, where a stone beacon tower stood until modern times. The excavations showed extensive industrialisation of the region for its clay and iron from Caesar's day to the Napoleonic Wars. We may yet find fortifications around the palisaded Norman camp at *Hastingaport* nearby.

Early spellings suggest the name Icklesham may have been *ecclesia-ham* – 'church settlement' – but isca- and Ex- names are also suggestive of ancient Dacian cantons, confirmed by the neighbouring Guestling Thorn. Stones found on the coast below Icklesham in the last century are elaborate tracery consistent with continental ecclesiastical architecture unknown otherwise in Saxon England. These have yet to be tested for age or origin. Neighbouring Wickham or '*vicus*-ham' suggests a Roman mercantile settlement between the Icklesham church and Iham. Where other Fécamp Abbey churches in the Brede Valley are staunchly Norman, the church at Icklesham may have been founded much earlier by Saint-Denis.

Some suggest Icklesham was a minster of St Wilfred in the 8th century. Wilfred brought continental reformed Christianity to coastal Sussex. He frequently travelled to Rome and promoted Benedictine reforms. Wilfred is said to have taught Sussex locals to fish, which probably meant teaching tidal fish traps and salt-curing for export. Wilfred's episcopal seat was at Selsey – 'salt-island'. A Gallic port and market at the Brede Basin would provide additional salt and fish exploitation and export.

Scene 48: *Hastenga*   11th c. Frankish church   Ruin of St Leonard's
at Iham 1794

St Leonard's Church on Iham hill, now Winchelsea, was initially an alien cell of Fécamp Abbey in the 12th century parish of *Hastingas*. The tower offered views over the valley, the estuarine Rye Camber and the Channel toward Gaul, and a beacon guided navigation to the port and provided defensive communications with surrounding watchtowers. The building left behind when the Normans go to battle at Scene 48 of the Bayeux Tapestry resembles an 11th century Frankish church above a steep ridge, consistent with St Leonard's location and features. Only a few stones now remain.

The Bayeux Tapestry also shows construction of a motte with raised wooden platform and a stone watch tower or signal beacon at Scene 45. A man-made mound much like the motte depicted in the tapestry still rises on the south side of Iham hill where the Normans might have anticipated an attack from the neighbouring Icklesham ridge, and an ancient stone watch tower or signal stood on the seaward cliff of Iham.

Scene 45: Motte and tower   Man-made mound at Iham   Ancient tower at Iham
at the Hastings camp

Roman roads provide another archaeological basis for thinking the Brede Basin more important to events of 1066 than formerly appreciated. Roman roads were for imperial military use. We find roads where the military wanted roads. There are plenty of Roman era roads around the Brede Basin, and the trackways along the ridgetops were paved with iron slag as well. There are engineered descents and stonework roadbeds and causeways either side of the Icklesham ridge, leading across the basin to the Udimore ridge to the north and across Pannel River to the south. Another road led across a bridge at Sedlescombe, the limit of tidal inundation.

The pattern of Roman roads indicates the whole basin may have been developed on imperial industrial principles from Caesar's day forward to maximise production of ships, chandlery, weaponry, salt, pottery, salt-foods and other military requirements for continental armies. The *Classis Britannia*, the Roman navy in Britain, had its base in the Brede Basin until the rebellion of Carausius led to reorganisation of coastal defence. The ruins of Anderidos loomed above the landscape until the 12th century and then disappear from history, perhaps reused to build Norman fortifications.

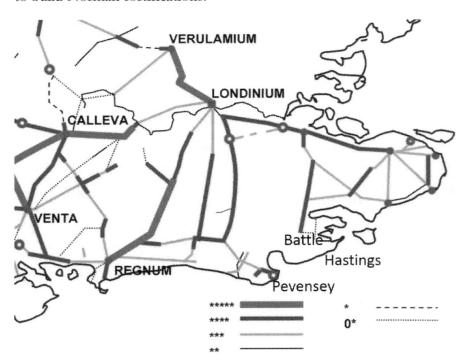

Roman roads of Sussex and Kent, R. Whaley, *Roman Road Abstracts* (2009).

Once the medieval geography and coastline are better understood, the Victorian legend that Duke William landed at modern Pevensey and marched to modern Hastings becomes untenable. The locations make no sense for landing a fleet or marching an army. Between the headlands of Eastbourne and Hastings a thousand years ago was a wide tidal wash and deep inland saltmarsh leading into the dense forest of the Weald. The extent of this geographic obstacle can be measured by the Roman roads that circumvent it. If the Norman army had landed at Pevensey, they should have marched to Winchester, the royal seat of the kings of Wessex, not to Hastings or Battle.

Relocating the events of the Norman Conquest to the Brede Basin represents a big challenge to 1066 romantic histories, but makes much better sense of the historical, geographic, toponymic and archaeological record. The Brede Basin has far superior claims in terms of navigation and logistics. Duke William would rationally prefer the familiar Norman heavy cargo port with plentiful spring water for men and horses. The port was used by Norman navigators for centuries and was the rightful possession of Fécamp Abbey from 1017. The terrain offered a sheltered harbour, defensible fortifications, plentiful fish and game, forage for horses, timber, firewood, charcoal bloomeries, good metalled roads, and convenient cross-Channel beacon communication with Gaul.

If we reconsider the geography of the Norman landing, camp and fortifications, we might also reconsider the site of the battle, disputed now for over thirty years. The 13th century *Chronicle of Battle Abbey* and the E manuscript of the *Anglo-Saxon Chronicle* say the abbey stands at the spot where the Normans gained victory. No traces of an 11th century battle have been found by archaeologists after decades of exploration at Battle to support these assertions. A single axe blade was found several miles away, more likely lost by a woodsman than a 1066 defender of England.

The *Chronicle of Battle Abbey* provides clues to another site for the original battlefield. The founding monks tried to move the site from the battlefield at *Hurst* as it was arid, inconvenient and lacked stone. Hurst can only mean a lowland site, not a hilltop. King William denied the request, saying he would provide wine in place of water and bring stone from Caen with his ships, but long delays building Battle

Abbey raise suspicions about his later enthusiasm for the project. He died without giving the financial support and endowments he had initially promised to the monks building Battle Abbey. One view is that the Battle Abbey Chronicle was completed by a foreign propagandist cleric brought in to improve the abbey's financial prospects at a time when forgeries and fanciful histories were undergoing a boom.

Initial progress on the abbey was certainly unenthusiastic and halting. The founding monks are said to have built only a few rooms after 1070 before becoming discouraged. The first abbot of St Martin de Bello occupied a temporary site in 1076. The royal charter for the establishment of Battle Abbey issued only after 1085, as territorial disputes were being negotiated and settled by Domesday Book. Professional masons from the continent finally completed the building of the abbey for the Marmoutier order so it could be consecrated in 1094, after King William's death, on a hilltop surrounded by good arable land. It did not prosper until much later in the 12th century.

If there was no battlefield at Battle then why is the abbey sited on Battle Hill? The answer is quite simple when viewed from the perspective of mariners on the sea and defenders on the land. Where the abbey was positioned at the top of Battle Hill made it centrally visible to all ships as they sailed into either the port in Rameslege or the narrow channel to Hooe on the Pevensey Levels. Medieval abbeys were customarily sited where they would be visible to mariners coming into port. Clerics also had responsibility for watching to determine if fleets approaching were friendly or hostile from their high towers. Mariners and merchants were expected to be generous for their safe The site of the abbey also provides an excellent signal station, linking Eastbourne's signal tower to those in the Brede Basin. Battle can be seen from both Brede and Udimore church towers through a gap in the great ridge.

Another explanation for placing Battle Abbey away from the battlefield of *Hastingas* may be that the battlefield was in the estate of Fécamp Abbey. The Abbey of St Martin de Bello may have been forced to take its place at Battle when they received their charter in 1085 because King William would not dispossess the favoured monks of Fécamp Abbey to found a new monastery for a competing order from Marmoutier.

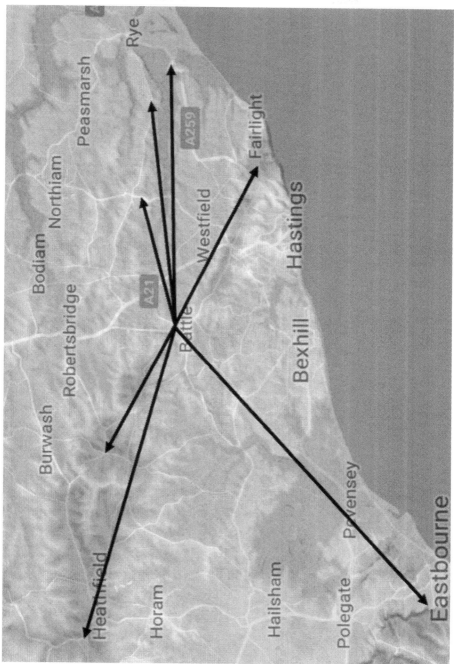

Battle Abbey sightlines to Fécamp Abbey cells in the Brede Basin and surrounding churches suggest a strategic signal station for defence of coastal ports. The abbey could oversee ships sailing into the Brede Basin and coastal vessels on the Pevensey Levels.

In favour of this theory, Battle Abbey sits a league west from the Roman bridge below Sedlescombe, the limit of former tidal reach in the estuarine Brede River. This road and bridge seems a likely western boundary for *Rameslege*. Battle Abbey was endowed with a circular soke of a league, just about reaching the bridge and encompassing the canal that once ran from Sedlescombe to somewhere near Battle.

The *Carmen* offers additional clues to aid a search for the battlefield. Both armies were on the march when they met, indicating the battle lies near a Roman road or ancient ridgeway road. Harold's forces were urged on through the night, which would require a good road, and the duke is mounted and his army on the march when the envoy returns, also implying a road. The duke could see the king's approaching banners from the point on the road where he met the envoy, consistent with a ridgeway road offering vistas around the valley.

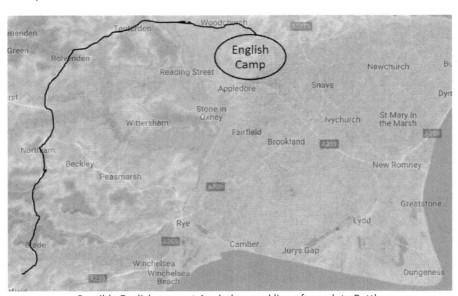

Possible English camp at Appledore and line of march to Battle

The Anglo-Saxon Chronicle, manuscript D, says that King Harold mustered his large army at *haran apuldran*. This was translated romantically in 1861 as 'hoary apple tree'. It was better translated in 1731 as 'estuary at Appledore', which is much more likely. In medieval navigation *harena* or *arena* meant a sandy anchorage or basin suitable for grounding the round-bottomed coastal raiding and trading vessels, *carinas*, named at line 319 of the *Carmen*. Appledore was then a small peninsula below the Roman road at the edge of the great tidal basin of the Rye Camber. A Roman road led across tidal causeways at Tenterden, Northiam and Brede to the cape of Hastingas. Appledore was an ideal place for muster of local land armies and sea-borne warriors. Travel by coastal transport was faster, safer, and allowed much better carriage of men and materiel.

We cannot know exactly where the battle occurred without archaeological discovery of the battlefield. What we can do is make better sense of the clues left to us about the location.

According to the *Carmen*, the English came forth out of the woods suddenly while the duke was still ordering his forces. The English rushed together to take a nearby hill adjoining a valley, rugged and uncultivated, before Duke William could fully position his cavalry. The English formed their shield wall, with nobles on the summit of the hill. The duke halted his army's advance below the steep hill, beginning the battle with his archers and crossbowmen. During the French Feint the greater part of the English mob remained on the ridge in formation while those that followed the feint into the valley were slaughtered on the steep slope below.

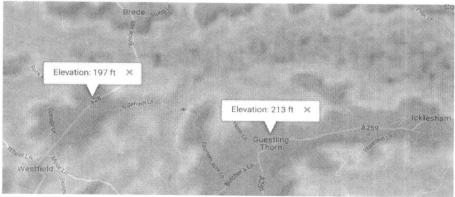

The battlefield of 1066 may be near Westfield or Guestling Thorn by the Brede Basin. While modest hills above the flood plain now, they were steeper and taller in 1066.

When the shieldwall had been broken and the Gauls had taken the ridge, Duke William could see King Harold fighting in a dense crowd on the summit of the hill above. This may indicate the hill of the battlefield is rather more modest in height than has been supposed. Westfield and Guestling Thorn rise near the ancient isthmus below the Weald that separated Hastingas from the hinterland. The hill might be the great ridge above Hastings too, where Ore gained a church after the battle. Any of these places would justify the Norman identification with *Hastingas*, the Saxon identification with *Senlac,* and the Nordic identification with *Helsingiaport.*

As Shakespeare reminds us in *Henry V*, Normans named battles for the nearest fortification. The battlefield should be a hill not far from ancient *Hastingecaestre*, the undiscovered settlement 'swallowed up by the sea' after the 12th century. Westfield is an Anglicised variant of Guestfield. It was likely the market field for the fortified Romano-Dacian settlement at Guestling Thorn. It would be worthwhile exploring for ancient *Hastingacaestre*, possibly at Guestling Thorn, and then seeking the battlefield around nearby hills.

Even now the bones of thousands of men and horses, uncounted buckles, harnesses, clasps, broaches, shards of broken weapons and armour must leave their trace for archaeologists to find. According to the *Carmen* the Norman dead were buried the morning after battle with a swiftness hinting a sandy mass grave on a floodplain. Archaeological investigation at Battle Abbey continues despite disappointing results, but perhaps if nothing more is found, the search might move three to five miles southeast. Consistent with the description in the *Battle Abbey Chronicle*, the place names below the ridge bordering the western end of the Brede Basin often include *hurst,* and the ruggedness of the terrain has left the area largely uncultivated even today.

APPENDIX IV

ROYAL, PAPAL, URBAN AND ECCLESIASTICAL JURISDICTIONS

The medieval involvement of pope, prelates and clerics in royal, urban and commercial affairs will be confusing to those with modern political sensibilities about divisions between church and state and between religion and commerce, or even those who think states are sovereign and independent. No such distinctions can be drawn in the medieval or any earlier era. Christian kings were chosen by God through his vice-regent the pope. Kings were consecrated with holy oil that they might be vice-regents of God's earthly affairs, cooperating with bishops and popes. A king's first duty was to protect the Universal Church and promote Romanised Christianity. Prelates and secular clerics served kings as agents of God, directed exploitation of royal industries such as salt, mines and mints, promoted mercantile markets, fairs and ports, and administered the royal chancery and exchequer. At lower levels clerics supported manorial administration by earls, and urban secular administrators such as reeves. Local priests and clerical orders also manned watchtowers and maintained signal beacons and bells to provide an early warning network to rally defenders in case of attack. Clerics were also military auxiliaries to aid defence in times of conflict.

To ensure alignment of economic interests and cooperation, early kings endowed the church and religious orders with valuable estates, ports and emporia in exchange for secular services. The sees, abbeys and minsters enabled the spread of Christianity, but they also kept strategic resources that earned gold and silver revenues from manorial nobles who might rebel. Both kings and prelates profited from taxation and trade, concentrating wealth and power and in state and church.

Historians who believe the early church was principally about devotion to God and contested theology miss the main thrust of how the church was practically organised and administered to promote trade, hereditary wealth and royal power. The geographic pattern of carefully targeted early minsters recreated Dacian, Hellenic and Roman imperial trade routes, and spread mercantile trade in parallel with the orthodox doctrines of Christianity. Early Christian envoys of the pope rarely preached the gospel to the people; they converted kings and chieftains, asked for urban minsters, sees and ports, and sought royal recruits to clerical ranks to enhance the church's power and prestige. Christianity was only spread to the common people once it had prospered from royal cooperation and trade.

The cooperation of church and state goes back much earlier than Christianity. The first stone temples were built at Sumerian saltworks in the eastern Mediterranean when salt was 'white gold', before coins were widely minted by salt-cementation of gold and silver. The stone temples preserved salt blocks from moisture which would corrupt salt's purity, preservation and weight, so served a very practical purpose. Stone also projected strength and superiority as quarries and masonry required great investments of slave labour. Priests controlled saltworks in the Sumerian, Greek, Roman, Germanic and Dacian empires for centuries before Christianity emerged and targeted the same saltworks for early Frankish, English and Danish Christian minsters.

Salt was currency for widespread trade, but salt was also essential to food preservation, hygiene, metallurgy, tanning and dying, so a critical enabler of urban survival, industry and trade. When coins came into use mints were naturally sited at the same secure stone temples at the saltworks and ports. Precious metal coins from trade could be assayed, melted down and reminted for domestic use in co-located facilities. Ports, saltworks, mints and markets are all synergistic contributors to creating, spreading and taxing wealth.

As Christianity spread, churches, minsters, abbeys and monastic cells were also stationed wherever salt and money might change hands. Stone temples were built to the Christian God, but still offered secure storage of salt and treasure, still ran markets and fairs. Christian secular clerics promoted systematic royal exploitation of land, labour and resources. They kept the records and books of both the church and the state, recording contracts, property holdings, tenancies, market trade, customs duties, taxes and tithes.

Popes, bishops and abbots were intimately involved in royal and secular politics within early Christian realms, influencing marriages and succession among rival claimants. Emperors and kings in turn chose bishops and abbots and validated the edicts of church councils. Because of their power and access to wealth, church primates were often members of the king or overlord's immediate family.

Medieval Christians believed that hierarchical ranks of man were ordered by God, from pope and kings down to slaves. Christian on Christian slavery is an uncomfortable topic for many today, but it is important to appreciate that the medieval church was not opposed to slavery. The English Church owned a huge population of slaves for the work of its arable lands and industries. Christian on Christian slavery persisted in Britain for several more centuries after it was banned on the continent. What records we have decrying slavery in the 11th century only oppose the sale of slaves to pagans. Clerics were expected to work each day under the rule of Saint Benedict, but if well-educated this work could be as secular clerics, artisans or scribes. Menial labour was relegated to the lowly born settled on church lands under covenant or slaves.

A complex system of legal and financial principles evolved to respect separate royal and church hierarchies, jurisdictions, prerogatives, responsibilities, immunities and privileges. Laws were not national but were localised to urban, church and royal possessions. Which laws governed an individual was determined by whether the individual was a tenant on a manorial, ecclesiastical or urban estate, and whether he was a freeman, an urban burgess, a bondsman or a slave. The *Carmen* provides an excellent example of this separation of urban and royal jurisdiction in the settlement of the London siege. The London Charter of Liberties granted burgesses of London self-rule and hereditary property rights that allowed them to trade anywhere in England with the king's protection.

From the Donation of Constantine, the Christian church insisted that its clerics, lands and possessions should be free of royal taxation. This privilege came into Britain in the 7th century as Saint Augustine brought England back into communion with the Roman church. A charter of King Ina dated 704 decreed all churches and monasteries in his kingdom of Wessex free from secular impositions and taxation. Similar royal privilege was common throughout Britain and the continent and zealously preserved by bishops, abbots and clerical estates. The church's prosperity was supposed to fund Christian outreach to the native population, but it often meant clerics came from elite families of the realm lived the most comfortable lives and provided the most comfortable hostels for pilgrims and merchants. Privileged monastic orders maintained their social position by a monopoly on teaching advanced numeracy and literacy, much like elite universities in later centuries. Parents committing a child to the church were expected to endow enough wealth for his or her upkeep and education, limiting access to the relatively wealthy.

Royals had to cooperate with the church if they wanted legitimacy. In early medieval Europe royal legitimacy could only be secured by the Christian rite of royal consecration with the consent of the pope and bishops. All Christ's disciples were made ministers, but only Saint Peter received the spiritual keys and the power to lock and unlock the gates of heaven from Christ.[184] As Saint Peter's spiritual heirs, Roman popes jealously preserved this power over Christian kings. The symbol of the Holy Apostolic See is the crossed keys of Saint Peter, and the Shrine of Saint Peter remains the most holy site in Rome, still associated with royal authority. It was the alter of Saint Peter in Westminster that received the burial of King Edward and by which King William was consecrated, conveying Roman sanctity.

Any king not consecrated with papal consent was deemed a tyrant. A lord could win a war, inherit a realm or be elected king by nobility and prelates, but he would not be recognised beyond his borders as king without the rite of consecration. A king might marry but could not make his wife queen without the rite of consecration.

---

[184] Matthew, 19:19; and see Isiah 22:21-22 for the Old Testament precedent. Throughout the Bible there are examples where there are many ministers to kings but only ever one keyholder. Jesus calls the apostle Peter 'pope' when he hands to him the spiritual keys of the gates of heaven and his church on Earth. An additional Judiac implication endowed Peter with the power to 'bind and loosen' or to allow or prohibit as church doctrine and orthodoxy. Matthew 16:19.

Gaining papal or archiepiscopal consent for consecration usually required foundation of an abbey or generous gifts to the church. These endowments proved the intention of a king to rule as a faithful Christian king and meet all obligations owed to the church and the pope. Any lord taking a crown or realm by violence was keen to propitiate his bishops, abbots and the pope to secure consent for consecration, and this helps explain some early charters leading up to 1066. England was far from Rome, but two early Anglo-Saxon kings were buried in the Chapel of St Peter in the basilica at Rome, evidencing strong ties.

Violence against church possessions or clergy, misappropriation of the church's wealth, war against a fellow Christian king, unauthorised consecration of a bishop or royal, or marriage in violation of a papal edict might all be punished by papal excommunication. Papal excommunication denied the excommunicant lord the services of the secular clergy and Christian burial rites. Heirs became illegitimate, ineligible for succession. Priests and clerics in a land where the lord was excommunicant might also be barred from providing religious or secular services generally to the nobles and people to provoke rebellion among the Christian faithful. Rival lords were invited by excommunication to wage war for their own gain as taking land or possessions from excommunicants to give to canonical Christians was both profitable and admirable. Excommunication could be withdrawn if the offending lord showed repentance and gave generous gifts to the church as evidence of his remorse and intention to be faithful to the church in future.

Popes attempted to maintain discipline among medieval royals by applying the twin levers of consecration and excommunication – Christ's authority 'to lock and unlock the gates of heaven' - to regulate royal legitimacy and succession. This is particularly evident in the 11th century. It may seem absurd now when nationalism is widely prevalent that a pope in Rome had much direct influence in distant England and Gaul, but the evidence is there in the historical records and patterns of events.

It was the pope who encouraged King Aethelred II to marry Emma of Normandy in 1002, after decades promoting truce between England and Normandy as Christian realms that might defend the church against the pagan sea-army attacks. Emma's consecration as queen ensured her sons precedence over Aethelred's elder sons. The founding of Eynsham Abbey soon followed, with its abbot the son of the powerful Ealdorman Aethelmaer and generous endowments. King Aethelred's confirmation of Ealdorman Aethelmaer's endowment charter of 1005 granting Rameslege and other estates to Eynsham Abbey formed part of the settlement. The port canton had been seized from Saint-Denis and given to Wulfwyn, a kinswoman of Aethelmaer. Giving the port canton to Eynsham Abbey returned it to privileged status and control of the church.

King Aethelred then promised the vast manor of Rameslege and its port to Fécamp Abbey in 1015 in gratitude for sanctuary, but the gift also gave the powerful and privileged Norman abbey an economic stake in preservation of his realm and protection of his sons' hereditary claim. Norman fleets had long depended on oak, weapons, iron and salt from the port a single tide away opposite their coast. The Norman naval campaign to retake the Mediterranean from the Saracens might not have been as successful without the salt-foods, iron, and oak of Rameslege for Norman ship-builders.

King Cnut executed a charter confirming the liberties of St Paul's church in London in 1017 as his first act. The liberty of the emporium may have been pledged to secure London aldermen and papal approval of his consecration as King of England. The *Carmen* describes how King William was forced to cede similar privileges of autonomy to London's citizens by his first act fifty years later to secure his own uncontested consecration. London had been protected by Rome since Pope Gregory the Great through Saint Augustine restored the English church to communion with Rome. London remained semi-autonomous by these royal charters of conquerors despite military conquest of hinterland England.

Similarly, King Cnut may have secured Queen Emma's consent to marriage and the pope's consent for her consecration as queen of England with the 1017 charter confirming Fécamp Abbey possession of Rameslege in fulfilment of King Aethelred's earlier promise. When King Cnut confirmed the Fécamp Abbey's rights in *Bretda* by charter sometime between 1028 and 1034, he also conferred two-thirds of the tolls of *Wincenesel* on the abbey. By promoting the powerful and privileged Norman abbey he promoted trade with Normandy and the Holy Roman Empire and secured royal revenues and expert Norman secular clerical administration of the port for himself.

After securing the Baltic as emperor of three kingdoms Cnut the Great went directly to Rome, down the fluvial Slavo-Dacian trade route. He negotiated trade privileges with his mother's kinsmen, the Holy Roman Emperor and the pope, pledging his royal daughter Gunhilde by Queen Emma in marriage to the son of the emperor. King Cnut secured good relations with the pope and empire, assuring security for trade from his three kingdoms to the east.

The 1034 pilgrimage of Duke Robert of Normandy, William the Bastard's father, capped a campaign of reconciliation to rescind excommunication for violence against church prelates and Fécamp Abbey during civil strife after his brother's death. Generous endowments to Rome and foundation abbeys won him consecration, the soubriquet Robert the Magnificent, and also bought recognition of son William as Duke Roberts's royal heir, despite the boy's illegitimate birth.

King Edward granted Fécamp Abbey the reversion of the port of Steyning in 1044 to be effective on Bishop Aelfwine's death shortly after he was consecrated king of England. This may have been gratitude for almost three decades of sanctuary in Normandy, but the gift strengthened the interest of the Norman abbey in the preservation of his English realm, expanded trade with Normandy, and the gained him secular clerics to reform the royal chancery and exchequer on continental principles. As King Edward had not started the refounding of Westminster at this early date, he may have relied on Fécamp Abbey for his royal treasury, at least until the treasuries at London and Rameslege were looted by Godwin in 1051 and 1052.

Duke William and Mathilda of Flanders were excommunicated in 1051 for their marriage contrary to an interdict of the pope for consanguinity, a dispute finally resolved after seven years with the aid of Lanfranc, then abbot of Bec. Their reinstatement to communion with the church required endowment of two new papally privileged abbeys at Caen, which became the ducal capital.[185] Lanfranc was

---

[185] The Abbey of Saint-Étienne for men the Abbey of Saint-Trinité for women were jointly founded by Duke William of Normandy and Mathilda of Flanders as penance for their marriage to lift their excommunication, restoring the legitimacy of their sons' succession to the duchy as royal heirs. Lanfranc, then prior of Bec, negotiated

installed as the first abbot of the newly built and papally privileged abbey, training secular clerics for ducal administration and cementing good relations with the pope in Rome. Caen became the new ducal seat, chancery and exchequer.

King Harold refounded Waltham Abbey with generous gifts from the mid-1050s, perhaps as his own chancery and exchequer as *subregulus* or perhaps to influence Rome in favour of his eventual succession.

King Harold was excommunicated as a tyrant for seizing the English crown and his unauthorised coronation by the uncanonical Stigand, who was also excommunicated yet again. Pope Alexander II thereby undermined Harold's legitimacy as an English king, denied Harold the services of secular clerics for royal administration, promoted English rebellion among the faithful, and disinherited Harold's heirs. The English Church had been alienated from Roman canon law authority since 1052, so the excommunications may have had negligible effect locally. Nonetheless, excommunication signalled to the ambitious king of Norway and duke of Normandy that they might overthrow Harold with the support of the pope and church.[186]

The principles of property tenure were also very different in the 11th century. The king held all royal demesne within his realm by royal prerogative, ceding possessory tenures to his nobles in exchange for military service, judicial administration and tribute. There were few hereditary tenures, although sons might expect to retain their father's lands by rendering similar services and tribute. The exceptions were estates granted in writing by charters under customary conditions. The conditions depended on whether the gift of land was to the native church, remaining under the control of the king, or to a papally privileged religious order, deemed within the jurisdiction of the Holy Apostolic See in Rome, extra-terrestrial from royal demesne. The law

---

the settlement and became the first prior of Saint-Étienne.

[186] Josef Stalin sarcastically asked how many army divisions the pope had, but in medieval times the pope's ability to mobilise ambitious or avaricious kings and their mercenary armies made up for any lack of warriors in the church or Rome.

that applied in any borough or market depended on whether it was royal demesne, domestic church land, or papally privileged abbey land.

The generosity of early Christian kings and lords endowing the church also influenced geography and economic development. The story of the first Christian king in almost every European realm will have three things in common: (1) Approached by a missionary from a pope a pagan tribal lord converted to Christianity and was consecrated the first Christian king of his realm. (2) He endowed an abbey founded in the Holy Apostolic See and privileged by the pope at a trading port to be a Roman-law emporium, usually an island, cape or peninsula a day's ride distant from the royal seat in the hinterland. (3) He established a see for a bishopric in the royal seat with generous secular liberties such as markets or fairs so that the church might prosper as it spread Christianity and trade within the kingdom.

The medieval Roman Church motivated royals to co-operate by mobilising thousands of literate and numerate priests and monks for tax collections and urban, mercantile and commercial development. These clerics enhanced royal power and authority by bringing efficient systems for communications, education, industrialisation and secular administration, in addition to sending priests to convert and serve the faithful by providing Christian rites and rituals. Early royal and church co-operation seems ideally designed to reinforce centralisation of royal power and promote Christianity through the assured prosperity of both king and church. The system worked well, if slowly, corruptly and sometimes violently, to create the European nations familiar to us in the modern era. Early Christian port cantons and episcopal sees are now the familiar commercial and political capitals of Europe.

While the legal claims of the Holy Apostolic See, the native church and royals appear archaic and confused now, they were jealously guarded and often violently enforced in medieval times. Each jurisdiction had laws, prerogatives, obligations, privileges and immunities established by canon law, royal charter, national law, and custom and usage. Each pope, royal, noble, bishop and abbot knew precisely the extent of his claims and privileges. Infringements were hotly resented.

Possessions held by religious orders with papal privilege were jurisdictionally protectorates of the Holy Apostolic See in Rome, ruled under a common legal and commercial framework derived from

Roman mercantile law. The name *Rameslege* - 'Rome's lowey' - is a toponymic expression of Roman lingual and legal jurisdiction at the great port canton in Sussex. Romney – 'Rome's island' – marked the beginning of Roman jurisdiction. The river *Limne* – 'border river' – demarked the border between king's demesne and ecclesiastical estate.

Holy Apostolic See estates in medieval times had the legal extraterritoriality and inviolability now reserved for diplomatic embassies and mandated territory ceded to multinational bodies like the United Nations. Lands endowed to orders in the Holy Apostolic See were immune from legal or financial claims of the king and manorial lords in perpetuity, and also immune from direction or financial claims of the native church and archbishops.[187] The king was obliged to protect church possessions and liberties from his own manorial lords and foreign enemies alike by consecration oath, charters, and sometimes written laws. In return all burgesses, citizens and magistrates in a privileged port or borough were sworn directly and personally loyal to the king, and were obliged to provide services to the king and defensive works to their borough. Revenues of ports, crafts, industries, saltpans, mints and markets were shared between the church and the king, and skilled secular clerics from privileged orders oversaw collection of revenues for the port or urban reeve.

Privileged orders under protection of Rome often came into conflict with bishops and archbishops in the native church and jealous manorial lords. Privileged orders were expected to share their wealth only with the pope and king. In theory abbots were directed only by the pope, although in practice they were often close relatives of manorial lords or kings. Bede recounts an emissary from Pope Gregory accompanying Saint Augustine into Gaul in 595 to demand

---

[187] The exemption from native church heirarchy helps historians identify ancient Holy Apostolic See possessions. Omission of known settlements and ports from church financial accounts suggests possession by privileged orders of the Holy Apostolic See. Possessions and parishes of Fécamp Abbey and other possessions of the Holy Apostolic See are not detailed in Church of England financial accounts until the 13th century, although they are recorded in the *Taxatio* of Pope Nicholas II. Possessions of privileged abbeys and London are largely omitted from Domesday Book as exempt from royal taxation.

payment of arrears to Rome from a recalcitrant bishop. The mission of Erminfrid to King William in 1070 included the calculation and remission of arrears to Rome from the English Church withheld by Stigand. These were made good by King William, perhaps from dispossession of Stigand's massive personal wealth and estates.

Resentment and conflicts arose frequently. Manorial lords resented the clerical wealth and privileges they did not share. Royal or papally privileged orders were often targeted to fund revolts to depose a disliked king, or raided and looted when the bishop or abbot died and before a replacement could be settled, or seized as profits of war. Godwin's serial raids against port possessions at Berkeley, Bosham, Plumstead, Sandwich, Steyning and Rameslege, and Harold's looting of the vacant sees of East Anglia and Wells are part of this wider and older pattern. Normans did it too. William de Braose tried to take tolls and church revenues from the port at Steyning after the Norman Conquest, as did his heirs, leading to several suits by the abbots adjudicated by Norman kings.

Urban tribute, market tolls, customs levies and thelony (*gablo, vectigalia, portoria* and *telonei*) provided shared royal and clerical revenues to preserve the mutual interest of kings and church in protection and promotion of trade at boroughs and ports. The two-thirds share of *telonei* - thelony – of the port of *Wincenesel* in King Cnut's second Rameslege charter to Fécamp Abbey and King William's demand of only *vectigalia* – market tolls – from Winchester at line 630 in the *Carmen* suggest division of these revenues could be negotiated. The importance of these revenues helps explain why secular clerics serving as royal chaplains were customarily appointed to York, Winchester and London, the great trade emporia of medieval England.

Privileged port cantons of religious orders under Holy Apostolic See dominion were generally kept isolated and highly secure from inland realms to avoid conflict between foreign migrants, merchants and craftsmen in the port and natives in the hinterland. This also kept the port safe from hinterland brigands and manorial lords. Visiting envoys, pilgrims, merchants or mariners would have 'liberty of the port' within the port city's fortified walls, but they were not allowed further inland without royal consent. This segregation resembles the ancient Veneti arrangements for the port used by Julius Caesar, keeping the *mercatores* – merchantmen - from the hinterland. Segregation preserved the hinterland realm from foes, spies, traitors, thieves and foreign adventurers coming from abroad. Medieval mariners were apt to raid opportunistically wherever they saw vulnerability, so restricting them to port cantons kept the inland realm hidden and more secure.

The accommodation agreed between early popes and Christian kings to keep trade routes and royal realms secure provided the model still in use for modern shipping ports and airports today. Sailors, pilgrims and merchants could expect the same protection of church law and more or less the same regulation of market commerce in *Hastingaport* or *Londonwick* as in Paris, Cologne or Ravenna, a major advantage for prosperous trading across Europe. One of England's earliest laws gave merchants and ships of the Frankish empire the same rights in London as freemen of the city, recognising that London's merchants enjoyed similar privileges at the Saint-Denis fair in Paris. Privileged ports in all Christian kingdoms had common privileges to mint coins, trade in foreign currency, lend at interest, and otherwise promote economic development and trade consistent with coordination from Rome.

Those living in hinterland regions were not permitted to enter a port without authorisation of their manorial lord and a bishop – a 'passport'. Pilgrimage was therefore restricted to those of some wealth as a manorial lord was required to refuse a passport if absence would leave a family without sufficient means for support. By contrast, burgesses of port cantons could generally trade abroad in other port cantons or emporia freely anywhere in Christendom. A passport provided access and protection at any port administered by the church on the route of a pilgrimage or mercantile voyage. If an offence was committed in the hinterland, a manorial lord was obligated to return a citizen to his home city for trial under municipal law.

An attestation to a charter of King Edward the Confessor quoted in a later Cinque Ports charter suggests a papal legate for ports: *Hiis testibus venerabili patre Roberto Portuense Espiscopo, sacro sanctae Romanae ecclesiae* - 'These things are witnessed by the venerable father Bishop Robert of Portus of the Holy Church of Rome.' In the mid-11th century the bishop of Portus may have served as the papal legate to intercede with the English king for protection of ports in England, perhaps instigating the institution of the privileged Cinque Ports.

One of the prerogatives of a Roman-privileged canton was

sanctuary. Kings and manorial lords could not enter without consent, even in pursuit of fugitives. The fugitive might remain free so long as he did not offend within the port or borough. This explains why deposed royals, fugitives and rebels flee to port cities or other Roman-privileged abbeys in medieval times. King Aethelred, Queen Emma and their children sought sanctuary at Fécamp Abbey in Normandy in 1013 and 1014. King Aethelred and Edmund Ironside took refuge in London in 1016. Queen Emma, Earl Sweyn and Earl Godwin all sought refuge at different times in Bruges. In the *Carmen*, the rebels surviving the battle of Hastings flee to London at line 642, hoping to live there by its liberties. Any king or manorial lord pursuing with violence would risk excommunication offending prelates or the pope.

The *Carmen* alludes to the constraint of sanctuary in its account of King William's dealings with both Winchester and London. King William admits at line 628-29 that it would be shameful to enter and pillage the see of Winchester as the dower estate of Queen Edith. Winchester also held the Roman-privileged abbey founded by Alfred the Great at New Minster. King William demands only market tolls and a pledge of loyalty, both legitimate royal claims on a privileged borough. He had his troops circle the walls of London, and his siege engines threaten doom at its barbicans, but he did not actually enter to eradicate the rebels. King William finally negotiates a truce with the rebels, accepting merely a pledge of loyalty and conceding that London might continue to enjoy citizen self-rule, preserving its historic liberties as a protectorate of Rome and port commonwealth.

King Cnut similarly respected the extraterritorial jurisdiction of historically privileged boroughs. He may have chosen the Benedictine Saint Botolph (died c. 680) as his instrument to collect royal levies on urban trading by locating churches dedicated to the Anglo-Dacian saint outside the gates of privileged boroughs and at bridges and fords approaching privileged estates. During King Cnut's reign more than 70 churches were dedicated to St Botolph, more than any other medieval saint in England. These churches collected customs levies and provided merchant hostels, giving rise to Botolph's modern association as a patron saint of travellers. King Cnut may have chosen Saint Botolph for royal levy collections because Botolph was also celebrated and revered in Denmark or simply as a Dacian jest. One obvious derivation of the saint's name is 'boat wolf', appropriate to a Dacian sea-king taking a bite of royal tribute out of English commerce.[188] Saint Boat-Wolf would be an apt choice of saint for the Danish, an inside joke quite literally at the English expense. There were four Saint Botolph churches founded outside the four gates of London at Aldgate, Aldersgate and Bishopsgate, and on the strand at Billingsgate.[189] King Cnut even gathered Saint Botolph's remains and had them reinterred in a great tomb in Bury St Edmunds, which he also refounded as a privileged order.

Botolph and his brother Adolph fled East Anglia in their youth when the region fell to pagans and London's first Roman Catholic bishop, Mellitus, fled into exile. Both Botolph and Adolph were ordained at a Frankish Benedictine order on the continent. Adolph became bishop of Utrecht in Freesia and Botolph returned to East Anglia to gain a port minster from the Christian King Anna. Utrecht can be reached from East Anglia on a single tide, creating an ideal maritime trading route for the mercantile Benedictine brothers to exploit. Utrecht had once held the Roman Empire monopoly on cross-sea trading to East Anglia. The customs house there collected Roman levies on all trade along coastal routes from the north and south as well. Botolph massively increased 7th century sea-borne trade from the Wash region as proven by coin finds, and he promoted wider regional prosperity through cooperation between regional and continental kings. Great abbeys at iron and salt-rich Peterborough, Thorney, Ely and Waltham were founded with his guidance, and Bury St Edmunds, once Romano-Dacian *Villa Faustini*, grew newly rich as an emporium for trade between Ouse ports and London. Botolph may have founded the school that became Cambridge University to train secular clerics for royal administration. Botolph's later minster at *Icanho* – 'fluvial promontory of the Iceni' – or *Icinos* – 'port-mouth of the

---

[188] A wolf's head was the customary totem for the stem of Viking ships and a wolf-skin was the battle standard of both Pontic and Nordic Dacia.

[189] Thelony – customs tolls - was collected by King Aethelred at Billingsgate in London from 978, probably on the site of the Saint-Denis cell at Londonwick under earlier kings This may give a date for the dispossession of Saint-Denis. Billingsgate gets its name from *bulla*, a lead tax disc proving customs levies had been paid on market goods, redeemable for unsold goods when leaving a port.

Iceni' – became a magnet for other aspiring clerics.[190] The Venerable Bede's own abbot Saint Coelfrith learned Benedictine practice from Botolph at Icanho.[191] Freesia, East Anglia and Lindsey would not remain prosperous for long after Botolph's death. They were all wasted, with their great abbeys and minsters looted, burned and ruined in wars among jealous rival British kings and sea-army attacks.

Native church bishoprics, and minster towns below them, remained in the dominion of a king. Under the king's protection they might be free of legal and financial claims of subsidiary manorial lords such as earls. Revenues from administering boroughs, markets and fairs supported the local charitable and religious works of the church and were shared with the king and native church hierarchy in exchange for the king's protection. This arrangement helped to consolidate royal power by streaming the gold and silver of urban taxes and commercial tolls to the king, while denying gold and silver to manorial lords who might rebel against the king. The system also helped consolidate the church's power by enriching the native church hierarchy.

The system failed where earls became more powerful than the king and dispossessed the church, as in the case of Godwin and his sons under the weak King Edward. Then church, port and urban privileges might be degraded, and the earls might enrich themselves at the expense of both the church and the king. Eadmer, a monk of Christ Church at Canterbury at the turn of the 12th century, wrote in his *Historia Novorum in Anglia* that Godwin was 'the bitter enemy of the

---

[190] The minster of *Icanho* or *Icinos* is probably at Downham Market or Mildenhall on the estuarine Ouse, then tidal as far as Cambridge.

[191] Bede was a son of Franks who immigrated to Northumbria to aid the founding of the abbey at Monkwearmouth where Bede was born. Bede's *Historia ecclesiastica gentis Anglorum* is biased favouring Anglian Northumbria. He omits any mention of Botolph and denigrates religious practice in East Anglia as the see at Elmham was then a rival to York for elevation to archiepiscopal status. The East Anglian king may have been Gregory the Great's original target for the mission of Saint Augustine to the Angles. Bede's diplomacy and selective history prevailed; York won the honour of the Anglian archiepiscopacy.

church of Canterbury', and many other accounts noted that Godwin and his sons looted diocesan sees, churches and abbeys. Eadmer says that before the Danish occupation of England in 1016 there were forty-two religious foundations, but they then suffered greatly, with the worst oppression occurring under the reign of Edward the Confessor. King Edward might have remained faithful to the church, but he had no nobles or troops loyal to him after the rebellion of 1052 reinstated Godwin and his sons with more power than ever. Looting the church and abbeys was then largely unchecked. It was a practice Godwin must have taught to his sons. The diocesan treasury of the vacant see of East Anglia was looted when Harold became earl there in 1045, before Stigand was appointed to the see. Harold opportunistically looted the diocesan treasury of the vacant see of Wells in 1060, before Giso could be appointed to the see. Violence against the church was one factor in the northern thegns rebellion against Earl Tostig in 1065.

Lacking hereditary lords and nobles, Roman-privileged urban and port boroughs were run as republican corporate commonwealths with municipal laws, administration and defence all provided by covenant with burgesses and citizens, similar to Hellenic or Dacian self-rule commonwealths. *Munera* – the root of the word municipal – were the obligations of urban citizens to provide tribute, loyalty, public works and urban defence in return for urban privileges and royal protection. Citizenship in urban and port boroughs was not granted by birth but by covenant, signalled in the *Carmen* by the use of *colonis* for residents in Rameslege, Westminster and London. Once citizenship was granted, merchant citizens could trade anywhere free of manorial tax and toll and claim the king's protection and trial by their own municipal law. The designation 'law-worthy' was both a valuable municipal licence and source of protection, even across national borders. English merchants were 'law-worthy' at the Saint-Denis Fair in Paris from the 8th century, and shipmen and merchants of the Frankish empire were similarly 'law-worthy' in early medieval London. Both Angli and Franci burgesses are made law-worthy in the Charter of London Liberties after 1066.

The municipal magistrate of urban settlements before the conquest was the reeve or portreeve.[192] The title derives from the Roman practice of tax farming, as a reeve was literally a harvester of

---

[192] Mayor was an office introduced after the conquest.

taxes. The word was preserved in the Old Norse and English as reeve. The ancient royal exchequer was called the *saccarium* from the verb *saccare* meaning 'to sack or plunder', suggesting raiding and tax collection might be difficult to distinguish. King Cnut's initial reforms creating the Huscarls as royal agents for tax collection combined a military threat with royal prerogative to collect taxes. By the mid-11th century reeves were the senior magistrates, appointed by the king as officers of the king to collect rents, taxes and tolls, organise civic defence, oversee wall and bridge building, and maintain public order. Reeves swore an oath of loyalty to the king but they were also obliged by oath to protect and act for the common profit of the borough or port where they served.

The church provided the clerical manpower, systems, and communications networks for the complex requirements of royal and urban financial administration. Clerics were the medieval bankers, watchmen, scribes, lawyers and accountants of royalty and nobility. Clerics were trained in writing, recordkeeping and accounting at royal foundation abbey schools and deployed to urban boroughs, ports, markets, fairs, city gates, border posts, royal courts and other places where detailed recordkeeping was an essential function. The royal chancery and exchequer were usually sited at a royal foundation abbey with a school, as at Winchester, Westminster and Waltham. The king's offices were staffed with clerics keeping royal records and royal accounts for the king. Royal chaplains wrote writs, charters and laws for the king. Kings might find it near impossible to administer their kingdoms without chaos if the clerics refused them secular clerical services because of excommunication.

Manorial lords often coveted the wealth of ports, boroughs and abbeys, and resented the immunities of arrogant urban burgesses from manorial tax and toll. The reeve Togred was disciplined by King Edgar in 960 for taxing the clerics and lands of Saint-Denis at Rotherfield and *Portus Hastingas et Peuenisel*. He was forced to hand deliver King Edgar's charter confirming restoration of the abbey's property and gold to the abbey in Paris and lay it on the altar the three martyrs himself to prove his own and King Edgar's contrition for the offence against the most powerful Carolingian abbey and, indirectly, the pope. The unrest and civil strife during King Aethelred's reign may have triggered the later dispossessions.

Likewise, King Cnut must have been asked to reconfirm and restore possession of the manor of *Bretda* to Fécamp Abbey as provided in the second Rameslege charter in his reign. It seems probable that Godwin had presumed to take the manor of *Bretda* as Godwin had already successfully taken Berkeley, Bosham and Plumstead and perhaps other church port possessions in the south of England. Unless there was a dispute with Godwin this charter would not have been necessary.

Godwin showed a particular enmity for *Pefenesea* or *Peuenesea* later: he raided *Peuenesea* in 1051 on his way into exile in Bruges and raided *Pefenesea* twice more in 1052, the second time 'taking all the ships that were put in there' to supplement his mercenary fleet from Flanders and Harold's fleet from Ireland. *Wincenesel* may have been the cell for collection of anchorage tolls and customs at *Pefenesea*, as Boston was the island cell for collecting tolls at the vast sandy anchorage in the western Wash. That ships 'put in' or sheltered there indicates somewhere in the 11th century seascape rather than landscape. The *Anglo-Saxon Chronicle* hints that profits from raiding the port may have been applied by Godwin and Harold to 'entice to them all the land-folk by the sea-coast and also upward in the land' and as they proceeded 'ever alluring forth with them all the boatmen that they met.' The looting of the royal treasuries by the rebels would have confirmed King Edward's resolve to found Westminster as a new royal foundation abbey.

The Normans avenged the treachery of Hastingas by laying waste the region in 1066 after securing their camp. Wasting was the traditional punishment for local disloyalty. They wreak havoc, loot and kill the *plebs* – commoners – in the surrounding countryside, justifying the deaths at line 147 of the *Carmen* because 'they denied your rule' and at line 153 as 'the tribe of treachery'. *Plebs* at line 147 contrasts with *colonis* at line 127, suggesting that those settled on the land in 1066 were regarded by the invading Normans as either traitors who had forfeited mercy for their share in the rebellion or Godwinist retainers settled by Godwin and Harold on lands violently seized from Norman colonists.

After their 1052 restoration to titles, wealth and power by the powerless King Edward, Godwin and his sons purged England of Anglo-Norman and Anglo-Frankish lords, courtiers, bishops and clerics, leaving only a handful to the royal court and William as bishop in London. Stigand appointed himself the uncanonical archbishop of

Canterbury and withheld from Rome the monies normally paid from the Church of England. Anglo-Danish rebels who had supported Godwin were rewarded with lands dispossessed from outlawed Gauls and the Huscarls were rewarded with reinstatement of the Heregeld tax. Godwin, his sons and Stigand all became enormously wealthy, as recorded in 1086 in Domesday Book, suggesting many of the possessions and treasures of those killed or driven into exile were retained for their own profit.

The dedication of King Edward's remaining life to service of the church after 1052 may have been his attempt to ward off excommunication for his failure to protect the church and privileged abbeys of his realm. King Edward's correspondence displays an awareness of this failing and emphasises his personal devotion and generosity. He pledged a tenth of his royal revenues to his new abbey at Westminster and generously endowed building at Bury St Edmund's where Abbot Baldwin, formerly a monk of Saint-Denis, might plead his case to influential clerics on the continent and Rome.

Viewed from the perspective of Rome and the pope, the mission led by Abbot John of Fécamp Abbey to recover the abbey's possessions in England in 1054 becomes more interesting. It may have been a suit to King Edward for better royal protection and restoration of privileged possessions and also an early test of Earl Harold following his succession to his father's titles and lands in Wessex and Kent. King Edward supported Abbot John's claims to restoration of the abbey's lands and ports, and added the further gift under seal of lands around Eastbourne, including *Caestre* (Pevensey Castle), but King Edward could not enforce his will or deliver possessions against Earl Harold's entrenched opposition and occupation. Earl Harold refused to relinquish the abbey's possessions at Rameslege or Steyning or to make restitution for his father's past violence against the abbey. Earl Harold continued opportunistic violence against the church, raiding the vacant see of Wells as soon as the bishop died, dispossessing valuable estates and looting the diocesan treasury as he had done at Elmham in 1044. Had Earl Harold shown more generosity to the Norman abbey in 1054, and curbed his violence against the English Church and religious foundations thereafter, King Harold's fate and the judgement of Pope Alexander II might have been very different in 1066.

Given a Godwin family history of raiding church, abbey and diocesan treasuries, denying tribute to Rome, dispossession of lands and ports, and violence against clerics and prelates, Pope Alexander II might reasonably fear losing all remaining possessions, revenues and authority in England to King Harold in 1066. To counter the risk of permanent loss of England from communion with Rome the pope excommunicated King Harold, inviting attack from Christian realms abroad as a holy service to the pope. If the church were to regain and secure its possessions, revenues and authority in England, then the pope would need a king on the throne consecrated to Christian submission to Rome, someone who could ensure restoration and reform of the English Church. King William and Archbishop Lanfranc efficiently provided exactly what Rome needed.

The dominion, liberties and immunities of ecclesiastical jurisdictions are also important to the narrative of civic administration described in the *Carmen* for Dover, Canterbury, Winchester and London as King William sought to secure civic dominion over all of England after the military battle had been won. The *Carmen* provides a great deal of concise, knowledgeable detail about the jurisdictional status of these places and the political accommodations each reaches with the king.

In keeping with the medieval laws of war, William succeeded to royal demesne by defeating King Harold in battle and declaring himself king of England by Harold's grave at line 595. William still did not have the submission of ecclesiastical estates, boroughs and ports until the English burgesses, bondsmen and magistrates in those polities took oaths of loyalty and duty to him as their new king in exchange for his royal protection. It is this process of urban and ecclesiastical submission that completes the Norman Conquest after the battle. The very fine details provided in the *Carmen* reveal that the author had a deep grasp of England's early medieval ecclesiastical history and the political accommodations required between the English king and the church.

When King William marched from *Hastingaport* five days after the battle his first objective was Dover. By legend King Lucius was the first Briton to become a Christian convert about the year 180, receiving envoys from Pope Elutherius. Keeping to the pattern of first Christian kings, Lucius built a minster for the legates from Pope Elutherius in

Dover Castle,[193] endowed the minster with toll and custom of the port below, and granted further minsters for two of the legates at Winchester and London, the two most important emporia of the Romano-Belgae and Romano-Frisians. Whether or not the legend has a factual basis in Romano-British history, it was widely believed in medieval times as the true history of the earliest establishment of the Christian church in Britain.

Christianity in communion with Rome was famously restored to Britain by the mission sent from Gregory the Great with St Augustine in 595. Augustine converted King Aethelberht of Kent, whose queen was a Gallic Christian already, and as with all first Christian kings, King Aethelberht gave Augustine an archiepiscopal see at Canterbury to promote the church not only in his kingdom of Kent but throughout the entire diverse island with its many rival kingdoms.[194]

Dover is King William's first urban objective after the battle, and Canterbury, Winchester and London follow next in the narrative. Dover is taken as a royal possession by right of conquest, having been possessed long before 1066 by Godwin, and later Harold, by self-appointment as constables of Dover Castle. Canterbury quickly yields in canonical duty, encouraging a widespread rush to send tribute and swear loyalty. Winchester and London, however, are both reluctant to yield until offered generous privileges, perhaps in recognition of Rome's ancient claims to the emporia.

Godwin became the first Constable of Dover Castle sometime before his death in 1053, and Harold succeeded to the new office. Some suggest a confederation pre-dating the Cinque Ports was created by Godwin following the rebellion in 1052, when Godwin suborned all

---

[193] Matthew Paris wrote of Dover Castle as the 'lock and key of the whole kingdom', which was fitting as the Roman god Portus was the god of locks and keys, and ports represent both access and vulnerability. Two crossed keys are the emblem of the Holy Apostolic See.

[194] Augustine may have been intended by Pope Gregory to begin his mission in East Anglia, where the kings had been Christian for some time, but was diverted to Kent by King Aethelberht's Gallic foster-father and father-in-law, King Charibert of Neustria.

the ships and ship-warriors of the south coast to his fleet before
proceeding to besiege King Edward at Westminster. Interpretation of
Hellocis as 'strait-places' at line 504 of the *Carmen* may give us a regional
name for the earlier arrangement. His appointment of himself as
constable of Dover Castle secured the strategic fortress to Godwin's
manorial rule as earl of Kent. Norman sources say delivery of Dover
Castle was a condition of Earl Harold's oath of vassalage to Duke
William in 1064, suggesting the Normans resented Earl Harold
retaining command in Dover after Godwin's death. After the conquest
King William gave possession of Dover to his half-brother Odo,
bishop of Bayeux, perhaps initially meaning to restore some form of
ecclesiastical possession. Later rebellions and divisions between the
brothers saw the strategic castle and port retained by the king.

Dover's burgesses hurried to meet and submit to King William in
1066 as he marched toward the port at lines 599-602. The burgesses
have been criticised by some historians for yielding so readily to King
William, but as either a royal or manorial domain of King Harold the
castle was justly delivered to its new lord by right of conquest. The
burgesses brought the keys to the castle's gates. The king accepted the
keys and their oaths of loyalty, but then dispossessed the burgesses of
their homes and settled his retainers in them. This was probably done
to avenge the affront to Count Eustace in 1051, and punish the
arrogant burgesses for disloyalty to King Edward in 1052, but the
Carmen alludes to another purpose. As word spread of this harsh
example to other urban boroughs, the magistrates from all over
England swarmed like flies to bring tribute and oaths of loyalty to the
new king to preserve their historic privileges and royal protection.

Canterbury is the next objective after Dover. Canterbury was the
archiepiscopal seat of the Church of England, established by Saint
Augustine, with authority over all other episcopal sees and English
foundation minsters and abbeys. The pope's letter to the English
clergy confirming King William as the rightful heir and requiring the
English clergy's allegiance in canonical duty might have been persuasive
in Canterbury if the threat of the Norman army a day's march away was
not enough. Canterbury brought the 'first tribute' but then other urban
settlements swiftly followed: 'All brought gifts and reconfirmed their
loyalty'. As mid-October was the traditional date for remission of
tribute to the king under a convention dating back to Roman tax
farming, the new king had timed his conquest well.

After a month in Dover only two urban hold outs remained: Winchester and London. The historic immunities of these emporia are closely associated with both the Elutherian mission to King Lucius and the Gregorian mission to King Aethelberht. Papal protection and Roman influence may explain the generous negotiated settlements reached ultimately with both urban emporia.

The Old Minster at Winchester was established as the see of Wessex in the 7th century. The borough also became the royal seat of descendants of King Cerdic of Wessex and the traditional place for dowry of English queens. As an episcopal see of the Church of England, Winchester should have been compliant with the submission of Canterbury and the direction of the pope in canonical duty to yield to King William. Unfortunately, the bishop of Winchester was Stigand, the excommunicant, uncanonical archbishop of Canterbury and lifelong partisan of Anglo-Danes in general and the Godwin family in particular. He had insisted on holding the see in duality with Canterbury after seizing the archbishopric in 1052. He had retired to Winchester to protect himself in sanctuary there in 1066, implying Winchester retained an historic papal privilege of sanctuary where Canterbury was royal demesne.

Besides the diocesan see, there was another religious foundation in Winchester which complicated jurisdiction between king and Holy Apostolic See. Alfred the Great, anointed king of the West Saxons as a child in Rome, had established a privileged abbey for a religious order within the Holy Apostolic See, called the New Minster, which closely neighboured the episcopal see at Old Minster. King Alfred had thus confused jurisdiction for the borough between the Church of England, subject to royal rule and direction from Canterbury, and the Holy Apostolic See, subject only to the pope. The bard of the *Carmen* is clearly knowledgeable about this duality. In the narrative that begins at line 620, he uses the plural for primates (bishop and abbot collectively) and asserts the dower-right of Queen Edith as King Edward's widow as a bar to violence against the sanctuary.

King William agreed that it would be shameful to waste the borough at lines 628-29, as entering violently would offend both of Holy Apostolic See inviolability and the dower-right of the queen. He ceded the primates of the two minsters and the queen immunity from *tributa* – royal taxes, but required payment of *vectigalia* – market tolls at line 630, and demanded their pledge of loyalty. The queen and two primates acceded to his demands and his dominion as king, providing an important example of ecclesiastical and royal accommodation at lines 633-34: 'And likewise both primates gave assent to the king's command for they brought the gifts of the queen and their own together.' *Dona* – gifts – are different than *tributa* – taxes, as they are deemed voluntary and imply no continuing obligation. Norman kings later forced the abbot and monks of New Minster to relocate outside the borough, resolving the confusion of papal and royal jurisdiction in the wealthy market town and diocesan see.

The king's army then turned to London, where rebels had fled to seek sanctuary in the richest and most powerful borough in England. In defiance of the conquest at Hastingas and the submission of other urban boroughs, a great council convened in London and selected the half-Saxon and half-Slavo-Hungarian child Edgar to be their king, meaning him to be a mere figurehead with no real authority. King William regarded the ploy as 'unworthy' at line 659, presumably because the boy cannot be consecrated king without the pope's consent, but also perhaps because the boy lacked any experience of war, owned no land or treasure, commanded no warriors, and could provide no meaningful leadership and protection commensurate with the obligations of a king.[195]

Like Winchester, London also had a confusion of ecclesiastical jurisdictions, and these may be important to the narrative in the *Carmen* that follows. Saint Mellitus was a companion of Saint Augustine and accompanied him to England to restore Christian communion with Rome. He converted King Saeberht of the East Saxons to Christianity, and like all early royal converts, King Saeberht founded an abbey at the port island of Thorney and an episcopal see for the native church with the revenues of the emporium of London. The abbey consecrated to Saint Peter was known as West Minster, spelled as *Guest* at line 667 in the *Carmen*. The episcopal see consecrated to Saint Paul was within the ancient walls of the Roman emporium, sometimes called East Minster. Mellitus was ordained the first bishop to the new see at St Paul's

---

[195] Aethling is a modern honorific assigned by romantic Victorians to the boy. He signed no charters and was never given royal regard in the 11th century prior to the conquest to justify such a title.

church in 604. According to Bede when St Augustine re-established communion of the English Church with Rome, Pope Gregory retained the see of London as subject to direct papal authority, excluding it from the wider English Church.[196] The *Carmen*'s use of *colonis* for the rebellious citizens of London at line 631 and also for the founders of Westminster at line 667 indicates the bard was aware of the distinctive ecclesiastical status of both boroughs. William stops at Westminster, where the palace is royal demesne, rather than offend the pope by invading privileged London.

Bede's reproduction of the letter from Pope Gregory to Saint Augustine provides that the bishop of London will always be chosen by his own synod and the bishop can only receive the pall of his office from the pope. These conditions for London indicate that even from the 6th century the pope saw mercantile London as different to all other sees in England and sought to preserve self-rule in the city. By the time Bede wrote in the 8th century London had become 'an emporium of peoples of all the world, coming by land and sea'. If papal consent was still required for London's bishop, then the new Archbishop Robert's refusal to ordain Spearhafoc in 1052 becomes an important test of papal influence in King Edward's England. Spearhafoc's refusal to relinquish the see to Bishop William and his looting of the diocesan treasury during Godwin's revolt are Anglo-Danish rejections of papal authority.

Holy Apostolic See protection of London may have secured the city to some extent from the rivalries of competing tribal monarchs. Defeated royals often sought sanctuary within its walls. The distinctive status of London as a mandated canton may also explain why William the Norman, bishop of London, was uniquely able to return from exile after Godwin and Harold's revolt in 1052, and why Frankish burgesses remained protected there from the purges elsewhere. Recognition of a distinctive and privileged jurisdiction makes sense of line 688, in which King William offers London 'a better separation'.

The combination of royal and papal protection of London proved a powerful impetus to emigration of skilled tradesmen and merchants from other Christian realms, just as British Empire

---

[196] *Historia ecclesiastica gentis Anglorum* (I:29).

protection and English law would promote multi-cultural, skilled immigration and commerce in the 19th and 20th centuries to distant Hong Kong and Singapore. This special status of London as a Roman-privileged emporium helps explain the charter for the bishop of London as King Cnut's first act in 1017 and the London Charter of Liberties as King William's first act in 1067.

By contrast, the metropolitan of York was established as subject to the authority of the see of Canterbury, creating a unified Church of England over the kingdoms of Northumbria and other diverse kingdoms in the 7th century, before unification of England as a kingdom. York did not become an archbishopric until late in the 8th century, after Bede had promoted it with his Northumbrian-biased and selective history.

The siege and negotiations for London are light-hearted in the *Carmen*, as Normans delighted in the use of cunning as well as force. Both King William and the wily magistrate of London were determined to win by guile, and arguably both succeeded. King William stationed his army around the city, dug mines under the walls, and placed a siege engine at the barbican, but ultimately, he understood that he would impoverish himself by destroying his mercantile capital. Threatening doom, he offered the Norman-born portreeve a crafty way out that would force rebels to remain trapped within the sanctuary of the city's walls or swear oaths of loyalty to gain reinstatement to their lands. King William secretly offered the portreeve a 'better means of separation' of the urban jurisdiction from the royal demesne, with himself as a submissive figurehead king in place of the boy-king Edgar. The boy could be as easily disregarded in December 1066 as he had been in January when King Harold took the crown. Lines 690-691, always unsatisfactory before, now make perfect sense and probably raised a laugh among medieval audiences in on the joke: 'Merely call him king, he said, but by the prerogatives of royal power, as Edgar now commands, he instead might rule in total submission.'

Understanding the nature of the offer also clarifies the motivations for the London Charter of Liberties. This writ-charter is the earliest document to grant rights and protections to the citizens of a city - the original civil rights act. The protections in this writ are that the burgesses will remain 'law-worthy' with rights of inheritance for their heirs. These were the same privileges historically asserted by the arrogant tribes of Roman-privileged coastal Neustria, the Gallo-

Dacians who inter-married with Rollo's Norsemen and taught their fierce children to speak *Romana* and worship the Christian god.

The written assurance may have been sought and drafted by William the Norman, bishop of London, in much the same spirit as the Gallo-Dacians demanded a written law preserving their privileges before they swore loyalty to Carolingian kings. The bishop had been royal chaplain to King Edward so was familiar with the form of English royal writs. He was long afterward venerated for securing London's deliverance and liberties in 1066 with an annual procession of mayor and aldermen to his tomb in Old St Paul's church.

Still in the possession of the Corporation of London, a translation of the Old English text reads:

> William the king, friendly salutes William the bishop and Godfrey the portreeve and all the burgesses within London, both Frankish and English. And I declare that I grant you to be all law-worthy, as you were in the days of King Edward; And I grant that every child shall be his father's heir, after his father's days; And I will not suffer any person to do you wrong; God keep you.

This scrap of vellum changed the world. The charter had enormous constitutional implications for the kingdom of England, limiting the royal prerogatives of King William and all future kings. It proved citizens could unite to collectively demand power and privilege, setting an example copied in other mercantile emporia in England and abroad. A few generations later barons would unite to demand greater powers from the king and enshrine these in Magna Carta. Preservation of London's liberties became clause 9, and is still law. The charter itself was revoked in 1693 on grounds of London's treason against James II.

London, then as now, was arrogant toward the hinterland, multi-cultural and tolerant of skilled and unorthodox immigrants who could contribute to communal prosperity. Its commercial interests, then as now, were more closely aligned with the wealthy mercantile urbanites of continental trading capitals than with English agrarian provincials. In the *Carmen*'s narrative London's residents quickly agreed 'either side', citizenry and aldermen, to renounce the weak child-king in favour of the strong Norman king. The oaths of the rebels cleared the way for William the Conqueror's consecration as king and assured him royal legitimacy.

The London Charter of Liberties and face of the Great Seal of William I, both still held in the London Metropolitan Archives

The consecration itself as described in the *Carmen* evidences a unification of the Nordic and Frankish traditions. The king first seeks communion with the Universal Church, consistent with the Frankish ordo for royal consecration. But what follows next is from the Dacian tradition: the king is elected by the nobility – England's military elites – and that election is confirmed by the prelates and aldermen, the church and mercantile elites. If we accept the DNA evidence of Dacian migrations to Nordic, Frankish and British mercantile cantons from antiquity, then we can now derive a parallel continuity tracing Dacian rule of law. The Nordic, Frankish and British traditions converge in the consecration of King William. As with all Dacian truces, one element was the ceding of a self-ruled commonwealth, London.

King William displayed his gratitude for divine favour to the pope and church in many ways. He entertained the papal envoy

Erminfrid to depose the uncanonical Stigand in favour of Lanfranc and to agree the past-due contributions the English church owed to Rome. King William confirmed all possessions and liberties of Fécamp Abbey in England in 1072 for the care of his soul, King Edward's soul, and all his royal predecessors and successors. He gave the first vacant bishopric in England to Remigius of Fécamp Abbey, commander of the ship and clerical warriors that accompanied the Norman fleet. In 1085 King William provided Fécamp Abbey a further charter confirming possession of Steyning and providing lands at *Beriminstre* (Bury above Arundel) in compensation for losses at Rameslege. Fécamp Abbey's royal influence and possessions were finally eroded by disputes between England and Normandy that would only grow with nationalist division and religious separation between the English Church and the popes in Rome.

Soon after the conquest Fécamp Abbey built a church at Ore, atop the southern headland of the cape of Hastingas, dedicated to Saint Helen, the Anglo-Dacian mother of Saint Constantine. Its tower overlooked the Channel to Normandy and also the great port in the Brede Basin. As wife of the Emperor Constantius the young Helen became the Empress Helena, the first Christian member of the imperial ruling family and mother to the emperor who founded the Universal Church under authority of Roman popes. Constantine as sole emperor institutionalised the Christian faith within the Roman Empire and was the author of the administrative, financial, monetary, civic and military reforms that shaped medieval European kingdoms. Saint Helen was a potent symbol of Britain in communion with Rome and a Europe united in Christianity.

King William founded a further abbey for the care of his soul and to fulfil a battlefield vow to a monk of Marmoutier Abbey. He gave the newly established abbey lands and liberties, although not until many years later. The Abbey of St Martin de Bello at Battle was finally consecrated in 1094 after King William's death and received custody of many of the holy relics he had carried into battle against King Harold.

St Helen's Ore on the Great Ridge above Hastings

Battle Abbey was destroyed during the Reformation, when an English king once again severed communion with Rome, but the foundations remain etched in stone. The church of Saint-Martin-de-Bataille stood on the eastern heights of Battle Hill, visible above the great port of the Brede Basin and the lesser channel leading to Hooe through the Pevensey Levels. The gleaming spire of the white Caen stone church would be a grand expression of royal and ecclesiastical authority seen by all mariners and merchantmen as they came into port. The abbey also provided an ideal signal station for securing the south coast of England, communicating by beacons to high points all around the coast. If you visit Battle today and climb up to the viewing deck on the roof of the gatehouse, reopened in 2016, you can still see down the great valley to the royal manor of Court Lodge at Udimore, the Norman fortified camp at Icklesham, and the entrance to the great port between Rye and Winchelsea, whose calm basin and steep heights embraced a Norman invasion fleet in 1066.

SEAL OF WILLIAM THE CONQUEROR

ABOUT THE TRANSLATOR

Kathleen Tyson had a career in global financial markets before developing an interest in medieval history in 2013. She took a sabbatical in 2015 and received an MA (Merit) in Medieval History in 2017 from King's College London. She enjoys speaking about the Norman Conquest and her researches into earlier history and geography, and is open to invitations.

Email enquiries, comments and invitations to:

CarmenAndConquest@gmail.com

Follow further research and discussion:

CarmenAndConquest.blogspot.co.uk

96062111R00180